HOUGHTON MIFFLIN

English

Authors
Robert Rueda
Tina Saldivar
Lynne Shapiro
Shane Templeton
C. Ann Terry
Catherine Valentino
Shelby A. Wolf

Consultants
Jeanneine P. Jones
Monette Coleman McIver
Rojulene Norris

 HOUGHTON MIFFLIN   BOSTON • MORRIS PLAINS, NJ

California • Colorado • Georgia • Illinois • New Jersey • Texas

Acknowledgments

For each of the selections listed below, grateful acknowledgment is made for permission to excerpt and/or reprint original or copyrighted material as follows:

Published Models

Adapted from *Before the Storm* by Jane Yolen, paintings by Georgia Pugh. Text copyright ©1995 by Jane Yolen. Illustrations copyright ©1995 by Georgia Pugh. Reprinted by permission of Boyds Mills Press.

"The Billy Goat and the Vegetable Garden" from *Señor Cat's Romance and Other Favorite Stories from Latin America* by Lucia M. González, illustrated by Lulu Delacre. Published by Scholastic Press, a division of Scholastic Inc. Text copyright ©1997 by Lucía M. González. Illustrations copyright ©1997 by Lulu Delacre. Used by permission.

"Build a Bird Feeder" from *Science Wizardry for Kids* by Margaret Kenda and Phyllis S. Williams. Copyright ©1992 by Margaret Kenda and Phyllis S. Williams. Reprinted by arrangement with Barron's Educational Series, Inc., Hauppauge, NY.

"The Great Hair Argument" from *Ramona and Her Mother* by Beverly Cleary. Text copyright ©1979 by Beverly Cleary. Used by permission of HarperCollins Publishers.

Acknowledgments are continued at the back of the book following the last page of the Index.

Printed in the U.S.A.

ISBN: 0-618-03079-4

56789-VH-06 05 04 03 02 01

TABLE OF CONTENTS

Part 1

Grammar, Usage, and Mechanics

Unit 1 The Sentence 31

SECTION 1 Narrating and Entertaining

Unit 7 Writing a Personal Narrative 258

SECTION 2 Explaining and Informing

Unit 9 Writing Instructions 326

Unit 10 — Writing a Research Report 354

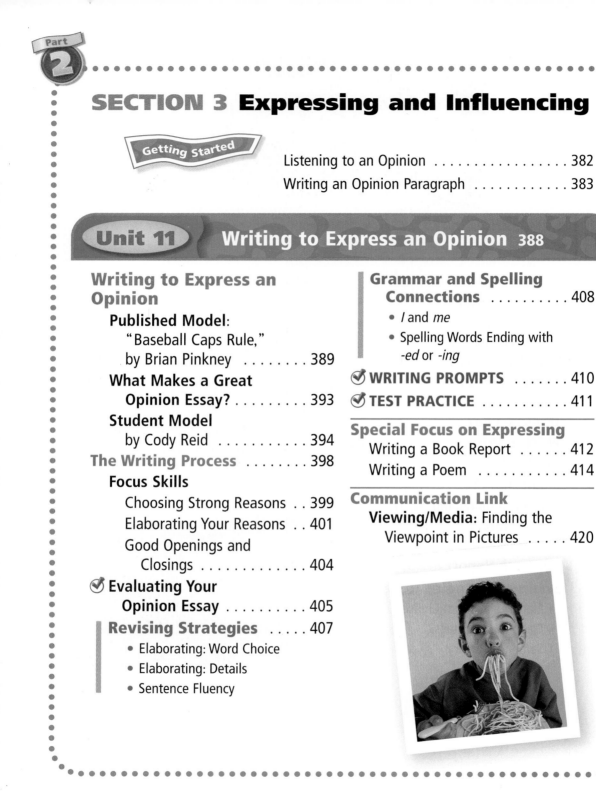

Part 2

SECTION 3 Expressing and Influencing

Getting Started

Unit 11 | Writing to Express an Opinion 388

Unit 12 · Writing to Persuade 422

Part 3 Tools and Tips

Getting Started

Listening, Speaking, and Viewing

A Day in the Life of a Student

Learning from Each Other

Each of you is a one-of-a-kind person. The things you know and the things you can do make you different from anyone else. Because you're each special, just think what you can all learn from each other!

Together we can write a mystery, explain why it rains, speak Spanish, catch a fly ball, name a dinosaur, and raise goldfish.

Learning from each other will make everything you do easier and more fun. Your teachers and classmates can help you solve problems and think of new ideas. They can make you proud to do your best. How can you learn from each other? LISTEN, SPEAK, and LOOK! Speaking lets you share what you know. Listening and looking, or viewing, help you learn from others. Here are the most important purposes for speaking, listening, and viewing.

Speaking	Listening and Viewing	Examples
to entertain	to enjoy yourself	telling a story, listening to a poem, watching a movie
to give information	to get information	giving a message, listening to instructions, looking at pictures in a school book
to persuade	to form an opinion	explaining why you want something, listening to a report, looking at an ad

Think and Discuss

- Look back at the picture on page 1. What is each student's purpose for listening, speaking, or viewing?
- At what other times do you speak, listen, and view during the day?

What's Wrong with This Discussion?

These students are trying to choose a story to act out, but they are not using good listening and speaking skills. What's wrong?

Think and Discuss

- What is each student doing wrong in this discussion?
- What could the students do to improve their discussion?

What's Right with This Discussion?

The students are still choosing a story to act out. How have they improved their listening and speaking skills?

Think and Discuss

- What has each student done to improve his or her listening or speaking skills?

Being a Good Listener and Speaker

Whether you are with your family, your friends, or your classmates, listening and speaking connect you with other people. To keep those connections strong, follow these rules for listening and speaking.

When You Speak

- Wait your turn. Don't interrupt!
- Look at your listeners.
- Speak loudly and clearly enough for your listeners to hear and understand you.
- Don't speak for too long. Give others a chance.
- Ask others what they think about your ideas. Say what you think about theirs.
- If you disagree, politely explain why.
- Don't have side conversations.
- Every so often, sum up the ideas that the group has shared.

When You Listen

- Find a quiet place for your discussion. Get rid of or block outside noises. Don't make noise yourself.
- Look at the speaker.
- Listen carefully, and think about what you hear. Don't daydream.
- Silently sum up what you hear.
- If you don't understand, ask a question.
- If you are confused, say in your own words what you think the speaker meant.

Try It Out Choose one of the sentences below. Decide whether or not you agree with it. Discuss your opinions in small groups.

- Playing computer games is better than playing sports.
- Winter is the best season of the year.
- Cats make the best pets.

Being a Good Viewer

Good viewers use their eyes to learn. Here are some ways.

When You View

Viewing Places and Things

► First, sweep your eyes over the whole place or thing you are viewing.

► Then take a longer look at the most interesting or important parts.

► Finally, look more closely at those parts. What details do you see?

Viewing People

► When other people speak, watch their hands and faces for clues that help explain what they are saying or show what they are feeling.

► When you speak, watch the faces of your listeners for clues about what they are thinking or feeling.

► When someone shows you how to do something, watch the person's actions carefully so that you can copy him or her.

Viewing Still or Moving Images

Pictures and diagrams are often called *images*. Images can move, as in cartoons, or they can be still, as in photographs.

► Look for the most important part of the image. What catches your eye?

► Look more closely. What do the details tell you?

► Is the purpose of the image to entertain? persuade? give information?

► What audience is the image for? children? adults? everyone?

Try It Out With a small group, act out part of a well-known story without speaking or using props. Have the rest of the class guess the story.

The Writing Process

What Is the Writing Process?

The writing process takes you step by step from a blank sheet of paper to an interesting piece of writing. The writing process gives you many chances to make your writing better.

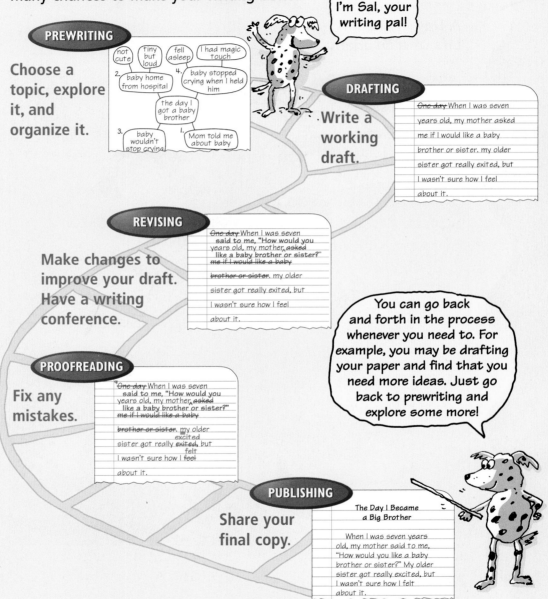

I'm Sal, your writing pal!

PREWRITING

Choose a topic, explore it, and organize it.

not cute · tiny but loud · fell asleep · I had magic touch

2. baby home from hospital   4. baby stopped crying when I held him

the day I got a baby brother

3. baby wouldn't stop crying   1. Mom told me about baby

DRAFTING

Write a working draft.

~~One day~~ When I was seven years old, my mother asked me if I would like a baby brother or sister. my older sister got really exited, but I wasn't sure how I feel about it.

REVISING

Make changes to improve your draft. Have a writing conference.

~~One day~~ When I was seven said to me, "How would you years old, my mother ~~asked~~ like a baby brother or sister?" ~~me if I would like a baby~~ ~~brother or sister.~~ my older sister got really exited, but I wasn't sure how I feel about it.

You can go back and forth in the process whenever you need to. For example, you may be drafting your paper and find that you need more ideas. Just go back to prewriting and explore some more!

PROOFREADING

Fix any mistakes.

~~One day~~ When I was seven said to me, "How would you years old, my mother ~~asked~~ like a baby brother or sister?" ~~me if I would like a baby~~ ~~brother or sister.~~ my older excited sister got really ~~exited,~~ but felt I wasn't sure how I ~~feel~~ about it.

PUBLISHING

Share your final copy.

The Day I Became a Big Brother

When I was seven years old, my mother said to me, "How would you like a baby brother or sister?" My older sister got really excited, but I wasn't sure how I felt about it.

Looking Ahead In this section, you will learn about the writing process while you write a description. To get ready, you will first read a description that was published in a book.

Jane Yolen wrote this description of a hot, sticky summer afternoon. What details help you feel the uncomfortable weather?

A Hot Summer Day

adapted from *Before the Storm,* by Jane Yolen

It was a hot summer day, the air crackling with heat, and Strider lay panting by the barn door. His tongue hung out of his mouth like a big wad of pink bubble gum, and the noise he made was as snuffling as a train.

My brother, Pete, was reading a book about the frozen North. My sister, Sara, was coloring. Each crayon grew soft and mushy in her hand.

I just sat on the swing in the chestnut tree. It was too hot even to consider swinging.

A squirrel ran in front of Strider, then up a tree. Strider raised one ear and shifted his head slightly. Then he closed his eyes. It was *that* hot.

more ▶

Mama stuck her head out of the door. "Lemonade!" she called. Only I got up, my shorts leaving a wet perspiration mark on the swing seat.

The lemonade glass was cool in my hand. I put it against my forehead. That was almost better than drinking. "Bring me some, too, Jordie," Sara called out.

"Me, too," Pete said, never looking up from his book. I got two more glasses and held them against my cheeks. I almost didn't want to give them up.

Then I went around the side of the house where the hose lay curled like a snake in the short grass, one end already tight around the faucet. It was hard to do, but I turned on the water and held the hose as it uncurled with the power of the flow.

Pop! The water sprayed out, catching me by surprise. First it was hot, from the hose lying all day in the sun. And then it turned colder than the frozen North in Pete's book. I shivered.

Strider rose slowly to his feet, shaking off lazy flies. Then Sara came, flinging away her paper and the last of the soft crayons. Pete looked up from his book, his eyes squinty from staring over patches of deep snow. "Me first!" he called. "I'm the oldest."

We took turns: Pete running through the spray like a runner winning a race.

Then Sara on her knees, laughing, and shaking off the water like Strider scattering flies.

When it was my turn in the spray, Pete held it first low on my legs like a strong waterfall, then high on my head like a gentle rain. I looked up and let it patter down, drinking until I was deliciously cold inside and out.

Reading As a Writer

Think About the Description

- Reread the first two paragraphs on page 9. What details show how hot it was?
- Reread the paragraph on this page that begins *When it was my turn.* Which details help you feel and hear the water?

Think About Writer's Craft

- Jane Yolen makes comparisons using *like* or *as.* Two examples are *His tongue hung out of his mouth like a big wad of pink bubble gum* and *the noise he made was as snuffling as a train.* What other comparisons does she use?

Think About the Picture

- The picture on page 9 shows how hot the kids are. Look at the colors the artist used. Which colors help you feel the heat?

Looking Ahead

Next, you will see how one student, Jermaine Boddie, used the writing process to write a description of his dog, Nikki. You will also write your own description.

Using the Writing Process

What Is Prewriting?

Before you start to write, you first choose a topic, think what you will say about it, and plan your writing. You think about your **purpose** and **audience**. Why will you write this paper? Who will read or listen to it?

You also think about how you will **publish** or **share** what you will write with your audience. This will help you decide how you will write it.

How Do I Choose a Topic?

Here are a few ways to find an idea to write about.

Ways to Think of Topics		
Try this!	**Here's how.**	
Remember your experiences or those of others.	You won the prize for funniest costume at a party.	• Write a **personal narrative** about what happened.
Read a book.	You enjoyed a book about a camping adventure.	• Write a **research report** about places to camp near you.
Reread your journal.	You wrote a journal entry about a trip to the zoo.	• Write your **opinion**, or what you think, about zoos.
Use your imagination.	What would it be like to be two inches tall?	• Write a **story** about a person who is two inches tall.

Write a Description

Choosing a Description Topic

Learning from a Model Jermaine made a list of things he could describe for his classmates and thought about each thing.

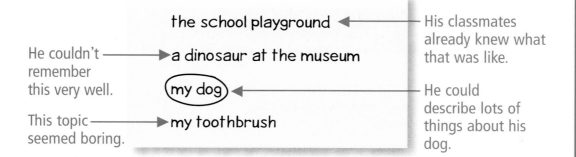

the school playground ← His classmates already knew what that was like.

He couldn't → a dinosaur at the museum
remember
this very well.

(my dog) ← He could describe lots of things about his dog.

This topic → my toothbrush
seemed boring.

▶ Choose Your Topic

Think about your **purpose** and **audience**. Think about how you will **publish** or **share** your description.

❶ List four or five things that you could describe, such as a special place, a favorite toy, or a pet. Use the chart on page 12 for help.

❷ Discuss your topics with a partner. Which ones does your partner like? Why?

❸ Ask yourself these questions about each topic.
- Can I look at this before I write about it?
- Can I describe it using at least three of my five senses (sight, sound, touch, taste, and smell)?

❹ Circle the topic you will write about.

Keep all your work for your description in one place, such as a writing folder.

Tech Tip
See page H35 for ideas for using a computer to write.

What Is Exploring?

When you explore your topic, you remember events, find facts, and think of details about your topic.

How Do I Explore My Topic?

This chart shows different ways to explore a topic.

Exploring Strategies	
Try this!	**Here's how.**
Brainstorming a list	Pink Bicycle loud, shiny horn smooth blue seat thick wheels reflectors
Clustering	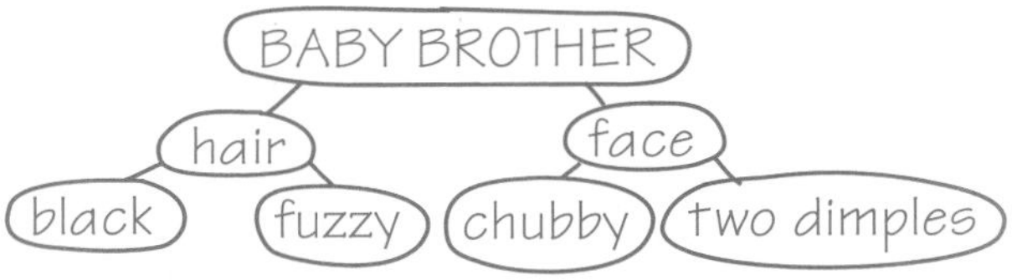 BABY BROTHER hair face black fuzzy chubby two dimples
Making a chart	The River at Night Sounds | water rushing, crickets Smells | fishy, gasoline
Drawing and labeling	 yarn for hair sock
Asking *Who? What? Where? When? Why? How?*	Clown Mystery Who? a clown What? got lost from his circus

See page H46 for more graphic organizers.

Exploring a Description Topic

Learning from a Model Jermaine observed his dog, using most of his five senses. He paid special attention to how she looked, sounded, felt, and smelled. Then he listed details about Nikki in a Sense Chart.

Looks	Sounds	Tastes	Feels	Smells
buff-colored ears	bark scares my sister		nose feels rough	breath like burnt toast
brown spots on back				smells good after bath
brown tail				

▲ Jermaine's Sense Chart

► Explore Your Topic

❶ **Make** a Sense Chart for your topic.

❷ **List** details under each sense that is important to your topic.

❸ **Use** words that tell how your topic looks, sounds, tastes, feels, or smells. The words below might give you some ideas.

Sight	Sound	Taste	Touch	Smell
sparkling	roar	stale	damp	rotten
striped	squeal	buttery	chilly	fishy
violet	pop	mild	spongy	sweet
slim	whisper	creamy	tingling	faint
wrinkled	sputtering	spicy	smooth	sharp
puffy	crunchy	peppery	mushy	lemony

What Is Organizing?

After you think of details about your topic, you choose the ones that you want to use. Then you put them in the order that you will write about them.

How Do I Organize My Writing?

Group facts, events, or ideas. Put together details that tell about the same fact, event, or idea.

Choose the best order. Decide what order you should use to tell about your details. Look at the ideas in the chart below.

Ways to Organize	
Try this!	**Here's how.**
Time order First Next Last	Tell events in the order they happen.
Place order	Describe things from top to bottom, side to side, near to far, or far to near.
Comparison and contrast	Tell how two things are alike. Then tell how they are different. You can also describe the differences first instead of last.
Question and answer Q? A . . . Q? A . . .	Ask a question and tell the answer. Then ask another question and answer that.
Logical order	Group details that tell about the same idea. Put the groups in an order that makes sense.

Organizing a Description

Learning from a Model Jermaine numbered each group of details in the order that he would write about them. He added another detail that he wanted to use.

① Looks	④ Sounds	Tastes	② Feels	③ Smells
buff-colored ears	bark scares my sister		nose feels rough	breath like burnt toast
brown spots on back				smells good after bath
brown tail				
big eyes				

▲ **Jermaine's numbered Sense Chart**

▶ Organize Your Description

❶ **Reread** your Sense Chart.

❷ **Number** your groups of details in the order that you will write about them.

❸ **Add** any more details you think of. Use exact words.

What Is Drafting?

When you draft, just get your ideas on paper.

- If you think of other details, add them.
- Don't worry about mistakes. You can fix them later because this is a **working draft**.
- Remember your purpose and your audience as you write.

How Do I Draft My Paper?

Write sentences and paragraphs. Look at the details you wrote when you explored and organized your paper. Use them to write sentences in a **paragraph**.

> A paragraph is a group of sentences about one main idea.

Write a beginning and an ending. Begin with an interesting sentence that tells a main idea about your topic. Write an ending that sums up what you think or feel about your topic.

Make connections. Use connecting words to tie your ideas together.

Ways to Make Connections	
Try this!	**Look at these examples.**
Tell the order of events.	before, after, finally, then, next, until, when, often
Link causes and their effects.	because, as a result, so that, therefore, if…then
Tell where something is.	above, around, down, here, there, beside, inside, outside, over, under
Link likenesses and differences.	however, although, in contrast, in the same way
Link a new idea to another one.	also, too, another, in addition

Drafting a Description

Learning from a Model Jermaine wrote a draft of his description. He thought of a good way to begin. Then he looked at his Sense Chart. He wrote sentences, using the details in the order that he numbered them in his chart. As he wrote, he thought of more details and added them.

My dog, Nikki, is a lovabul cocker spaniel. Nikki is ~~little~~ short

she has brown spots on her back and a brown tail. She has

buff-colored Ears. Her eyes are big. Her nose feels rough.

After she takes her bath, she smells good, but before she

takes a bath, peeyew! When she is eating, her breath smells

like burnt toast. Her bark ~~scares my little sister~~ is sure to

frighten you, but Nikki would never hurt anyone. She just

wants to be friendly!

▲ **Jermaine's working draft**

▶ Draft Your Description

Don't worry about fixing mistakes now.

❶ **Begin** by saying something interesting about your topic.

❷ **Use** your Sense Chart to help you write your working draft.

❸ **Write** sentences that tell the details about your topic. Skip every other line.

❹ **End** by telling what you think or feel about your topic.

What Is Revising?

When you revise, you add or take out words to make your paper clearer or more interesting. Ask yourself the big questions. Don't worry about mistakes yet.

How Do I Make Revisions?

Don't erase! Make changes on your draft. Don't worry if your paper looks messy. You can make a clean copy later. Here are ways to make changes.

Revising: The Big Questions
- Did I say what I wanted to say?
- Did I tell enough and use details?
- Did I organize the facts, events, or ideas in a clear order?
- Did I write in an interesting way that is right for my audience?

Ways to Make Revisions	
Try this!	**Look at these examples.**
Cross out words that you want to change or take out.	The wind ~~blew~~ howled outside our tent.
Use carets to add new words or sentences.	dainty gray A cat sat on the front steps.
Draw circles and arrows to move words, sentences, or paragraphs.	Dip your brush in the green paint. Wet your brush first.
Use numbers to show a new order.	② A baby horse can walk soon after it is born. ① A mother horse usually has one baby at a time. ③ It can see right away.
Add strips of paper, or "wings," to show long parts to be added.	My old bike is too small. I've grown four inches since I got it! My knees come up too high when I pedal. That makes it hard to ride.

Revising a Description

Learning from a Model Jermaine reread his draft. He crossed out some words that were not clear and added more exact words. He added a comparison to help his audience "see" Nikki's eyes.

My dog, Nikki, is a lovabul cocker spaniel. Nikki is ~~little~~ short ^and about two feet long^

she has brown spots on her back and a brown tail. She has ^floppy^

buff-colored Ears. Her eyes are ~~big.~~ ^as big as bouncy balls from a toy machine^ Her nose feels rough.

After she takes her bath, she smells ~~good,~~ ^fresh^ but before she

takes a bath, peeyew! When she is eating, her breath smells

like burnt toast. Her bark ~~scares my little sister~~ is sure to

frighten you, but Nikki would never hurt anyone. She just

wants to be friendly!

▲ **Jermaine's revised draft**

▶ **Revise Your Description**

Reread your description. Use the Revising Checklist to help you make changes. Use a thesaurus to find exact words.

Don't worry about fixing mistakes yet!

Revising Checklist

✔ Did I begin with something interesting about my topic?

✔ Where do I need to add sense words or details?

✔ Did I put the details in an order that makes sense?

✔ Does my ending tell what I think or feel about my topic?

📖 See the Thesaurus Plus on page H60.

What Is a Writing Conference?

In a writing conference, you read your paper to one or more listeners to find out if it is clear and interesting. You can read it to a friend, your teacher, someone in your family, or someone else you know.

How Do I Have a Writing Conference?

These guides will help you.

Guides for a Writing Conference	
When You're the Writer...	**When You're the Listener...**
• Read your paper aloud. Read clearly and slowly. • Listen carefully to what your partner says. • Take notes to remember any questions or suggestions. • After the conference, make any other changes you want.	• Listen carefully as the writer reads. • Retell what you have heard. • Then say something that you like about the paper. • Next, ask questions you have about the paper. • Finally, share any ideas you have that might make the paper clearer or more interesting for the audience. • Choose words that won't make the writer feel bad.

Your details help me really see your topic.

You use exact verbs, such as *ramble* and *splatter*.

Tell exactly what you liked about your partner's paper.

Having a Writing Conference

Learning from a Model Jermaine had a conference with his classmate Matt.

▶ Have Your Writing Conference

① **Have a writing conference** with a partner or a small group. Follow the guides on page 22.

② **Use** your notes from your conference to make any other changes you want.

What Is Proofreading?

When you proofread, you correct mistakes. You check that you used words correctly, wrote complete sentences, and started the first line of a paragraph a few spaces from the left. That is called **indenting**.

How Do I Proofread?

Choose from these ideas to help you proofread.

- Use proofreading marks.
- Proofread for one skill at a time.
- Hold a ruler or a strip of paper under each line as you check it.
- Read your paper aloud to yourself. You may hear mistakes.
- Circle any word that might be misspelled. Check spellings in a class dictionary.

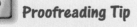

HELP?

Proofreading Tip

Remember **CUPS** when proofreading.
Capitalization
Usage
Punctuation
Spelling

Proofreading Marks		
Try this!	**Here's when.**	**Look at these examples.**
¶	to indent the first line of a paragraph	¶It was a snowy Monday in February. School had just been called off.
∧	to add letters, words, or punctuation marks	The hamster is smaller than ^the guinea pig.
⸜	to take out words, sentences, and punctuation marks or to correct spelling	They had ~~went~~ gone about two miles.
/	to change a capital letter to a small letter	Most Sea Horses live close to shore.
≡	to change a small letter to a capital letter	The new coach's name was mr. Green.

Proofreading a Description

Learning from a Model Jermaine made more changes to his description after talking with Matt. Then he proofread it.

¶My dog, Nikki, is a ~~lovabul~~ *lovable* cocker spaniel. Nikki is ~~little~~ short *and about two feet long.* she has brown spots on her back and a brown tail. She has *floppy,* buff-colored ~~E~~ears. Her eyes are big. *as big as bouncy balls from a toy machine* Her nose feels rough. *Her fur is soft.* After she takes her bath, she smells ~~good,~~ *fresh* but before she takes a bath, peeyew! When she is eating, her breath smells like burnt toast. Her bark ~~scares my little sister~~ *sounds like a souped-up motorcycle. It* is sure to frighten you, but Nikki would never hurt anyone. She just wants to be friendly!

▲ **Jermaine's proofread draft**

▶ **Proofread Your Description**

Use the Proofreading Checklist to help you proofread your description. Use the proofreading marks shown on page 24.

Proofreading Checklist

✔ Did I indent each paragraph?
✔ Did I write complete sentences?
✔ Did I begin each sentence with a capital letter and use the correct end mark?
✔ Did I correct any spelling errors?

📖 Use the Guide to Capitalization, Punctuation, and Usage on page H51 and the Spelling Guide on page H56 for help.

What Is Publishing?

When you publish your writing, you share it with your audience.

How Do I Publish My Writing?

Here are ideas for publishing and sharing your writing.

Helping Hands

Write It
- Send your paper as a letter or an e-mail to friends or family.
- Post your paper on the Internet.
- Put your paper with your classmates' papers to make a class book.

Say It
- Read your paper aloud from the Author's Chair.
- With friends, act out your paper.
- Record your paper on audiotape. Add sound effects.

Show It
- Add photographs, maps, drawings, or charts to your paper.
- Draw a comic strip to show with your writing.
- Make a poster to show with your paper.
- Show slides about your topic while reading your paper aloud.

Tech Tip
Make a multimedia presentation. See page H41 for ideas.

How Do I Reflect on My Writing?

When you reflect, you think about what you wrote. What did you do well? What could you do better next time? What are your goals for the next time you write?

You might want to keep a collection of your favorite papers.

Publishing a Description

Learning from a Model Jermaine made a neat, correct final copy of his description. Later, he put it on poster paper with pictures of Nikki and showed it to his classmates.

Jermaine Boddie

My Dog, Nikki
by Jermaine Boddie

My dog, Nikki, is a lovable cocker spaniel. Nikki is short and about two feet long. She has brown spots on her back and a brown tail. She has floppy, buff-colored ears. Her eyes are as big as bouncy balls from a toy machine. Her nose feels rough. Her fur is soft. After she takes her bath, she smells fresh, but before she takes a bath, peeyew! When she is eating, her breath smells like burnt toast. Her bark sounds like a souped-up motorcycle. It is sure to frighten you, but Nikki would never hurt anyone. She just wants to be friendly!

> Your details help me see, feel, smell, and hear Nikki. Great job!

> Your beginning and ending tell me how you feel about Nikki.

▶ Publish Your Description

❶ **Make** a final copy of your description. Use good handwriting.

❷ **Add** a title. Publish or share your description. Look at page 26 for ideas.

Will you keep this description? Use the paragraph on page 26 to help you reflect on your writing.

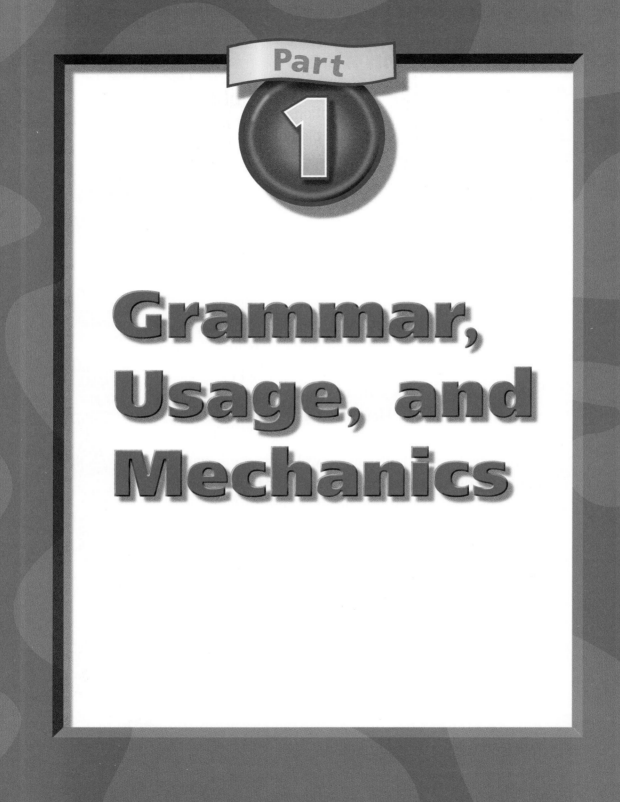

Part 1

Grammar, Usage, and Mechanics

What You Will Find in This Part:

Informal Language

When you talk with your friends or your family, you may not worry about using every word correctly. That's fine. When you write notes for yourself, it doesn't matter if every word, capital letter, or end mark is correct. YOU know what you mean.

Ideas for Show and Tell

photos of camping trip

~~my stamp collection~~

demonstrate making piñata

...ut a mouse named ...nd father in a ...say to keep out ...does not do what ...loves to nap on the soft velvet. One day, the case where he is sleeping gets packed on a truck. When Gigio wakes up, he is on a plane! The rest of the story tells how Gigio finds his way home.

My Opinion: This story is really funny! Sometimes Gigio uses Italian words like <u>ciao</u>! They're fun to learn. The The pictures are really cute.

Formal Language

In school and many times outside of school, though, you need to talk and write in a more formal way. This part of the book will help you learn to use formal language when you need it.

The Sentence

Stop the bus.
This isn't going to be
boring after all.
The tigers are so close!
Who brought a camera?

1 What Is a Sentence?

DOGS BY GAIL GIBBONS

Read the sentences below. Whom or what are the sentences about? What happens?

A happy dog wags its tail. An angry dog sometimes bares its teeth.

—from *Dogs*, by Gail Gibbons

A **sentence** is a group of words that tells a complete thought. It tells who or what, and it tells what happens.

Not Sentences	Sentences
My best friend.	My best friend found a dog.
Barks all night.	The dog barks all night.

My best friend tells who or what. It does not tell what happens. *Barks all night* tells what happens. It does not tell who or what. How do you know that the words on the right are sentences?

Try It Out

Speak Up Which groups of words are sentences? Which groups are not sentences? Why?

1. Buddy does many tricks.
2. Buddy barks.
3. Big paws and floppy ears.
4. He sleeps all day.
5. His favorite rubber ball.
6. Plays with the cat.
7. They never fight.

Read the two groups of words after each number. Write the group of words that is a sentence.

Example: Live in the water.

Beavers live in ponds.   *Beavers live in ponds.*

8. Good swimmers.   **10.** Beavers steer with their tails.
   Beavers swim fast.   Can swim under the water.
9. They have flat tails. **11.** A thick coat of soft fur.
   Look like paddles.   Their fur keeps them warm in cold water.

12–15. Read these notes for a report on beavers. Write each group of words that is a sentence.

Example: • Beavers work hard.   *Beavers work hard.*
          • Together in small groups.

- Beavers cut down trees.
- Very strong front teeth.

- Beavers make houses out of twigs.
- Made of big twigs and small stones.

- Mud from the river.
- Mud holds the twigs together.

- Young beavers stay warm.
- Warm all winter long.

WRITING • THINKING • LISTENING • SPEAKING

INFORMING

Writing Wrap-Up

Write a List of Facts

Write three sentences about your favorite animal. For example, you might write, *Whales eat tiny shrimp called krill.* Then read your list of facts to a partner. Have your partner identify the sentences.

Writing Good Sentences

Writing Complete Sentences Good writers use complete sentences to make their meaning clear. Sometimes you can fix a sentence that is not complete by adding it to a complete one.

This parakeet comes from Australia.
And is called a budgie.
} This parakeet comes from Australia and is called a budgie.

Apply It

1–4. Rewrite the captions on this poster. Fix each incomplete sentence by adding it to a complete sentence.

The Budgie

The Budgie is a good bird!

Years ago budgies lived only in the wild. But later became pets too.

Tame budgies can learn to say words. And even sentences.

Wild budgies are mostly green. And have yellow faces.

Budgies use their sharp beaks. To crack seeds and to climb branches.

A complete sentence tells who or what, and it also tells what happens. Your writing will be easy to understand if you use complete sentences.

The writing below has some incomplete sentences.

> The macaw is a beautiful bird in the parrot family. Has the brightest colors of all the parrots. Likes to eat fruit.

The writer fixed the sentences by telling who or what.

> The macaw is a beautiful bird in the parrot family. It has the brightest colors of all the parrots. The macaw likes to eat fruit.

Remember that you can sometimes fix an incomplete sentence by joining it to a complete sentence.

A macaw can learn to talk.
But usually just screeches.
} A macaw can learn to talk but usually just screeches.

Apply It

5–10. Rewrite these paragraphs from a first draft of a report about parrots. Fix each incomplete sentence.

Revising

The macaw is a large parrot. Has a big beak. That strong beak is needed. To crack hard nuts for food. Only one other kind of parrot has such a large beak. Is called the cockatoo.

Be careful when you go near macaws! They sometimes bite other animals. And people too. Can be tamed. Need many things to chew on so they won't bite their owners. They make very nice pets.

2 Statements and Questions

Think of a riddle to try out on your classmates. Use a question to ask the riddle and a sentence that tells to answer it.

Riddle: Why did the coach spill the lemonade?

Answer: Something was wrong with the pitcher.

Every sentence begins with a capital letter. There are four kinds of sentences. Statements and questions are two kinds.

- **A sentence that tells something is a statement.** It ends with a period.

    Statements: Tyler runs every morning.
    He jogs around the lake.

- **A sentence that asks something is a question.** It ends with a question mark.

    Questions: How far does Tyler run?
    Can he run a mile?

Try It Out

Speak Up Is each sentence a statement or a question? What mark should end each sentence?

1. Megan is my neighbor
2. What is her best sport
3. It is softball
4. She can play with us
5. Can she pitch
6. Megan can catch

Write *statement* if the sentence tells something. Write *question* if the sentence asks something.

Example: Carlos is my best friend.   *statement*

7. Where is Carlos?
8. We like to play soccer.
9. Would you like to play?
10. Can you kick the ball?

11. Will you come to the game?
12. You can meet us later.
13. My brother is coming too.
14. I will find Carlos.

15–20. This sports interview has two missing capital letters and four missing or incorrect end marks. Write the interview correctly.

Example: Reporter: when is your next game
   Reporter: When is your next game?

Proofreading

A Talk with the Coach

Reporter: your team won again. Were you
             surprised

Coach Brag: Why should I be surprised? My team
             is the best?

Reporter: How do your players keep winning. what is
             their secret?

Coach Brag: It is no secret. They have the best coach

Writing Wrap-Up WRITING • THINKING • LISTENING • SPEAKING

EXPRESSING

Write an Interview

Think of someone you would like to know more about. It could be a friend, a family member, or anyone. Write three questions you would like to ask that person. Have a partner make up statements for the answers. Act out the interview for your class.

3 Commands and Exclamations

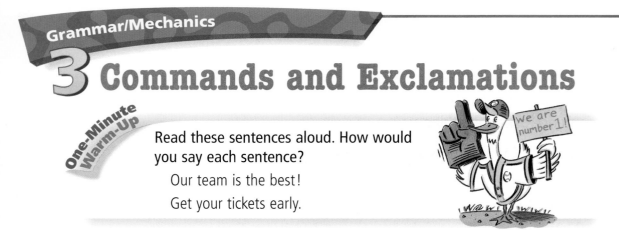

Read these sentences aloud. How would you say each sentence?

Our team is the best!

Get your tickets early.

You have learned about two kinds of sentences, statements and questions. Two other kinds of sentences are commands and exclamations.

- **A command is a sentence that tells someone to do something.** It ends with a period.

  Commands: Please hold my bat.
  Watch the ball.

- **An exclamation is a sentence that shows strong feeling, such as excitement, surprise, or fear.** It ends with an exclamation point (!).

  Exclamations: She hit a home run!
  Our team won the game!

Try It Out

Speak Up Is each sentence a command or an exclamation?

1. Baseball is great!
2. Please play with us.
3. Pick up the bat.
4. Here comes the ball!
5. Hit the ball hard.
6. It is over the fence!

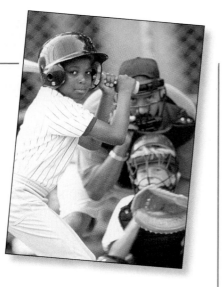

Write each sentence correctly. The word in ( ) will tell you if the sentence is a command or an exclamation.

Example: she is a great pitcher (exclamation)
She is a great pitcher!

7. paul caught the ball (exclamation)
8. throw the ball to first base (command)
9. please hand me my helmet (command)
10. i hit a home run (exclamation)
11. swing the bat higher (command)
12. rita got a base hit (exclamation)
13. we are winning (exclamation)
14. meet me after the game (command)

15–20. These signs have two missing capital letters and four missing end marks. Write the signs correctly.

Example: support your team *Support your team.*

Proofreading

Come to the playoff game it will be so exciting!

Buy your ticket in the school office

please bring a friend You will have a great time

Writing Wrap-Up

WRITING • THINKING • LISTENING • SPEAKING

INFORMING

Write a Sign

Write a sign for a special day at your school or an event in your town. Include commands and exclamations. Draw a picture for your sign, using bright colors. Then read your sign to a small group. Ask volunteers to name the end marks.

4 The Subject of a Sentence

Read the sentence below. Whom or what is the sentence about?

> The big waves crashed against a rocky reef far away.
>
> —from *Iguana Beach*, by Kristine Franklin

- You know that a sentence is a group of words that tells a complete thought. **The subject is the part of a sentence that tells whom or what the sentence is about.** The subject usually comes at the beginning of the sentence.

  The subject of the first sentence below is *Sam.* What are the subjects of the other sentences?

  > Sam walked to the beach.
  > He brought a towel.
  > The rocky beach looked crowded.
  > Some people sat under umbrellas.

- The subject can be one word or more than one word. You can always find the subject of a sentence by asking, *Whom or what is the sentence about?*

Try It Out

Speak Up What is the subject of each sentence?

1. The ocean looked pretty.
2. Some big waves splashed.
3. Two young girls played in the sand.
4. They made a castle.
5. Beautiful shells lay on the sand.

Write each sentence. Underline the subject.

Example: The owl hooted loudly.   *The owl hooted loudly.*

6. My family went on a vacation.
7. We stayed in a cabin.
8. The cabin was in the woods.
9. Joey saw a baby rabbit.
10. I heard an owl.
11. A red squirrel ran up a tree.
12. My older sister walked to the lake.
13. Two frogs jumped into the water.
14. Melissa jumped in after them.

15–22. Write this e-mail message. Underline the subject of each sentence.

Example: The weather is hot! *The weather is hot!*

---

e-mail

To: Austin
Subject: Vacation
　　We started our vacation with Grandpa today.
His farm has a big red barn. Four cows sleep there.
One brown cow has a calf. The calf ate grass from my
hand. Hens live on the farm too. I found six eggs this
morning. Fresh eggs taste great!

Writing Wrap-Up　WRITING • THINKING • LISTENING • SPEAKING

DESCRIBING

Write a Post Card

　　Write a post card describing a special place you know. Make sure
that each sentence has a subject. Then put your post card in a class
mailbox. Take your turn picking a card to read to the class. Can your
classmates guess who wrote the post card?

---

5 The Predicate of a Sentence

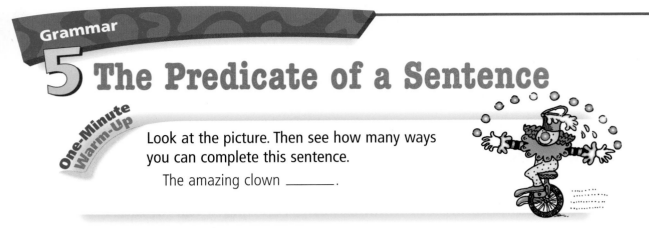

Look at the picture. Then see how many ways you can complete this sentence.

The amazing clown _____.

Every sentence has two parts. The subject is one part of a sentence. The other part of the sentence is the predicate. **The predicate is the part of a sentence that tells what the subject does or is.** The predicate can be one word or more than one word.

Subject	Predicate
Jessica	won a prize.
The crowd	clapped.
She	is happy.
Her brother	rode on the rides.
He	had fun.
The children	ate a lot of food.

Try It Out

Speak Up What is the predicate of each sentence?

1. People hurry to the fair.
2. Music floats through the air.
3. A man sells balloons.
4. The clown is funny.
5. Jillian laughs.
6. We bought a ticket for a ride.
7. The ride was scary.

Write each sentence. Underline the predicate.

Example: Emily takes swimming lessons.
Emily <u>takes swimming lessons</u>.

8. Josh goes with her.
9. They take lessons together.
10. Each lesson lasts an hour.
11. The two children listen.
12. A coach teaches Emily.
13. Another coach watches Josh.
14. They follow the safety rules.
15. Josh dives from the board.
16. He dives well.
17. Emily cheers.

18–25. Write this sportscast. Underline the predicate of each sentence.

Example: The diver waits her turn.   *The diver <u>waits her turn</u>.*

Kim climbs the ladder. She steps onto the diving board. Her face looks calm. The crowd waits. Kim dives. Her body flips twice in the air. The dive is perfect. This young girl has talent!

WRITING • THINKING • LISTENING • SPEAKING

NARRATING

Write a Story About Yourself

Write a paragraph about something you like to do, such as playing a favorite game or drawing pictures. Each sentence should have a subject and a predicate. Read your story to a partner. Does your partner like to do the same thing?

6 Correcting Run-on Sentences

One-Minute Warm-Up

Buy your tickets here trains leave every hour.

Can you find two sentences in this sign? Where should you put a period and a capital letter?

- **Two or more sentences that run together are called run-on sentences.** Use end marks and capital letters correctly to keep sentences from running together.

  Wrong: Have you ridden on a train it is fun.
  Right: Have you ridden on a train? It is fun.

- Do not use a comma to separate two sentences.

  Wrong: Erin likes trains, she takes train trips.
  Right: Erin likes trains. She takes train trips.

Try It Out

Speak Up How can you correct these run-on sentences?

1. The train is fast the wheels are loud.
2. The train goes to cities it makes many stops.
3. Where else does it go it travels everywhere.
4. Erin sits by a window the world rushes by.
5. Does Erin see many farms once she saw cows.
6. She saw a big tractor a dog ran after it.
7. Erin waved to a farmer, he waved back.

Write two sentences for each run-on sentence.

Example: I have a garden it is big.   *I have a garden. It is big.*

8. Would you like to see it do you have time?
9. My garden is rocky I rake out the rocks.
10. I need to pull the weeds, they grow so fast.
11. Some weeds are big I dig them out.
12. I planted flowers, which ones do you like?
13. Do you want to smell them they smell sweet.

14–18. This part of a magazine article has five run-on sentences.
Write the article correctly.

Example: Sunflowers are huge some sunflowers are ten feet tall.
        Sunflowers are huge. Some sunflowers are ten feet tall.

Proofreading

Giants of the Garden

Have you ever seen sunflowers they look
like giant daisies. Sunflowers are a source of
food for birds and people sunflower seeds are
good to eat. The seeds taste like nuts you can
roast them or eat them raw. Make sure you
remove the shells first! There is oil inside the
seeds, people use it for cooking. Do you like
salads then try a salad with sunflower sprouts.

Writing Wrap-Up   WRITING • THINKING • LISTENING • SPEAKING

EXPLAINING

Write Instructions

Write a list of instructions on how to prepare your favorite kind of
food. Then read your instructions to a partner. Have your partner act
them out. Work together to check for run-on sentences.

Writing Good Sentences

Fixing Run-on Sentences You already know how to fix a run-on sentence by breaking it into two sentences. You can also add a comma (,) and the word *and* to make one complete sentence.

Wrong: Gardening teaches science it is a great hobby too.

Right: Gardening teaches science, and it is a great hobby too.

Apply It

1–6. Revise this part of a letter to a school principal. Fix the six run-on sentences by adding a comma (,) and the word *and*.

Revising

Dear Mrs. Koval,

    I have an idea for our class I will tell you about it. Our class is learning about plants we are growing some flower seeds. We could learn even more with our own garden. My friend's class planted a garden the flowers won first prize at the Science Fair.

    Outside our classroom is an old field. No one uses the land it is full of weeds. Flowers would grow well there the field would look beautiful. The whole class would work on the garden the parents would help too. Would you think about this idea?

               Sincerely,

               Austin Barnes

Combining Sentences Too many short sentences make writing sound choppy. Good writers use sentences of different lengths. Sometimes two short sentences have ideas that go together. You can combine them to make one longer sentence. Use a comma (,) and the word *and, but,* or *or* when you combine two sentences.

The flowers grew fast.   The flowers grew fast, but
The weeds grew faster.   the weeds grew faster.

Apply It

7–10. Write each pair of sentences as one sentence. Use the word in ( ) to combine the sentences.

Revising

Science in Bloom

Melissa dug a hole. Brian put in a plant. (and)

The plants need water. They will dry up. (or)

We must weed often. The weeds will take over! (or)

Two plants were short. The others grew tall. (but)

Enrichment

Sentences!

Sentence Scramble

Players: 2

Materials: You need 25 index cards. Write on them the words *the, children, big, ran, in, after, them, a, parrots, little, saw, to, but, and, some, old, an, castle, were, with, and, the, we, monkey, they.*

To play: Take turns making sentences with the cards. Say where capital letters and end marks should be. Ask your partner if your sentence is correct.

Scoring: Each word in a correct sentence earns 2 points. Subtract 5 points for each run-on sentence. The player with the highest score wins.

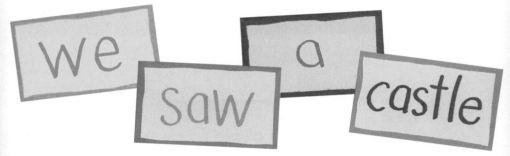

Invent a Cereal

You work at a cereal company. Your job is to invent a new cereal. It must be healthful and also fun to eat. Write an ad for your cereal. Use commands and exclamations to get people to buy it.

Try some Crunchies. They are great!

Crunchies

Challenge Write an ad that has all four kinds of sentences. Make the first sentence a question, the second a statement, the third an exclamation, and the fourth a command.

1 **What Is a Sentence?** *(p. 32)* Read the two groups of words after each number. Write the group that is a sentence.

1. Many dark clouds.
   The sky turned dark.
2. The sun disappeared.
   The sun away.
3. Hurt my ears.
   I heard thunder.
4. It rained all day.
   Water for the flowers.
5. I wore my raincoat.
   Boots by the door.
6. Splashed in puddles.
   My feet got wet.

2 **Statements and Questions** *(p. 36)* Write each sentence correctly.

7. what is the weather like at the South Pole
8. it is very cold all year long
9. has anyone ever been to the South Pole
10. an explorer named Amundsen reached it first
11. he and his men rode on dogsleds

3 **Commands and Exclamations** *(p. 38)* Write *command* if the sentence tells someone to do something. Write *exclamation* if the sentence shows strong feeling.

12. It is such a beautiful day!
13. Please come to the beach with us.
14. Put the towel under the umbrella.
15. Here comes a huge wave!
16. The water is freezing!

4 **The Subject of a Sentence** *(p. 40)* Write each sentence. Underline the subject.

17. Tara plays the piano.
18. She practices every day.
19. Mr. George Massey gives Tara lessons.
20. Her three brothers wait outside.

5 The Predicate of a Sentence *(p. 42)* Write each sentence. Underline the predicate.

21. A map is like a picture.
22. Most maps have symbols.
23. Symbols stand for real places or things.
24. Ana found her street on a map.

6 Correcting Run-on Sentences *(p. 44)* Write each run-on sentence as two sentences.

25. Mom tells stories some stories are about me.
26. One story is funny it is about my pet spider.
27. Does your family tell stories do you hear the same stories many times?
28. My uncle tells the best stories they are about his adventures as a sailor.

Mixed Review 29–34. This part of a science report has two missing capital letters and four missing or incorrect end marks. Write the report correctly.

Proofreading Checklist

Did you write these correctly?
✔ capital letters
✔ end marks

Proofreading

Amazing Animals

What animal can run the fastest. cheetahs are the fastest runners over a short distance. The cheetah is a member of the cat family. Its light brown fur is covered with small black spots, two black stripes run down its face. The cheetah can sprint more than sixty miles an hour on its long legs.

Cheetahs are wild animals They are quite gentle though. A ruler in Asia once owned one thousand tame cheetahs? Find out more about these amazing animals at your local library.

 **Test Practice**

Write the numbers 1–8 on a sheet of paper. Choose the correct end mark for each sentence. Write the letter for that answer.

1 Workers are fixing the road
   A .   **B** ?   **C** !   **D** None

2 Why do the stars twinkle at night
   F !   **G** .   **H** ?   **J** None

3 Please hang this poster on the door
   A !   **B** .   **C** ?   **D** None

4 I had such a scary dream last night
   F .   **G** ?   **H** !   **J** None

5 Bring the salad bowl to the dinner table
   A ?   **B** .   **C** !   **D** None

6 Mom and I will go to the library this afternoon
   F !   **G** ?   **H** .   **J** None

7 Should we draw with crayons or markers
   A ?   **B** .   **C** !   **D** None

8 Corey can hardly wait until summer vacation
   F .   **G** !   **H** ?   **J** None

Write the numbers 9–14 on your paper. Read the passage and look at the numbered, underlined parts. Choose the correct way to write each underlined part. If it is already correct, choose "Correct as it is." Write the letter for the answer you choose.

A spider uses its web to catch insects for <u>food the</u> spider's
(9)
web is <u>sticky insects</u> get trapped in it. The spider eats these
(10)
helpless <u>insects? but</u> the spider does not get trapped in its own
(11)
web. Do you know <u>why? Only</u> some threads of the web are
(12)
<u>sticky, Other</u> threads are not sticky. The spider knows the
(13)
<u>difference. it</u> stays off the sticky threads.
(14)

9 A food. the

  B food. The

  C food and. The

  D Correct as it is

10 F sticky? Insects

  G sticky. insects

  H sticky, and insects

  J Correct as it is

11 A insects but

  B insects, but

  C insects? But

  D Correct as it is

12 F why and only

  G why. Only

  H why? only

  J Correct as it is

13 A sticky. Other

  B sticky! other

  C sticky other

  D Correct as it is

14 F difference, It

  G difference? it

  H difference. It

  J Correct as it is

(pages 32–33)

1 What Is a Sentence?

Remember

- A sentence is a group of words that tells a complete thought.
- It tells *who* or *what*, and it tells *what happens.*

● Make these words into sentences. Use words from the box to complete each sentence.

barks	shines brightly	splash in the water
A little boy	sails into the air	Pretty shells

Example: The sun _____. *The sun shines brightly.*

1. Many children _____.
2. _____ are in a pail.
3. A balloon _____.
4. _____ plays in the sand.
5. A dog _____.

▲ Write *sentence* if the group of words is a sentence. Write *not a sentence* if it is not a sentence.

Example: I saw a puppet show.   *sentence*

6. Three puppets on strings.
7. The puppets sang a song.
8. On the stage.
9. Many people came to the show.
10. They liked the show.

■ Use each group of words to write a sentence.

Example: a paper bag puppet   *Maria made a paper bag puppet.*

11. small lunch bag
12. stuffed the bag
13. a funny face
14. string and yarn
15. buttons for eyes

(pages 36–37)

2 Statements and Questions

> **Remember**
>
> • All sentences begin with a capital letter.
> • A statement is a sentence that tells something. It ends with a period.
> • A question is a sentence that asks something. It ends with a question mark.

● Write *statement* if the sentence tells something. Write *question* if the sentence asks something.

Example: When did dinosaurs live?   *question*

1. Dinosaurs lived long ago.
2. Many dinosaurs were very large.
3. How big were they?
4. Some dinosaurs were seventy feet long.
5. How can I learn more about dinosaurs?

▲ Write each sentence. Use the correct end mark.

Example: What is a tiger   *What is a tiger?*

6. A tiger is a wild cat
7. It has orange fur with black stripes
8. Is a tiger as big as a lion
9. Where does a tiger live
10. A tiger lives in the jungle

■ Write each sentence correctly.

Example: have you ever seen a giant panda
Have you ever seen a giant panda?

11. what does a giant panda look like
12. it looks like a large bear
13. the panda has black and white fur
14. where can you find giant pandas
15. some giant pandas are in zoos

(pages 38–39)

3 Commands and Exclamations

Remember

- A command is a sentence that tells someone to do something. It ends with a period.
- An exclamation is a sentence that shows strong feeling. It ends with an exclamation point (!).

● Write *command* if the sentence tells someone to do something. Write *exclamation* if the sentence shows strong feeling.

Example: Throw the football. *command*

1. Start the game.
2. We are ahead!
3. Listen to the coach.
4. Wear your helmet.
5. Dave caught the pass!
6. This game is exciting!

▲ Write each command or exclamation correctly.

Example: help me build the doghouse (command)

Help me build the doghouse.

7. this doghouse will be great (exclamation)
8. get a hammer (command)
9. bring the nails (command)
10. fifi is running in circles (exclamation)
11. count the boards (command)
12. we finally finished (exclamation)

■ Write *statement, question, command,* or *exclamation* for each sentence.

Example: Today is the big race! *exclamation*

13. Will you enter the race?
14. Take along some water.
15. My parents will be there.
16. The race will be close!
17. When does it start?
18. I hope I win!

(pages 40–41)

4 The Subject of a Sentence

- The subject tells whom or what the sentence is about. Remember

● Write the subject of each sentence.

Example: The weather|is warm. *The weather*

1. Two robins|build a nest.
2. The children|picked flowers.
3. Dali|washed the car.
4. A yellow kite|floated by.
5. Dogs|played behind a rock.
6. We|planned a picnic for Amy.

▲ Write the subject of each sentence.

Example: My family likes the winter. *My family*

7. The wind feels cold.
8. We wear warm jackets and gloves.
9. Josh carries his sled to the park.
10. My little sister slides down the hill.
11. She laughs.
12. Our funny snowman has a big head.
13. Dad chops wood in the backyard.

■ Change the silly subject in each sentence to a subject that makes sense. Write the new sentences. Underline the subjects.

Example: Radio won a prize. *Jamal won a prize.*

14. My parents sing in the trees.
15. The dog mows the lawn.
16. Baby helps him rake the leaves.
17. Our new car has a pool.
18. The tree gave a pool party yesterday.
19. The young pencils played tag.
20. My favorite fruit is the summer.

(pages 42–43)

5 The Predicate of a Sentence

- The predicate is the part of a sentence that tells what the subject does or is.

Remember

● Write the predicate of each sentence.

Example: The sky|looks dark.   *looks dark*

1. Lightning|flashes.
2. Rain|begins to fall.
3. Thunder|rumbles in the sky.
4. Some people|run for cover.
5. The storm|is over quickly.
6. The sun|shines again.

▲ Write each sentence. Draw a line between the subject and the predicate.

Example: Uncle Steve is a circus clown.
Uncle Steve|is a circus clown.

7. His nose is big and red.
8. He juggles three balls in the air.
9. Funny cars chase him around the ring.
10. A black hat drops on the floor.
11. A large bird flies out of the hat.
12. All the people clap.

■ Write each sentence. Draw one line under the subject. Draw two lines under the predicate.

Example: The forest animals listened for danger.
The forest animals listened for danger.

13. A deer leaped over the logs.
14. Two small rabbits were afraid.
15. The gray squirrels ran up a tree.
16. Raccoons hid in a hollow log.
17. A chipmunk family dug a hole.
18. Some owls hooted.

(pages 44–45)

⑥ Run-on Sentences

- Two or more sentences that run together are called run-on sentences.
- Do not run sentences together.

Remember

● Write each run-on sentence as two sentences. The line shows where the first sentence ends and the second sentence begins.

Example: Birds are fun | do you like them?
Birds are fun. Do you like them?

1. What do birds eat | some birds eat seeds.
2. Robins often eat worms | owls eat mice.
3. Andy has a pet duck | it is big and fluffy.
4. My parrot talks | what does it say?

▲ Write each run-on sentence as two sentences.

Example: The city is busy it is very noisy.
The city is busy. It is very noisy.

5. People drive to work they honk their horns.
6. Buses pass by where are they going?
7. Workers build a bridge it is long.
8. A police officer blows her whistle a car stops.
9. Stores are open do you want to shop?

■ Some sentences below are run-on sentences. Write each run-on sentence correctly. Write *correct* if the sentence is correct.

Example: Some stars are very bright. *correct*

10. Stars are many sizes they are many colors.
11. Our sun is a yellow star is it very hot?
12. Some people see pictures in the stars.
13. Do some groups of stars look like animals?
14. One group looks like a bear another looks like a lion.

Nouns

What has ten eyes like
marbles, five black muzzles,
and lots of cuddly wool?

1 What Are Nouns?

Read the sentence below. What words name persons, places, or things?

> Finally the lights dim, a drum rolls, and the band launches into a lively tune.

—from *Big-Top Circus,* by Neil Johnson

A word that names a person, a place, or a thing is a noun.

cousin

town

tickets

Persons	My cousin and his friends are excited.
Places	They're going to the circus. It's in town.
Things	They saved their money for the tickets.

Try It Out

Speak Up One noun is underlined in each sentence. Find the other noun.

1. The clowns have funny <u>noses</u>.
2. Their hats and <u>shoes</u> are floppy.
3. Trained elephants do <u>tricks</u>.
4. Their long trunks spray <u>water</u>.
5. The <u>lions</u> and tigers are scary.
6. A young <u>girl</u> rides on a pony.
7. The people always love the <u>circus</u>.

Write the nouns in each sentence. Each sentence has two nouns.

Example: This city has an airport.   *city   airport*

8. A busy airport has many buildings.
9. Some children watch the airplanes.
10. A tall man carries a big bag.
11. Several women buy tickets.
12. Two girls walk to the gate.
13. Small shops sell gifts.
14. A plane rises into the sky.
15. That family is flying to another country.

16–25. This poem has ten nouns. Write the poem. Underline the nouns.

Example: The world looks strange from a plane.
The <u>world</u> looks strange from a <u>plane</u>.

An Airplane Ride
The airplane flies high in the sky.
The streets and towns are tiny.
Fields like patchwork quilts go by.
Rivers and lakes are shiny.
Could that be a truck down there?
It looks so small from up in the air!

Writing Wrap-Up

WRITING • THINKING • LISTENING • SPEAKING

CREATING

Write a Poem

Write a short poem naming some things you see every day. Each sentence should include one or two nouns. Then read your poem to a small group. Have them name the nouns you used.

2 Common and Proper Nouns

Name the people, places, and things in the picture. Then think of special names for each of the things you named.

- You have learned that a noun names a person, a place, or a thing. **A noun that names any person, place, or thing is called a common noun. A noun that names a particular person, place, or thing is called a proper noun.**

Common Nouns	Proper Nouns
My friend swam today.	Stacy swam today.
Her dog went with her.	Buddy went with her.
The lake was cold.	Pine Lake was cold.

- Proper nouns begin with capital letters. A proper noun, like *Pine Lake,* may have more than one word. Begin each important word in a proper noun with a capital letter.

Try It Out

Speak Up Is each noun a common noun or a proper noun?

1. Ash Road
2. country
3. Mexico
4. David Robinson
5. teacher
6. Thanksgiving

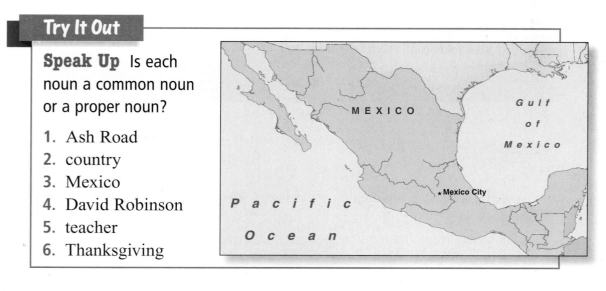

MEXICO

Gulf of Mexico

★ Mexico City

Pacific Ocean

Write each noun. Then write *common* after each common noun and *proper* after each proper noun.

Example: My family visited the Stone Museum.

family common   Stone Museum proper

7. The new museum opened in May.
8. This building has a large room with seats.
9. People can see the stars.
10. Jupiter, Saturn, and other planets can be studied.
11. The North Star does not seem to move.
12. A movie shows pictures of astronauts.
13. The first man on the moon was Neil Armstrong.

14–20. This online newspaper article has seven missing capital letters. Write the article correctly.

Example: jon learned about venus. *Jon learned about Venus.*

Proofreading

News

Do you want to know more about space? **Click Here**

Space Center Welcomes Children

The Freeman Space Center on foster road has a new room for children. Boys and girls watch a film about the planets. Then they take a make-believe trip to mars. Students from the prospect school enjoyed their journey. "We want to go again!" said diana fazio.

Writing Wrap-Up   WRITING • THINKING • LISTENING • SPEAKING

PERSUADING

Write a Contest Entry

Outer Space, Inc., is having a contest. The prize is a trip to Pluto. Write a paragraph explaining why you should win. Include proper nouns. Read your entry to a partner. Would your partner give you the prize?

3 Nouns in the Subject

Read the sentences below. What is each sentence about?

The park was cool, shady. A million red leaves were drifting off the trees.

—from *Pet Parade,* by Patricia Reilly Giff

You know that the subject of a sentence tells whom or what the sentence is about. The main word in the subject is often a noun.

Spencer watched an animal show.

Some **children** fed the ducks.

A little **girl** petted a goat.

Seals did tricks.

Two **boys** got wet.

Try It Out

Speak Up The subject of each sentence is underlined. What is the noun in the subject?

1. A <u>helicopter</u> landed.
2. <u>Two children</u> bought tickets.
3. <u>Sandy</u> wanted a ride.
4. <u>The pilot</u> waved.
5. <u>A woman</u> got on board.
6. <u>My older sister</u> sat down next to me.
7. <u>The helicopter</u> took off.
8. <u>The blue sky</u> seemed close.
9. <u>Big houses</u> looked tiny from the air.
10. <u>The ride</u> was too short.
11. <u>My father</u> waited for us at the gate.

Write the noun in the subject of each sentence.

Example: Green School held a field day. *Green School*

12. The first race started at one o'clock.
13. Adam wore his lucky sneakers.
14. The whistle blew loudly.
15. Teachers timed the race.
16. Peter ran fast.
17. Two girls passed Peter.
18. A tall boy moved ahead.
19. The race was close.
20. Carmen Alvarez was the winner!

21–26. Write these captions. Underline the noun in each subject.

Example: The year ends with a win! *The year ends with a win!*

Our Yearbook

The Tigers make the winning play.
A surprising result thrills fans!
Mark Samson gets an award.
The Bumblebees sting the Tigers.
Three sisters show off their medals.
Excited fans go wild with joy!

Writing Wrap-Up
WRITING • THINKING • LISTENING • SPEAKING

DESCRIBING

Write Captions

Think of some exciting things that happen in your school. Draw a picture of each one. Then write captions for your pictures. Use a noun in the subject of each sentence. Read your captions to a partner. Have your partner choose the drawing that goes with each caption.

Writing with Nouns

Elaborating Sentences You can make a sentence clearer by adding a noun that tells more about the subject. Put the noun and any words that go with it right after the subject.

Use a comma (,) before and after the words you add about the subject.

Elly throws the ball home.

Elly, our best shortstop, throws the ball home.

Apply It

1–3. Write more information about the subject of each yearbook photo. Choose the best group of words from the card. A caret (∧) shows where to add the words and the commas. The first caption is done for you.

Revising

, a quick runner,

, a strong batter,

, a fast swimmer,

, a good soccer player,

Brett, a quick runner, wins the race!

Felipe ∧ leads the team.

Julia ∧ slams a home run!

Patrick ∧ scores again!

Combining Sentences Sometimes two short sentences have the same predicate. You can put the sentences together by combining the subjects. This will make your writing smoother.

> Use the word *and* when you join two subjects.

Tamika ran fast.
Her brother ran fast. } Tamika and her brother ran fast.

Apply It

4–8. Read this article from a school newspaper. Combine each pair of underlined sentences.

Revising

Sports Fair Is a Success!

Students enjoyed the Sports Fair. Their families enjoyed the Sports Fair. All events started early in the morning. Cool weather made the day a success. Good teamwork made the day a success.

Many third graders took part in the events. Nicole performed in the tumbling show. Berta performed in the tumbling show. They did an exciting act. Frederico entered the pitching contest. Kristie entered the pitching contest. Frederico won third prize. All the students did their best. The teachers were proud. The students were proud.

4 Singular and Plural Nouns

Read the sentence below. What nouns name one person, place, or thing? What nouns name more than one person, place, or thing?

> As the wedding party moved through the forest, brightly plumed birds darted about in the cool green shadows beneath the trees.
>
> —from *Mufaro's Beautiful Daughters,* by John Steptoe

A noun that names only one person, place, or thing is a singular noun. A noun that names more than one person, place, or thing is a plural noun. Add *-s* to most singular nouns to form the plural.

Singular Nouns	Plural Nouns
Julie climbed a tree.	Julie climbed two trees.
She played on a swing.	She played on some swings.

Try It Out

Speak Up Is each noun below singular or plural?

1. brother
2. crayons
3. baseballs
4. trail
5. parade
6. painters

What is the plural of each underlined noun?

7. Two brothers rode to the park.
8. A girl walked her dogs.
9. One dog found a bone.
10. Ann bought a pretty balloon.
11. Three birds flew out of a nest.

Write each underlined noun. Then write *singular* or *plural* beside each one.

Example: Grandmother came to visit the girls. *girls plural*

12. She brought two <u>trunks</u> filled with old clothes.
13. Bethany showed the clothes to her <u>sister</u>.
14. They had a costume party with some <u>friends</u>.
15. Tina wore funny <u>shoes</u>.
16. Rita put on a straw <u>hat</u>.
17. Jon tried on an old <u>jacket</u>.
18. It had gold <u>buttons</u> down the front.

19–24. This invitation has four incorrect singular nouns and two incorrect plural nouns. Write the invitation correctly.

Example: Do you have a goofy hats? *Do you have a goofy hat?*

Proofreading

Come to a Costume Party!

When: Friday at 2:00 Where: Room 401
Bring all your friend!
Will you wear a crazy wigs or some donkey ears?
How many color can you paint your face?
A judge will choose the two best costume.
Both winner get a prize.
There will be a treats for everyone!

Writing Wrap-Up WRITING • THINKING • LISTENING • SPEAKING

CREATING

Write an Invitation

Plan a party. What will you do for fun? Write an invitation for the party. Use plural nouns in your sentences. Read your invitation to a partner. Have your partner name the plural nouns you used.

5 Plural Nouns with -es

Make up a story about this picture.
How many plural nouns can you include?

You know that you add -s to most nouns to form the plural. Add -es to form the plural of a singular noun that ends with s, sh, ch, or x.

Singular: class   brush   lunch
Plural: class**es**   brush**es**   lunch**es**

Try It Out

Speak Up What is the plural of each noun?

1. fox   2. sash   3. beach   4. address

On Your Own

5–10. This list has six incorrect plural nouns. Write the list correctly.

Example: Buy bunchs of grapes.   *Buy bunches of grapes.*

❏ Make two batchs of sandwiches.
❏ Wash all the dishs.
❏ Make two doll dress.

❏ Find both boxs of paints.
❏ Paint three toy bus.
❏ Rinse all the brushs.

Writing Wrap-Up

WRITING • THINKING • LISTENING • SPEAKING

INFORMING

Write a List

Write a list of silly things to do. Use the plural form of *inch*, *sandwich*, *fox*, and *class* in your sentences. Find a partner and read your lists to each other. How does your list compare with your partner's?

6 More Plural Nouns with -es

Three puppys are for sale.

Which word in the sign is spelled wrong? Do you know how to fix it?

You add *-s* or *-es* to most nouns to form the plural. If a noun ends with a consonant and *y*, change the *y* to *i* and add *-es* to form the plural.

Singular: penn**y**   cherr**y**
Plural: penn**ies** cherr**ies**

Try It Out

Speak Up What is the plural of each noun?

1. body   2. city   3. company   4. diary

Seattle, Washington

On Your Own

5–10. This part of an ad has six incorrect plural nouns. Correct the ad.

Example: Pick your own berrys!   *Pick your own berries!*

Proofreading

All familys love Hudson Farm. We have two ponyes for children to ride. Babies can pet lots of bunnyies and puppys. Adults can pick bunches of cherry. We give birthday partys too!

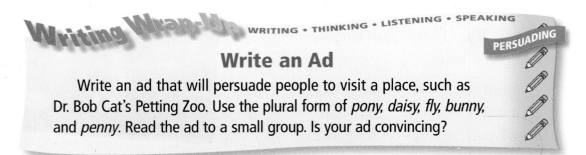

WRITING • THINKING • LISTENING • SPEAKING

Writing Wrap-Up

PERSUADING

Write an Ad

Write an ad that will persuade people to visit a place, such as Dr. Bob Cat's Petting Zoo. Use the plural form of *pony, daisy, fly, bunny,* and *penny*. Read the ad to a small group. Is your ad convincing?

7 Special Plural Nouns

Read the sentence below. Can you find the plural noun?

"Whoever heard of a cat that didn't like mice!"

—from *Martin's Mice*, by Dick King-Smith

Not every noun is made plural by adding *-s* or *-es*. Sometimes the spelling changes in a special way. How does the spelling of *goose* change when it is plural?

Singular: Marta fed one goose.
Plural: Otis fed two geese.

Look at the singular nouns below. How does the spelling of each noun change when it is plural?

Singular	Plural
one man	three men
a woman	five women
one child	many children
a mouse	a few mice
the tooth	several teeth
one foot	two feet

Try It Out

Speak Up Change each singular noun to a plural noun.

1. child
2. tooth
3. woman
4. mouse
5. foot
6. goose

Write each sentence correctly. Use the plural of the noun in ( ).

Example: The bus passed some _____. (goose)

The bus passed some geese.

7. The _____ waited for the bus. (child)
8. One child hopped on both _____. (foot)
9. A boy wiggled his two loose _____. (tooth)
10. A cat chased three _____. (mouse)
11. Many _____ were on the bus. (man)
12. A few _____ read newspapers. (woman)

13–18. This TV schedule has six incorrect plural nouns. Write the program correctly.

Example: Two mans raise giant mice.

Two men raise giant mice.

Proofreading

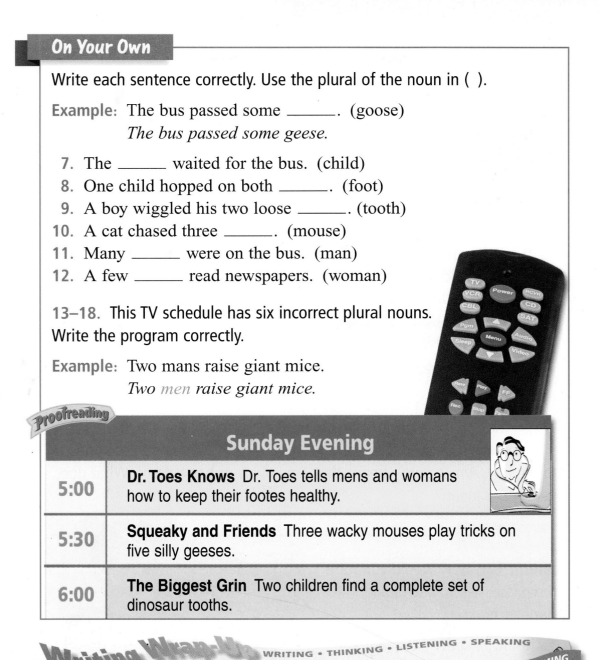

	Sunday Evening
5:00	**Dr. Toes Knows** Dr. Toes tells mens and womans how to keep their footes healthy.
5:30	**Squeaky and Friends** Three wacky mouses play tricks on five silly geeses.
6:00	**The Biggest Grin** Two children find a complete set of dinosaur tooths.

Writing Wrap-Up WRITING • THINKING • LISTENING • SPEAKING

INFORMING

Write a TV Schedule

Make up three TV shows. List the time and the title of each one. Use the plural form of *child, mouse, woman, foot,* and *goose.* Read your schedule to a small group. Ask the group to clap when they hear a plural noun.

8 Singular Possessive Nouns

Read the sentence below. Whose eyes sparkled?
How do you know?

John Henry's eyes sparkled as his voice quickened.

—from *When Jo Louis Won the Title*, by Belinda Rochelle

A **possessive noun** shows that a person or animal owns or has **something.** Add an **apostrophe** and *-s* (*'s*) to a singular noun to make it a possessive noun.

Singular Nouns	Singular Possessive Nouns
boy	boy's bike
Amy	Amy's game
cat	cat's paws

Look at the second column. *Boy's bike* means that the bike belongs to the boy. *Amy's game* means that Amy owns or has a game. What does *cat's paws* mean?

Try It Out

Speak Up How would you form the possessive of each underlined singular noun?

1. <u>horse</u>___ stall
2. <u>mother</u>___ boots
3. <u>Pablo</u>___ airplane
4. <u>neighbor</u>___ barn
5. <u>uncle</u>___ tractor
6. <u>puppy</u>___ food

Write each sentence correctly. Use the possessive of each noun in ( ).

Example: Mrs. Cohen read the _____ letter. (teacher)
Mrs. Cohen read the teacher's letter.

7. _____ school had an open house tonight. (Megan)
8. The teacher showed each _____ drawings. (child)
9. Ben drew a picture of his _____ farm. (cousin)
10. All the parents saw the _____ cage. (hamster)
11. There was a science fair in _____ classroom. (John)
12. The students in _____ class showed their art projects. (Tito)
13. _____ project won first prize. (Lin)

14–18. This letter has five incorrect singular possessive nouns. Write the letter correctly.

Example: Ms. Lee class has a fish.
Ms. Lee's class has a fish.

Proofreading

======= **Hamsters** =======

Dear Mrs. Weiss,
   Every teacher classroom needs a pet. My sister hamster, Peanut, just had seven babies. Hamsters cost ten dollars at my neighbor's pet store. Our class could have one of Peanuts babies for free! I would clean the hamsters cage. This was my mother idea.

                                        Hassan

Writing Wrap-Up   WRITING • THINKING • LISTENING • SPEAKING

PERSUADING

Write a Letter

   Choose the animal that you think would make the best classroom pet. Write a letter to your teacher. Give two or three reasons why this animal should be the class pet. Include singular possessive nouns. Then read your letter to a partner. Does your partner agree with you?

9 Plural Possessive Nouns

This caption is missing an apostrophe. Where should the apostrophe go?

Twins courage saves the day.

You know how to show that one person or animal owns or has something. How can you show that something belongs to more than one person or animal? Add just an apostrophe to a plural noun that ends in *s* (*s'*) to make it a possessive noun.

Plural Nouns	Plural Possessive Nouns
teams	two teams' bats
bunnies	bunnies' carrots
classes	classes' books

Try It Out

Speak Up How would you form the possessive of each underlined plural noun?

1. three babies__ toys
2. kittens__ fur
3. many nurses__ caps
4. three boys__ mother
5. foxes__ den
6. teachers__ maps
7. friends__ kites
8. parents__ room
9. two girls__ closet

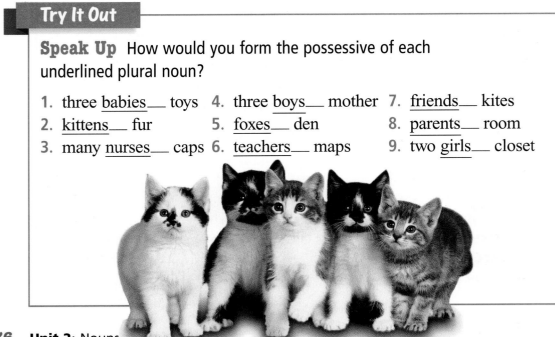

Write each sentence correctly. Use the possessive of each noun in ( ).

Example: My _____ garage is messy. (grandparents)
My grandparents' garage is messy.

10. Where is the _____ basket? (kittens)
11. The _____ collars are ripped. (puppies)
12. What happened to the _____ basketballs? (teams)
13. We can store the _____ trophies over there. (classes)
14. Help me find my _____ shovels. (uncles)
15. The _____ old beds are against one wall. (twins)

16–20. This journal entry has five incorrect plural possessive nouns.
Write the journal entry correctly.

Example: We rode in my parents car.   *We rode in my parents' car.*

Proofreading

Saturday, May 19
    I went to my grandparents house
today. My cousins were there. We all
played hide-and-seek with two ladys
dogs. The dogs chased us all over the
neighbors' yards! Then we played on my two cousins
computer. It was fun looking through Grandma's old photo
album. I saw my three aunts school pictures. Finally, we took
turns riding on two boys bikes.

WRITING • THINKING • LISTENING • SPEAKING

REFLECTING

Write a Journal Entry

Write a journal entry about a special day you spent with family or friends.
Include plural possessive nouns. Read your journal entry to a partner. What
did your partner like best about your day?

Using Exact Nouns

A noun names a person, a place, or a thing. Use exact nouns to make your writing clearer and more interesting.

Less exact noun: Katie waters her plant once a week.

More exact noun: Katie waters her beanstalk once a week.

Apply It

1–6. Rewrite this paragraph. Change each underlined noun to a more exact noun.

Revising

Without soil, we would not have fruit to eat. Animals would not have grass to eat. A young person would not have milk to drink. Without trees, we could not build things from wood. There would be no paper for people to write on. We would not have places for picnics.

Enrichment

Nouns!

Alphabeasts

You run a zoo with many different animals. Make an alphabeast book about the zoo. Think of animals for as many letters of the alphabet as you can. Create a page like the one here for each letter. Include a picture of the animal and write a sentence about it. Then staple your pages in alphabetical order.

E
elephant

Elephants have long trunks and short tails.

Challenge Use a singular or plural possessive noun in each of your sentences.

Silly Subtracting Poems

Copy this poem three times, leaving blanks for the nouns and numbers.

Complete each poem by choosing numbers and nouns for each blank. Use the nouns in the box if you wish. Make sure your plural nouns and your subtraction are correct!

fox	mouse	bus
baby	woman	fly
man	child	goose

I saw *(number) (noun)* sitting on a *(noun)*.
(Second noun above should rhyme with the number in the last line of the poem.)
(Number) (noun) left.
Then I saw *(number)*.

1 **What Are Nouns?** *(p. 60)* Write the nouns in each of the following sentences.

1. My class went to the fair.
2. The bus waited for the students.
3. Children ate their lunches.
4. The boys went to see the chickens.
5. Cute chicks hatched from eggs.
6. One girl won a puppet.
7. The teacher won a prize too.

2 **Common and Proper Nouns** *(p. 62)* Write *common* for each common noun and *proper* for each proper noun.

8. state
9. Ohio
10. cat
11. winter
12. Canada
13. Labor Day
14. Victoria Garcia
15. Post Road
16. puppet

3 **Nouns in the Subject** *(p. 64)* Write the noun in the subject of each sentence.

17. Marco entered his dog in a pet show.
18. Many people brought their dogs.
19. The dogs paraded around the room.
20. Judges looked closely at each dog.
21. The first prize was a blue ribbon.
22. Buddy won the blue ribbon!
23. The audience clapped for all the dogs.
24. The happy dogs barked loudly.

4 **Singular and Plural Nouns** *(p. 68)* Write the noun that completes each sentence correctly.

25. My father drives a (truck, trucks).
26. His truck has sixteen (wheel, wheels).
27. Dad drives the truck to a (dock, docks).

Go to www.eduplace.com/tales/ for more fun with parts of speech.

28. Several (ship, ships) came into the dock today.
29. Dad loaded many (barrels, barrel) into his truck.
30. Then he drove to a (store, stores).
31. Some (worker, workers) unloaded the truck.

5 **Plural Nouns with -es** *(p. 70)* Write the plural form of each of the following nouns.

32. glass	34. speech	36. ax	38. circus
33. marsh	35. business	37. inch	39. sandwich

6 **More Plural Nouns with -es** *(p. 71)* Write the plural of each of the following nouns.

40. family	42. canary	44. dairy	46. sky
41. ferry	43. mystery	45. blackberry	47. library

7 **Special Plural Nouns** *(p. 72)* Write the noun that completes each sentence correctly. Then write *singular* or *plural* beside each one.

48. A (man, men) bought some groceries.
49. The bag dropped on his two (foot, feet).
50. Several (woman, women) made a fruit salad.
51. One (child, children) ate all the blueberries.
52. The berries made all her (tooth, teeth) blue.
53. Two (child, children) set the table.
54. The cook brought in two roast (goose, geese).

8 **Singular Possessive Nouns** *(p. 74)* Change the singular noun in ( ) to the possessive form. Write each sentence correctly.

55. _____ book report is finished. (Sarah)
56. She put it on the _____ desk. (teacher)
57. Aaron wrote the _____ name under the title. (author)
58. He drew a picture with his _____ crayons. (sister)
59. The title of _____ book is Beast . (Elena)

60. She bought the book in her _____ store. (uncle)
61. Hideo did his report on his _____ computer. (neighbor)

9 **Plural Possessive Nouns** *(p. 76)* Change each underlined plural noun to the plural possessive form. Write each sentence correctly.

62. My <u>sisters</u> dolls come from different countries.
63. The dolls are on a shelf in my <u>parents</u> room.
64. Many of the <u>dolls</u> dresses are colorful.
65. Where are the <u>twins</u> dolls?
66. My <u>aunts</u> favorite doll comes from China.
67. Are your <u>friends</u> doll collections big?
68. They have thirty dolls at their <u>grandparents</u> house.

Mixed Review 69–75. This article in a camp newsletter has one missing capital letter, four incorrect plural nouns, and two incorrect possessive nouns. Write the article correctly.

Proofreading Checklist
Are these words written correctly?
✔ proper nouns
✔ plural nouns
✔ singular possessive nouns
✔ plural possessive nouns

Proofreading

These Campers Have Talent!

All of our familys had a great time at the Sunset Camp talent show. Davids tap dance won first prize. He can do amazing things with his foots! The three counselors wacky skit about a camp for mice won second prize. adam's poem about his two puppies' tricks won third prize.

Several of the camper served sandwichs and glasses of lemonade for lunch. Finally, everyone had a piece of cake.

✓ Test Practice

Write the numbers 1–8 on a sheet of paper. Read each group of sentences. Choose the sentence that is written correctly. Write the letter for that answer.

1 A Give these book to Ana.

  B How many page did you read?

  C Tim wrote a sad stories.

  D I read some nice poems.

2 F We had a party for our family.

  G Aunt Nora took a trains from Boston.

  H All of our cousin came.

  J Grandpa was the guests of honor.

3 A Those berrys look ripe.

  B Here are two red applees.

  C I ate a bag of peachs.

  D The oranges were juicy.

4 F We saw many gooses at the pond.

  G Some children were swimming.

  H Kyle put only his foots in the water.

  J Two womans were there.

5 A That dog had six puppies.

  B Did you see those foxs?

  C What do mouses eat?

  D I like riding horseses.

6 F This bikes tires are flat.

  G Kens' skates are new.

  H That girl's football bounced into the street.

  J My two cousins's school has a swimming pool.

7 A My sister's hair is short.

  B Tonys' eyes are brown.

  C That babies' smile is so cute.

  D Two of Pats teeth are loose.

8 F The third graders's play was a success.

  G The twins lines were funny.

  H The four dancers costumes were pretty.

  J Many of the students' parents came to the play.

Now write the numbers 9–25 on your paper. Read each paragraph. Choose the line that shows the mistake. Write the letter for that answer. If there is no mistake, write the letter for the last answer.

9 A   We have a new music
   B   teacher. Every week he
   C   teaches us a few song.
   D   (No mistakes)

10 F   The babies play well
   G   together. The babies's
   H   mothers are friends.
   J   (No mistakes)

11 A   Tonight we have
   B   company for dinner set an
   C   extra place at the table.
   D   (No mistakes)

12 F   Nikki saw a huge bug in
   G   the basement. It was
   H   almost three inches long.
   J   (No mistakes)

13 A   Why are these boxes
   B   so heavy? they are full of
   C   books for the school fair.
   D   (No mistakes)

14 F   Ryan led three ponies
   G   out of the stable. Then he
   H   put saddles on their backs.
   J   (No mistakes)

15 A   Steves lunch fell in a
   B   puddle. Lisa will share
   C   her sandwich with him.
   D   (No mistakes)

16 F   Wear long pants for
   G   the field trip we will
   H   be walking in tall grass.
   J   (No mistakes)

17
A Gary likes to collect
B stamps. He has stamps
C from many countrys.
D (No mistakes)

18
F Look at this old photo
G of my Grandma? What
H funny clothes she wore!
J (No mistakes)

19
A Troy picked lots of
B blueberry at the farm.
C Can we make a pie?
D (No mistakes)

20
F Last year Steffie was
G afraid of the water? Now
H she is a good swimmer.
J (No mistakes)

21
A Pablo saw the first star
B in the evening sky. He
C quickly made three wishs.
D (No mistakes)

22
F Vanessa did some new
G dance steps, and Gordon
H played a song on the piano.
J (No mistakes)

23
A The car is making a
B strange noise. Let's take
C it to the repair shop?
D (No mistakes)

24
F We saw bunnies at the
G pet shop. The bunnies'
H cage is near the fish tank.
J (No mistakes)

25
A Grandpa made fresh ice
B cream with a machine. All
C the childs came to taste it.
D (No mistakes)

Unit 1: The Sentence

What Is a Sentence? *(p. 32)* Read the two groups of words. Write the group that is a sentence.

1. A big red car.
   I enjoy car rides.
2. I look out the window.
   Can see everything.
3. The best seat.
   The front seat is best.

4. Cars zoom by me.
   Trucks with loud horns.
5. We go up the hills.
   Always love the bumps.
6. Interesting people.
   I wave at the people.

Kinds of Sentences *(pp. 36, 38)* Write each sentence correctly.

7. can you keep a secret
8. do not tell anyone
9. Kim told me her secret

10. it is a great secret
11. what is the secret
12. she got a new bike

Subjects and Predicates *(pp. 40, 42)* Write each sentence. Draw a line between subject and predicate.

13. Uncle Henry is a cook.
14. He works at my school.
15. He made soup today.
16. It tasted delicious.
17. A few children had a second cup.
18. Mr. Lee ate three cups!

Run-on Sentences *(p. 44)* Rewrite each run-on sentence as two sentences.

19. What is your favorite hobby I collect rocks.
20. Some rocks are smooth other rocks feel rough.
21. I label all my rocks this rock is very old.
22. Do you see that orange rock it comes from Arizona.
23. Grandma gave it to me she likes my collection.
24. Do you like this one you can have it.

 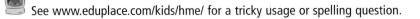

Unit 2: Nouns

What Are Nouns? *(p. 60)* Write all the nouns.

25. My cousins have a huge pool.
26. My sister is having a party.
27. Noisy children are under the umbrella.
28. Two boys are swimming in the water.
29. A neighbor serves lemonade.

Common and Proper Nouns *(p. 62)* Write *common* or *proper* for each noun.

30. Maine	32. pig	34. coat
31. book	33. Anita	35. Mill Road

Nouns in the Subject *(p. 64)* Write the noun in the subject of each sentence.

36. Many foods come from plants.
37. People eat different plant parts.
38. A fruit is part of a flowering plant.
39. A tomato is a fruit.
40. Carrots come from the root of a plant.

Singular and Plural Nouns *(pp. 68, 70, 71, 72)* Write the plural form of each noun.

41. beach	43. class	45. child
42. story	44. fox	46. foot

Possessive Nouns *(pp. 74, 76)* Change each underlined noun to the possessive form. Write each new group of words.

47. <u>Carrie</u> pencil
48. two <u>cousins</u> football
49. some <u>reporters</u> desks
50. the <u>classes</u> videos
51. a <u>fox</u> bark
52. <u>puppies</u> toys
53. a <u>boy</u> shirt
54. a <u>baby</u> blanket

(pages 60–61)

1 What Are Nouns?

• A noun names a person, a place, or a thing.

Remember

● Write the noun in each group of words.

Example: hat, ran, happy   *hat*

1. slowly, girl, tired
2. zoo, busy, early
3. bird, above, sleepy
4. muddy, played, aunt

5. under, lake, excited
6. funny, boat, up
7. farmer, near, sad
8. soft, truck, read

▲ Each sentence below has two nouns. Write each sentence. Underline the nouns.

Example: My teacher read to the class. *My teacher read to the class.*

9. The story came from my favorite book.
10. A king lived in a huge castle.
11. People from the town visited.
12. The queen showed each room.
13. Food was served on long tables.
14. The children played in the yard.

■ Write the nouns in each sentence. Then write *person, place,* or *thing* after each noun.

Example: Men and women do many jobs.
       Men—person   women—person   jobs—thing

15. Cooks prepare food.
16. Farmers grow fruits and vegetables.
17. Lifeguards watch swimmers at the beach.
18. Drivers take packages to cities.
19. Teachers show children how to read books.
20. Doctors and nurses help sick people.

(pages 62–63)

2 Common and Proper Nouns

- A common noun names any person, place, or thing.
- A proper noun names a particular person, place, or thing.
- Proper nouns begin with capital letters.

Remember

● Write the proper noun in each pair of words.

Example: boy
          Alex Wong   *Alex Wong*

1. Baker School
   school
2. Chicago
   city

3. street
   Main Street
4. state
   Texas

5. Elk River
   river
6. Mrs. Arnez
   teacher

▲ Make two lists on your paper. Write all the common nouns in one list. Write all the proper nouns in the other list.

Example: ocean

Common Nouns	Proper Nouns
ocean	

7. Pluto
8. Iowa City

9. umbrella
10. Lewis Ross

11. picture
12. avenue

■ Write each sentence, adding a proper noun for the word in ( ).

Example: Jason goes to _____. (school)
   Jason goes to Park School.

13. His school is on _____. (street)
14. One day _____ joined the class. (girl)
15. She came from _____. (state)
16. She and _____ became friends. (boy)
17. They played in _____. (park)
18. The children went to _____. (zoo)

(pages 64–65)

3 Nouns in the Subject

• A noun is often the main word in the subject.

Remember

● Choose a noun from the box to finish each sentence. Write each sentence.

Example: A _____ visits a farm. *A boy visits a farm.*

1. His _____ feeds the cows.
2. _____ moo loudly.
3. Three _____ eat oats.
4. _____ lay eggs.
5. The _____ should be painted.
6. The _____ tastes good.

corn	barn
Cows	horses
boy	grandfather
Hens	

▲ The subject of each sentence is underlined. Write the noun in the subject.

Example: Two <u>girls</u> planned a party. *girls*

7. <u>Brandon</u> made the popcorn.
8. <u>Cheryl</u> wrapped the presents.
9. <u>Her friend</u> brought the games.
10. One <u>boy</u> made party hats.
11. <u>Three red balloons</u> popped.
12. <u>The young children</u> had a good time.

■ Write the subject of each sentence. Underline the noun in the subject.

Example: Many bats are small and furry. *Many <u>bats</u>*

13. The animals fly like birds.
14. My older brother studied bats in school.
15. Insects are a favorite food.
16. The large wings are very strong.
17. All bats can hang upside down.
18. Most bats sleep during the day.

(pages 68–69)

4 Singular and Plural Nouns

> **Remember**
> - A singular noun names one *person*, *place*, or *thing*.
> - A plural noun names more than one.
> - Add *-s* to most singular nouns to form the plural.

● Write *singular* if the underlined word in each sentence is singular. Write *plural* if the underlined word is plural.

Example: The <u>forest</u> was quiet. *singular*

1. We slept in our <u>tents</u>.
2. One <u>girl</u> heard a noise.
3. She hid under her <u>blanket</u>.
4. Five <u>raccoons</u> played nearby.
5. They walked on our picnic <u>table</u>.
6. We had forgotten to put away the <u>eggs</u>.
7. Tomorrow we will go to the <u>store</u>.

▲ Write the plural form of each noun.

Example: ship *ships*

8. map
9. sailor
10. cloud
11. wave
12. ocean
13. shore
14. storm
15. captain

■ Change the singular noun in each sentence to a plural noun. Write the new plural noun.

Example: My brothers wrote a letter. *letters*

16. They took a trip with my cousins.
17. My uncle and my two aunts went along.
18. The train went through many towns.
19. My cousins looked out the window.
20. Many cows stood near a big barn.
21. They took a picture of the animals.
22. A boy waved to my cousins.

(page 70)

5 Plural Nouns with -*es*

- Add -*es* to form the plural of a singular noun that ends in *s*, *sh*, *ch*, or *x*.

Remember

● Read each pair of nouns. Write the plural form.

Example: boss   bosses   *bosses*

1. ditches
   ditch
2. dishes
   dish
3. fox
   foxes
4. gas
   gases

5. beaches
   beach
6. lashes
   lash
7. dress
   dresses
8. porch
   porches

▲ Write the plural form of each noun.

Example: mess   *messes*

9. ax
10. ranch
11. bush
12. church

13. walrus
14. wax
15. inch
16. waitress

■ Change each underlined singular noun to the plural form. Change each underlined plural noun to the singular form. Write the new sentences.

Example: Erica saw two <u>fox</u>.   *Erica saw two foxes.*

17. The foxes hid behind the <u>bush</u>.
18. Erica tripped over some big <u>branch</u>.
19. Did you see the <u>patch</u> on her leg?
20. She will have to use the <u>crutches</u>.
21. Erica cannot go to the <u>beach</u> for six weeks.
22. Her mother bought her the <u>dress</u> and a book.

(page 71)

6 More Plural Nouns with -es

Remember

- If a noun ends with a consonant and *y*, change the *y* to *i* and add -*es* to form the plural.

● Write each noun. Then write *singular* or *plural* beside each one.

Example: cities   *plural*

1. blueberry
2. countries
3. skies
4. fly
5. penny
6. daisies

▲ Use the plural form of each noun in ( ) to complete each sentence. Write the sentences.

Example: Laura read some _____. (story) *stories*

7. Each story was about animal _____. (family)
8. Some animals like to eat _____. (berry)
9. She learned about animal _____. (baby)
10. Baby dogs are called _____. (puppy)
11. Baby rabbits are called _____. (bunny)
12. Antonio read a story about _____. (pony)
13. Joshua found pictures of _____. (dragonfly)

■ Write the noun that correctly completes each sentence. Then write *singular* or *plural* beside each one.

Example: Sam lives in the (country, countries). *country   singular*

14. He picks many (blueberry, blueberries).
15. A (bunny, bunnies) watches him.
16. He has two (hobby, hobbies).
17. Sam collects pictures of (butterfly, butterflies).
18. He is learning to ride a (pony, ponies).
19. His town has one (library, libraries).
20. Sam reads (story, stories) about insects and horses.

(pages 72–73)

7 Special Plural Nouns

- Some nouns are made plural by changing the spelling in a special way.

Remember

● Write each noun. Then write *singular* or *plural* next to each one.

Example: children *plural*

1. tooth
2. woman
3. men

4. feet
5. goose
6. mice

7. child
8. women
9. teeth

▲ Use the plural form of the noun in ( ) to complete each sentence. Write the sentences.

Example: The _____ went to the farm. (child)
The children went to the farm.

10. Some _____ worked in the field. (man)
11. Two _____ painted the barn. (woman)
12. I fed some _____. (goose)
13. Field _____ ran across the road. (mouse)
14. We put our _____ in the pond. (foot)

■ Find the noun in each sentence that should be plural. Write each sentence correctly.

Example: A few child sat on the fence.
A few children sat on the fence.

15. Some goose started honking.
16. Two mouse heard the noise.
17. Several woman put some cheese on the ground.
18. Many child watched one mouse eat.
19. The mouse had two bad tooth.
20. It ran away on its four little foot.

(pages 74–75)

⑧ **Singular Possessive Nouns**

- A possessive noun shows ownership.
- Add an apostrophe (') and -s to a singular noun to make it show ownership.

Remember

● Write the possessive noun in each sentence.

Example: The family's lunch was ready. *family's*

1. Greg's friends ate lunch with us.
2. Mom poured soup into Camille's bowl.
3. Some soup spilled on Ben's fork.
4. Dad put a sandwich on Duane's plate.
5. Tina moved the baby's seat.
6. Roberto's napkin dropped to the floor.

▲ Change each underlined singular noun to the possessive form. Write each new group of words.

Example: <u>Ted</u> dog *Ted's dog*

7. <u>girl</u> balloon
8. <u>father</u> hats
9. <u>Ray</u> kite

10. <u>monkey</u> tail
11. <u>Mr. Kirk</u> house
12. <u>woman</u> letter

■ Rewrite each sentence. Use the possessive form of each underlined singular noun.

Example: The map that <u>Dad</u> has shows a path.
   Dad's map shows a path.

13. The path begins at the house that <u>Steve</u> owns.
14. The sister that <u>John</u> has leads the way.
15. The children see tracks that belong to an <u>animal</u>.
16. Kristin takes the hand that belongs to <u>Melissa</u>.
17. She points to a nest that belongs to a <u>bird</u>.
18. Everybody looks for the den that the <u>fox</u> has.

(pages 76–77)

⑨ **Plural Possessive Nouns**

- To show ownership, add just an apostrophe to a plural noun that ends in *s*.

Remember

● Read the two groups of words after each number. Write the group of words with the plural possessive noun in it.

Example: lions' den
lion's den   *lions' den*

1. father's book
   fathers' book
2. farmers' corn
   farmer's corn

3. clown's shoes
   clowns' shoes
4. horses' saddles
   horse's saddles

5. sailors' boat
   sailor's boat
6. coach's hats
   coaches' hats

▲ Change the plural noun in ( ) to the possessive form. Write each sentence correctly.

Example: Many people shop at my (brothers) store.
Many people shop at my brothers' store.

7. Mr. Chen buys baskets for his (daughters) bikes.
8. Austin looks at the racks of (boys) coats.
9. Mrs. Kane buys the (families) tents.
10. My two (friends) father buys a hammer.
11. Sara sees chairs for her (grandparents) house.

■ Write the possessive noun in each sentence. Then write *singular* or *plural* beside each one.

Example: Anita's dog is big and spotted.   *Anita's singular*

12. My sister's cat has orange fur.
13. Both girls' pets have funny names.
14. The dog's name is Lefty.
15. Pumpkin is the cat's name.
16. Lefty and Pumpkin chase my brothers' pets.

Unit 3

Verbs

Tug of war is no game for the timid. You grit your teeth, hold your breath, and TUG!

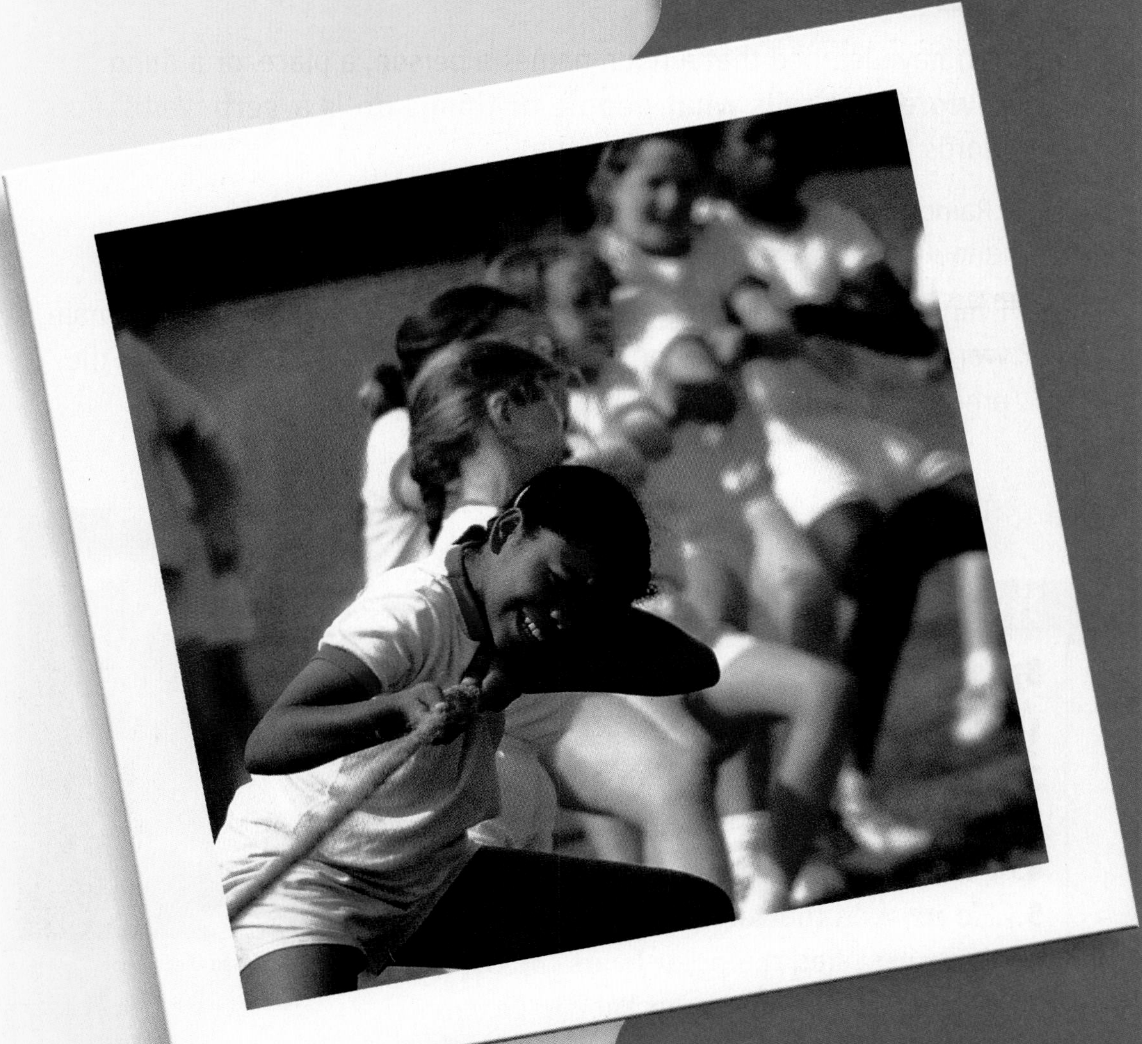

1 What Are Verbs?

Read the sentence below. What word shows action?

The miners of 1848 found the California hills pretty friendly.

—from *Striking It Rich: The Story of the California Gold Rush,*
by Stephen Krensky

- You have learned that a noun names a person, a place, or a thing. **A word that tells what people or things do is a verb.** Verbs are words that show action.

  Ramona bought a ticket.
  She rode on the bus.

- Every sentence has a subject and a predicate. You know that the main word in the subject is often a noun. The verb is the main word in the predicate.

  Subject   Predicate
  The driver   stopped at the library.

Try It Out

Speak Up What is the verb in each sentence?

1. Carmine flew to California.
2. He watched a movie on the airplane.
3. He stayed with his uncle.
4. Carmine visited many places.
5. He enjoyed the zoo in San Diego.
6. Carmine liked the polar bears the best.
7. One day he swam in the Pacific Ocean.

San Diego Zoo

Write the verbs.

Example: Erica works for a newspaper. *works*

8. She takes pictures for the newspaper.
9. One day a lion escaped from the zoo.
10. Police officers searched the streets.
11. Erica grabbed her camera.
12. She drove slowly through town.
13. Erica saw the lion in front of the pet store.
14. The lion snored very loudly.
15. Erica snapped a picture of the lion.
16. The picture made the front page.

17–25. Write this story beginning. Underline the nine verbs.

Example: The city scared the lion. *The city <u>scared</u> the lion.*

Lion on the Loose!

Leo pushed the cage door with one paw. The door swung open. He looked around Parkwood Zoo. The old lion walked out of the cage. He passed through the gates of the zoo. Then Leo saw something strange. Some big, shiny creatures raced past him. The creatures honked several times. Leo followed the creatures into the city.

Writing Wrap-Up WRITING • THINKING • LISTENING • SPEAKING

NARRATING

Write a Story Beginning

An animal has just escaped from a zoo. What happens after the animal leaves the zoo? Write the first paragraph of the story. Read your paragraph to a partner. Have your partner identify the verbs.

2 Verbs in the Present

Read the sentence below. Which word is the verb?

Snow falls to the earth in different ways.

—from *Weather Words and What They Mean,* by Gail Gibbons

Verbs show action in sentences. Verbs also tell when the action happens. **A verb that tells about an action that is happening now is in the present time.** Verbs in the present have two forms. The correct form to use depends on what the subject of the sentence is.

- Add *-s* to the verb when the noun in the subject is singular.

  The dog barks at the snowman. Jill laughs.

- Do not add *-s* to the verb when the noun in the subject is plural.

  The boys shovel. Their parents start the car.

Try It Out

Speak Up Is each subject singular or plural? What is the correct verb form for each sentence?

1. My cousins (loves, love) cold weather.
2. Gregory (make, makes) big snowballs.
3. Chris (get, gets) the sled.
4. The boys (race, races) to the park.
5. Their mother (take, takes) pictures.
6. Many children (slides, slide) down the hill.

Write each sentence. Choose the correct verb in ( ).

Example: The owl (hunt, hunts) at night.   *The owl hunts at night.*

7. A chipmunk (run, runs) under the rocks.
8. The horses (gallop, gallops) fast.
9. Rabbits (jump, jumps) into the bushes.
10. A bear (climb, climbs) trees.
11. Three worms (wiggle, wiggles) in the grass.
12. That monkey (swing, swings) on branches.

13–18. This online encyclopedia article has six incorrect verb forms. Write the article correctly.

Example: A koala move slowly from tree to tree.
  A koala moves slowly from tree to tree.

Proofreading

Web site

Koalas lives in Australia. Many eucalyptus trees grows there. The leaves makes a good meal for the koala. The koala eats at night. This furry, brown animal sleep in the trees during the day. A mother koala keep her new baby in her pouch. The older babies rides on their mothers' backs.

Back Forward

Writing Wrap-Up

WRITING • THINKING • LISTENING • SPEAKING

INFORMING

Write a List

Write a list of four animals. Next to each name, write a verb that tells how the animal moves. Use this list to write a sentence about each animal. Use verbs in the present time. Read your sentences to a group, leaving out the verbs. Can anyone guess the verbs?

3 More Verbs in the Present

Which one of these sentences has something wrong with it? How can you fix it?

Roscoe the Wonder Dog watch the children at the pool. Then he tries to jump into their tube!

- Most verbs in the present end with *-s* when the subject is a singular noun. Some verbs, though, end with *-es* instead of *-s*. Add *-es* to verbs that end with *s, sh, ch,* or *x* when they are used with a singular noun in the subject. Do not add *-es* when the noun in the subject is plural.

Singular	Plural
Rob tosses a ball.	The boys toss the ball.
My grandfather fishes.	The girls fish.
Emily mixes the salad.	Friends mix the salad.
Mother watches us.	People watch us.

- Some verbs end with a consonant and *y*. Change the *y* to *i* and add *-es* when you use this kind of verb with a singular noun.

    carry + es = carries   hurry + es = hurries

Try It Out

Speak Up What is the correct present time of each verb in ( )?

1. A boy _____ his red kite. (fly)
2. My sister _____ in the lake. (splash)
3. Father _____ me a game. (teach)
4. Aunt Victoria _____ the net. (fix)
5. Krista _____ the ball. (watch)

Write each sentence. Choose the correct verb in ( ).

Example: Mr. Hogan (teach, teaches). *Mr. Hogan teaches.*

6. The students (study, studies) history.
7. Maria (reach, reaches) for more paper.
8. Matt (try, tries) very hard.
9. Roberto (guess, guesses) the correct answer.
10. Tonya (finish, finishes) first.

11–15. This draft of a book report has five incorrect verb forms. Write the book report correctly.

Example: Each chapter catch your interest.
Each chapter catches your interest.

Proofreading

Title: The Pilgrims in America
Author: Sondra Gold

About the Book: This book teach us about the Pilgrims. Two chapters describe the voyage of the Mayflower. The next two chapters discusses the awful winter in Plymouth. The author finish with the first Thanksgiving feast.

My Opinion: The author mixs facts with her own ideas. She wishes all people could get along like the Pilgrims and the Wampanoag. I think this book carrys an important message.

Writing Wrap-Up

WRITING • THINKING • LISTENING • SPEAKING

EXPLAINING

Write an Explanation

Do you like working with numbers? Maybe you like reading best. Write a paragraph about your favorite subject. Explain why you think it is the best. Use the words *finish, try, guess, stretch,* and *hurry.* Read your paragraph to a partner. Does your partner agree with you?

4 Verbs in the Past

One-Minute Warm-Up

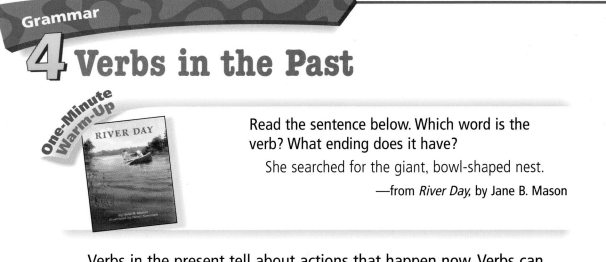

RIVER DAY

Read the sentence below. Which word is the verb? What ending does it have?

She searched for the giant, bowl-shaped nest.

—from *River Day,* by Jane B. Mason

Verbs in the present tell about actions that happen now. Verbs can also tell that actions have already happened. **A verb that tells about an action that has already happened is in the past time**. Add *-ed* to most verbs to show past time.

Present
Kelly **steers** the boat.

Past
Kelly **steered** the boat.

Present	kick	float	push	mix
Past	kicked	floated	pushed	mixed

Try It Out

Speak Up Which verb in each sentence shows past time?

1. Jesse (waits, waited) for the swan boat.
2. The boat (passes, passed) two ducks.
3. Jesse (watched, watches) the ducks.
4. The ducks (quacked, quack) loudly.
5. Jesse (enjoys, enjoyed) the sound.
6. He (tosses, tossed) some bread to the ducks.
7. The ducks (rushes, rushed) to the bread.

Swan Boat, Boston

Write *present* if the underlined verb shows present time. Write *past* if the verb shows past time.

Example: The children <u>fix</u> the doghouse.   *present*

8. Ling <u>patches</u> a hole in the roof.
9. Inez <u>sawed</u> the new boards.
10. Jeffrey <u>mixed</u> the paint.
11. Melissa <u>paints</u> the boards.
12. Josh <u>hammers</u> the boards into place.
13. The children <u>worked</u> for hours.
14. Finally, the children <u>finished</u> their repairs.

15–22. Read the paragraph to find the answer to this riddle. Then change the underlined verbs from present time to past time. Write the new verbs.

Example: Parents <u>visit</u> it.   *visited*

A Riddle

Birds <u>perch</u> on it. Branches <u>cover</u> it. Strong winds <u>rock</u> it. Squirrels <u>jump</u> onto it. Bugs <u>crawl</u> in it. Breezes <u>pass</u> through it. Children <u>climb</u> up to it. Friends <u>play</u> in it. What is it?

Answer: a tree house

Writing Wrap-Up   WRITING • THINKING • LISTENING • SPEAKING

CREATING

Write a Riddle

Write a riddle about a person, an animal, or a thing. Use verbs in the present time. Read your riddle to a partner and see if she or he can guess the answer. Then have your partner change the verbs to show past time.

5 More Verbs in the Past

Which verb below shows present time? Which verb shows past time?

"Hooray, a piñata!" Samson clapped his hands. "I love piñatas!"

—from *Hooray, a Piñata!* by Elisa Kleven

You can make most verbs show past time just by adding *-ed*. However, the spelling of some verbs changes in other ways when you add *-ed*.

- Some verbs end with *e*. Drop the *e* and add *-ed*.

  race + ed = raced   joke + ed = joked

- Some verbs end with a consonant and *y*. Change the *y* to *i* when you add *-ed*.

  cry + ed = cried   worry + ed = worried

- Some verbs end with one vowel followed by one consonant. Double the consonant and add *-ed*.

  stop + p + ed = stopped   hug + g + ed = hugged

Try It Out

Speak Up How is the past time of each verb spelled?

1. like
2. pat
3. marry
4. chase
5. smile
6. dry
7. drop
8. drag
9. copy
10. juggle

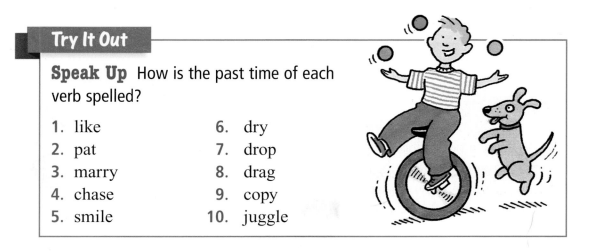

Write the correct past time of each verb in ( ).

Example: Tina _____ at the post office. (stop) *stopped*

11. A present _____ from her grandmother. (arrive)
12. A clerk _____ a box in front of her. (place)
13. Tina _____ home. (hurry)
14. She quickly _____ her present. (unwrap)
15. Tina _____ to open the present carefully. (try)
16. She _____ at the string. (tug)
17. A large clown puppet _____ at her. (stare)
18. The puppet _____ on strings. (move)

19–24. This journal entry has six incorrect verb forms in the past time. Write the journal entry correctly.

Example: Our parents claped for us.
             Our parents clapped for us.

Proofreading

Sunday, October 7
    Yesterday, Keesha and I planed a puppet show. We
invitted our parents. Keesha's puppet asked questions. My
puppet replyed with jokes. We copyied some of the jokes from
a TV show. Once the puppet stage tiped over. Our parents
kidded us about that. They loveed the show, though.

Writing Wrap-Up   WRITING • THINKING • LISTENING • SPEAKING

REFLECTING

Write a Journal Entry

Write a journal entry about a show you have seen, such as a
school play or a TV program. What happened in the show? Did you
enjoy it? Use verbs in the past time. Then find a partner and read your
entries to each other. Compare the shows you wrote about.

6 Verbs in the Future

Which sentence tells about an action in the past? Which sentence tells about an action that is going to happen?

Lightning flashed across the sky.

I will sleep under the covers tonight!

You know that verbs can tell about actions in the present or in the past. **A verb that tells about an action that is going to happen is in the future time.** Use the helping verb *will* to show future time.

Present	Clouds cover the sun.
	Rain fills the birdbath.
Past	Clouds covered the sun.
	Rain filled the birdbath.
Future	Clouds will cover the sun.
	Rain will fill the birdbath.

Try It Out

Speak Up Does the underlined verb show present time, past time, or future time?

1. This morning I <u>looked</u> out the window.
2. Rain <u>poured</u> from the sky.
3. I <u>keep</u> my boots in the closet.
4. Sarah <u>wears</u> her new raincoat.
5. We <u>will splash</u> in the puddles.
6. My cat Pepper <u>will stay</u> indoors all day.
7. He <u>will sleep</u> under my bed.

Write the correct future time of each verb in ( ).

Example: We _____ about weather in class. (learn)   *will learn*

8. Ming _____ his science project first. (present)
9. He _____ all about rain. (explain)
10. First, the sun _____ some of the water on the earth. (heat)
11. This water _____ a gas called water vapor. (become)
12. Tiny droplets of water from the water vapor _____ clouds. (form)
13. The droplets _____ larger and heavier. (grow)
14. Then they _____ as rain. (fall)
15. Cold weather _____ the droplets to snow. (turn)

16–24. This weather report has nine verbs in the future time. Write the weather report. Underline the verbs that show future time.

Example: The storm will last all day.   *The storm will last all day.*

WIND MAP

Heavy snow will begin by noon. It will end early tomorrow. About twenty inches of snow will fall. Strong winds will blow all night. They will cause huge drifts. Skies will clear on Monday. Then the temperature will rise to forty degrees. The snow will melt. Stay tuned to WSNO. Our reporters will inform you of any change in the weather forecast.

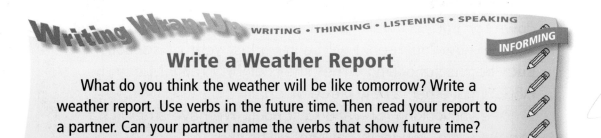

Writing Wrap-Up   WRITING • THINKING • LISTENING • SPEAKING

INFORMING

Write a Weather Report

What do you think the weather will be like tomorrow? Write a weather report. Use verbs in the future time. Then read your report to a partner. Can your partner name the verbs that show future time?

Writing with Verbs

Combining Sentences You know that combining sentences often makes your writing clearer. When two sentences have the same subject, you can put the sentences together. Join the two predicates and use the word *and* between them.

> Do not add a comma when you combine predicates.

I wrote Esther a letter.
I told her about school. } I wrote Esther a letter
and told her about school.

The subject of both sentences is *I.* You can combine the two predicates *wrote Esther a letter* and *told her about school.*

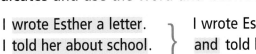

Apply It

1–6. Rewrite this part of an unfinished letter that a student started many years ago. Combine each pair of underlined sentences.

Revising

December 1, 1860

Dear Esther,

School starts tomorrow. We put away our farming clothes. We ironed our dresses. This year my little sister Lucy will walk with me to school. The walk is about two miles long. The walk takes about half an hour. I will have to slow down for Lucy. I walk fast. I like to run sometimes.

I am now fourteen. I will be in my last year of school. Lucy begins school, now that she is eight. I taught Lucy the ABCs. I gave her a new piece of chalk.

Are you looking forward to school? We have a new teacher. We wonder what she will be like.

You can combine some sentences in different ways. This gives you more choices when you write. Here are two ways to combine sentences.

Students make their own pens. ⎤ Students make their own pens
Students write on tree bark.   ⎦ and write on tree bark.

The writer decided to combine the predicates above and take out one of the subjects. This new sentence does not need a comma.

The writer could have decided to join the predicates and leave in both of the subjects. This new sentence needs a comma because it is made up of two complete sentences.

Students make their own pens, and students write on tree bark.

Apply It

7–12. Revise these captions. Combine each pair of sentences in two different ways.

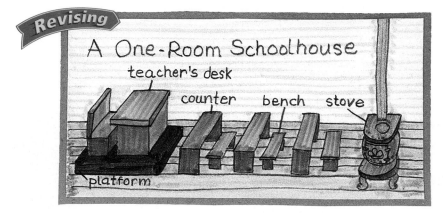

Revising

A One-Room Schoolhouse
teacher's desk
counter   bench   stove
platform

The teacher's desk is tall.
The teacher's desk stands on a platform.

Our stove burns wood.
Our stove warms the room.

We sit on benches.
We write on long counters.

7 The Special Verb *be*

How many sentences can you make out of the two lists of words below?

List 1 Father, bumpy, good, we, the, car, it, my, excited, a, bored, children, rainy, I, summer, road, baby

List 2 is, are, was, am, were

- The verbs *am, is, are, was,* and *were* are forms of the verb *be.* They do not show action. They tell what someone or something is or was.

- *Am, is,* and *are* show present time. *Was* and *were* show past time.

I am sleepy now.
Today we are in Maine.
It is a four-hour drive.

I was tired last night.
Friday we were in Vermont.
It was a long trip.

Subject	Present	Past
I	am	was
you	are	were
he, she, it	is	was
singular noun *(John)*	is	was
we, they	are	were
plural noun *(dogs)*	are	were

Try It Out

Speak Up Choose the correct verb for each sentence. Does the verb show present time or past time?

1. The porch light (was, were) on.
2. I (is, am) in the front seat of the car.
3. My brothers (is, are) in the back.
4. We (was, were) ready for our vacation.

On Your Own

Write each sentence. Choose the correct verb in ( ).

Example: I (is, am) in class.   *I am in class.*

5. Mrs. Schultz (is, are) the teacher.
6. We (are, is) excited about our reports.
7. Kevin (is, are) the class reporter today.
8. Nina (were, was) the reporter yesterday.
9. Your reports on Abraham Lincoln (was, were) terrific!

10–15. This chart has six incorrect forms of the verb *be*. Write the chart correctly.

Example: I were the tallest in the class.   *I was the tallest in the class.*

Proofreading

First Grade

I was seven years old.

My best subjects was reading and art.

My teacher were Mr. Diaz.

We was a noisy class then.

Third Grade

I am nine years old.

My best subjects is math and spelling.

My teacher are Ms. Mitchell.

We is quiet now.

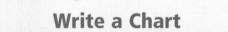

Writing Wrap-Up WRITING • THINKING • LISTENING • SPEAKING

COMPARING / CONTRASTING

Write a Chart
Write your own chart comparing first grade with third grade. Use the verb *am, is, are, was,* or *were* in each of your sentences. Read your chart to a small group. Ask the group to clap their hands when they hear a form of the verb *be*.

8 Helping Verbs

One-Minute Warm-Up

Which word on the ball will complete the sentence correctly?

The children _All_ lost their ball.

have
has

Sometimes the words *has* and *have* help other verbs to show past time. **Has and have are called helping verbs.**

- Use the helping verb *has* with a singular noun in the subject and with *he, she,* or *it.*

  Ana has played the game.   She has enjoyed it.

- Use the helping verb *have* with a plural noun in the subject and with *I, you, we,* or *they.*

  The boys have helped her.   I have watched.

Try It Out

Speak Up Choose *has* or *have* to finish each sentence correctly.

1. The game (has, have) started.
2. Allison (has, have) counted to ten.
3. She (has, have) peeked around a tree.
4. Reggie (has, have) run behind the house.
5. I (has, have) crawled under a big bush.
6. We (has, have) played hide-and-seek many times.

Complete each sentence correctly with *has* or *have*. Write the sentences.

Example: My school _____ visited the aquarium.
My school has visited the aquarium.

7. We _have_ seen a movie about seals.
8. Many fur seals _have_ traveled great distances.
9. One seal _has_ performed funny tricks for us.
10. We _have_ found a tank full of rays.
11. Some students _has_ bought books about sea life.
12. Tyrone _have_ picked out one about a giant manta ray.

13–18. This part of an e-mail message has six incorrect helping verbs. Write the message correctly.

Example: I has spotted a baby whale. *I have spotted a baby whale.*

Proofreading

e-mail	回目

To: Mark
Subject: Whale watching

    You has gone on a whale watch many times. Now I has done it too! Aunt Lilly have taken me twice. She has mailed you some pictures. Each trip have lasted six hours. We has watched several whales. They has come from hundreds of miles away.

Writing Wrap-Up   WRITING • THINKING • LISTENING • SPEAKING

EXPRESSING

Write an Opinion

Some whales have been hit accidentally by boats on whale watches. Do you think whale watches are a good idea or not? Write one or two paragraphs telling your opinion. Use the helping verbs *has* and *have*. Then compare your opinion with a partner's. Do you and your partner agree or disagree?

9 Irregular Verbs

Can you tell what is wrong with this caption? Do you know how to fix it?

Miles A. Minute had ran past Ima Cumming for the win!

Some verbs have a special spelling to show past time. They have another spelling when used with *has, have,* or *had.*

Present: Many people run in Boston's big race.

Past: William ran in the race last year.

With *has*: Megan has run in the race many times.

Present	Past	With *has, have,* or *had*
go	went	has, have, or had gone
see	saw	has, have, or had seen
do	did	has, have, or had done
run	ran	has, have, or had run
come	came	has, have, or had come

Try It Out

Speak Up Choose the correct verb for each sentence.

1. I had (saw, seen) the start of the race.
2. Wheelchair racers have (did, done) well.
3. Many racers (ran, run) all twenty-six miles last year.
4. One young man has (came, come) in first.
5. He (went, gone) home with a medal.

Write each sentence. Choose the correct verb in ( ).

Example: My class (saw, seen) movies of space flights.
My class saw movies of space flights.

6. Mrs. Rockett had (ran, run) the films for us.
7. The films had (came, come) from Kennedy Space Center.
8. Neil Armstrong had (went, gone) to the moon in 1969.
9. Edwin E. Aldrin, Jr., (went, gone) with him.
10. Reporters (did, done) stories about their trip.
11. Dad (saw, seen) the moon landing on TV.
12. Michelle has (saw, seen) moon rocks in a museum.

13–18. This part of a newspaper article has six incorrect verb forms. Write the article. Correct the underlined verbs.

Example: Now John Glenn has <u>goed</u> to space in the space shuttle.
Now John Glenn has gone to space in the space shuttle.

Proofreading

November 7, 1998—In 1962 John Glenn had <u>went</u> around Earth in a spacecraft. No other American had done that. Americans have <u>saw</u> him as a hero since then. In 1974 he <u>run</u> for the United States Senate and won.

Nine days ago, John Glenn <u>goed</u> into space again. This time he <u>done</u> it at age seventy-seven. Once again he has <u>came</u> back to Earth in good health.

Writing Wrap-Up

WRITING • THINKING • LISTENING • SPEAKING

INFORMING

Write an Article

You have just returned from a trip to the moon. Write an article about the trip for the school newspaper. Use the past time of the verbs *go, see, do, run,* and *come.* Read your article to a partner. Then work together to check that the verbs are written correctly.

10 More Irregular Verbs

gave, wrote, ate, took, grew

Pick a verb from the basket. Say a sentence with the verb. Then say the same sentence with *has, have,* or *had* before the verb. How many different sentences can you make up?

The verbs *give, write, eat, take,* and *grow* also have a special spelling to show past time. They have another spelling when used with *has, have,* or *had.*

Present: I grow tomatoes in my garden.

Past: Alexis grew carrots last summer.

With *have*: We have grown many pretty flowers.

Present	Past	With *has, have,* or *had*
give	gave	has, have, or had given
write	wrote	has, have, or had written
eat	ate	has, have, or had eaten
take	took	has, have, or had taken
grow	grew	has, have, or had grown

Try It Out

Speak Up Choose the correct verb for each sentence.

1. Grandpa (gave, given) me a camera for my birthday.
2. I (wrote, written) him a thank-you letter.
3. We have (grew, grown) sunflowers this year.
4. I (took, taken) pictures of the sunflowers.
5. Some insects had (ate, eaten) a few of the flowers.

Write each sentence. Choose the correct verb in ( ).

Example: Last year a farmer (grew, grown) watermelons.
Last year a farmer grew watermelons.

6. Amanda (took, taken) some of the watermelons home.
7. The children have (ate, eaten) them.
8. Ryan had (gave, given) some seeds to Grandma.
9. Grandma (wrote, written) to Ryan and Amanda.
10. One of her watermelons had (grew, grown) very large.
11. She (took, taken) it to the fair.
12. The judge has (gave, given) Grandma first prize.

13–18. This announcement at a state fair has six incorrect verb forms. Write the announcement. Correct the underlined verbs.

Example: The judge has <u>give</u> the prize for best watermelon.
The judge has given the prize for best watermelon.

Proofreading

I have <u>eat</u> many melons in my years as a judge. Yesterday I <u>written</u> in my journal about my search for the perfect melon. Today I ate some of Mrs. Vernon's giant watermelon. Nobody has <u>ate</u> better fruit. I have <u>gave</u> that melon the blue ribbon. Mrs. Vernon has <u>growed</u> watermelons only once before. She has <u>took</u> us all by surprise.

Writing Wrap-Up WRITING • THINKING • LISTENING • SPEAKING

DESCRIBING

Write a Description

You are a judge at a state fair. Write a description of the fruit or vegetable that won first prize, but don't say what it is. Use the past time of the verbs *give, eat, take,* and *grow.* Then read your description to a small group. Can anyone guess the fruit or vegetable?

11 Contractions with *not*

Make up silly rules for your classroom. Use one of these words in each of your rules:

don't   can't   shouldn't

Don't dance on the desks.

• Sometimes two words are put together and shortened to make a **contraction**. An apostrophe (') takes the place of any letter or letters that are left out.

Two Words
My radio **does not** work.

Contraction
My radio **doesn't** work.

Common Contractions with *not*			
is not	isn't	do not	don't
are not	aren't	does not	doesn't
was not	wasn't	did not	didn't
were not	weren't	could not	couldn't
has not	hasn't	should not	shouldn't
have not	haven't	would not	wouldn't
had not	hadn't	cannot	can't

• The contraction *won't* is special. It is formed from the words *will not*.

Try It Out

This machine isn't working right.

Speak Up What are the contractions for the word or words below?

1. were not
2. will not
3. did not
4. are not
5. is not
6. has not
7. cannot
8. was not

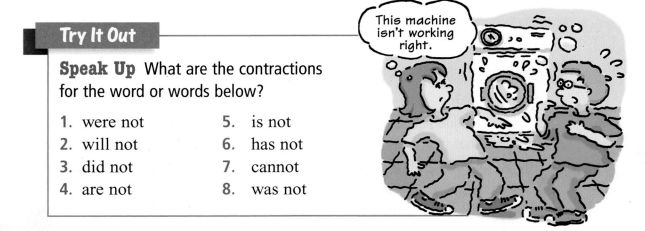

Write the contractions for the underlined words.

Example: We <u>are not</u> happy. *aren't*

9. The TV <u>is not</u> working.
10. We <u>do not</u> know what is wrong with it.
11. Ms. Cabot <u>could not</u> fix the TV today.
12. We <u>should not</u> have called her so late.
13. I <u>have not</u> seen my favorite animal show.
14. My father <u>has not</u> watched the news.

15–20. This part of a TV script has six contractions that have a missing apostrophe or an apostrophe that is in the wrong place. Write the script correctly.

Example: This hike has'nt been easy! *This hike hasn't been easy!*

The Wilsons Go Hiking

Eliza: I cant wait to eat. Our hike has given me a huge
appetite. I hav'ent been this hungry in a long time!
Jake: Sam does'nt look very happy. Aren't you feeling
well, Sam?
Sam: You wont believe this. I did'nt pack the food!
No wonder my backpack wasnt heavy.

Writing Wrap-Up WRITING • THINKING • LISTENING • SPEAKING

INFORMING

Write a List of Rules
Write a list of five safety rules for hikers or campers in the woods.
Use a contraction in each sentence. Then read your rules to a partner.
Work together to make sure your contractions are written correctly.

Using Exact Verbs

A verb can show action. Use exact verbs in your writing so that readers can picture in their minds the actions you write about.

Less exact verb:
Shauna runs to the bus stop.

More exact verb:
Shauna races to the bus stop.

Apply It

1–5. Use your Thesaurus Plus to find a synonym for each of the underlined verbs in the story below. Rewrite the story. Change each underlined verb to a more exact verb.

A synonym is a word with almost the same meaning as another word.

Revising

Zoe and Sam put a fancy bow on the top of their present. They put the present on Ryan's porch and ring the doorbell. The children don't want to be heard. They quietly walk down the steps. Back in the car, they see Ryan open the front door and quickly look around. The present is heavy, but Ryan's mom helps him lift it off the porch floor. They bump into a wall as they walk into the house.

Enrichment

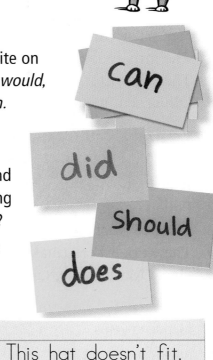

Verbs!

Contraction Cards

Players: 2

Materials: You need 14 index cards. Write on them the words *is, did, are, should, was, would, were, could, have, does, had, do, has, can.*

To play: Mix the cards and place them facedown in a pile. Take turns drawing a card. Add *not* to the word on the card and form a contraction. Write a sentence using the contraction. Is your sentence correct?

Scoring: A correctly written contraction earns a player 2 points. If the rest of the sentence is correct, the player scores another point. Play until someone scores 15 points.

can

did

should

does

This hat doesn't fit.

Pet Sitter

You are going on a vacation. A friend has offered to care for your pet. Write a list of instructions for your friend. Make each sentence a command.

Wash Al with a sponge.

Challenge Write a note that your friend might leave for you. Use verbs in the past time. Include the helping verb *have* or *has.*

Example: Al has enjoyed the sponge baths.

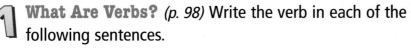

1 **What Are Verbs?** *(p. 98)* Write the verb in each of the following sentences.

1. Emma took a trip to Egypt.
2. Her sister Olivia went with her.
3. The girls rode camels.
4. Then the sisters visited the pyramids.
5. Olivia sent me a post card.

2 **Verbs in the Present** *(pp. 100, 102)* Choose the correct verb in ( ) to complete each sentence. Write the sentences.

6. A bee (fly, flies) to a flower.
7. Pollen (stick, sticks) to the bee's legs.
8. The bee (rush, rushes) the pollen back to the hive.
9. The worker bees (make, makes) honey.
10. Uncle Mario (take, takes) the honey from the hive.

3 **Verbs in the Past** *(p. 104)* Write the past time of each of the following verbs.

11. climb   13. fix   15. wish   17. look
12. touch   14. miss   16. lift   18. march

4 **More Verbs in the Past** *(p. 106)* Write the correct past time of each verb in ( ).

19. The wind _____ through the trees (whistle)
20. The rain _____ against the windows. (slam)
21. A cat _____ in the rain. (cry)
22. Dylan _____ to the front door. (hurry)
23. His cat _____ into the warm kitchen. (race)

5 **Verbs in the Future** *(p. 108)* Write the correct future time of each verb in ( ).

24. I _____ to the library tomorrow. (go)
25. Melissa _____ with me. (come)
26. We _____ on the bus. (ride)

See www.eduplace.com/kids/hme/ for an online quiz.

27. The librarian _____ us the latest books. (show)
28. Melissa _____ a book for her report. (get)
29. I _____ my book during the trip home. (read)

6 **The Special Verb** *be* *(p. 112)* Choose the correct verb for each sentence. Write the sentences.

30. A kitten (was, were) for sale.
31. Kittens (is, are) playful animals.
32. Ollie (is, are) black and white.
33. His paws (is, are) tiny.
34. Once Ollie (was, were) up on the roof.
35. He (was, were) scared.

7 **Helping Verbs** *(p. 114)* Complete each sentence correctly with *has* or *have*. Write the sentences.

36. Linda _____ been to a Mexican festival.
37. She _____ enjoyed the fireworks and bells.
38. Her grandparents _____ marched in the parade.
39. Some festivals _____ started before daylight.
40. Many Mexicans _____ worn colorful costumes.

8 **Irregular Verbs** *(p. 116)* Choose the correct verb in ( ) to complete each of the sentences below. Write the sentences.

41. Uncle Jack (went, gone) to Africa.
42. He (saw, seen) a herd of elephants.
43. The elephants had (ran, run) past his jeep.
44. My uncle has (did, done) work to save elephants.
45. Uncle Jack has (came, come) home.

9 **More Irregular Verbs** *(p. 118)* Choose the correct verb in ( ) to complete each of the sentences below. Write the sentences.

46. Uncle Jack (grew, grown) worried about the elephants.
47. The elephants had (ate, eaten) most of the young trees.
48. My uncle (gave, given) a speech about Africa.

49. The audience (took, taken) notes.
50. I have (wrote, written) a story about elephants.

10 **Contractions with *not*** *(p. 120)* Write the contraction for each word or words.

51. cannot
52. have not
53. should not
54. was not
55. do not

56. will not
57. did not
58. would not
59. had not
60. are not

Mixed Review 61–66. This book report has five incorrect verb forms and one contraction with a missing apostrophe. Write the book report correctly.

Proofreading Checklist
Did you write these words correctly?
✔ verbs in the present time
✔ verbs in the past time
✔ helping verbs
✔ contractions

Proofreading

Title A Change of Heart
Author Victoria Santiago
About the Book The author has written a book about her childhood in Chicago. The story tell about her life as a Mexican American. Victoria had come to the United States on her eighth birthday. At first she cryed every night for her home in Mexico. Victoria didn't like her new school either. She hadnt made any friends there. Then the girl next door stoped by for a visit. Soon the two girls was good friends.
My Opinion I has learned a lot about Mexican customs from this book. I liked the way it reminded me of my best friend.

✓ Test Practice

Write the numbers 1–8 on a sheet of paper. Choose the best way to write the underlined part of each sentence. Write the letter for that answer. If there is no mistake, mark the last answer.

1 Bill <u>eat</u> fruit every morning.

  A eating

  B eats

  C eated

  D (No mistakes)

2 Mom <u>give</u> me good advice.

  F gives

  G giving

  H given

  J (No mistakes)

3 Mia <u>finish</u> her book report.

  A finished

  B finishing

  C finishes

  D (No mistakes)

4 Tomorrow Dad <u>fixes</u> that broken chair.

  F fix

  G will fix

  H has fixed

  J (No mistakes)

5 My sister <u>were</u> sick for days.

  A are

  B am

  C was

  D (No mistakes)

6 Jackie has <u>see</u> that movie.

  F seen

  G saw

  H seeing

  J (No mistakes)

7 The corn has <u>grown</u> taller.

  A grew

  B growing

  C grow

  D (No mistakes)

8 Nathan <u>take</u> swimming lessons with me last year.

  F taking

  G taken

  H took

  J (No mistakes)

Now write the numbers 9–18 on your paper. Read each paragraph. Choose the line that shows the mistake. Write the letter for that answer. If there is no mistake, write the letter for the last answer.

9 **A** Felipe has went to the
  B museum many times. He
  C likes the paintings there.
  D (No mistakes)

10 **F** A puppy licked me.
  G I bent over and patted
  H the puppys head.
  J (No mistakes)

11 **A** Last year Jim lost four
  B tooths. He still has empty
  C spaces in his mouth.
  D (No mistakes)

12 **F** Our class cleaned the
  G park. We done hard work,
  H but it was worth it.
  J (No mistakes)

13 **A** Your costume really
  B scared me! Where did
  C you get that awful mask.
  D (No mistakes)

14 **F** I got a letter from
  G Tamika. Tonight I
  H will written back to her.
  J (No mistakes)

15 **A** Amy just fell off her
  B bicycle. Dan and Erin
  C have run to help her.
  D (No mistakes)

16 **F** How many book has
  G Jon read about space?
  H He knows all the planets.
  J (No mistakes)

17 **A** My brother practices
  B very hard on his clarinet.
  C He are an awesome
    musician!
  D (No mistakes)

18 **F** Sara hurryied to the
  G library. The book that she
  H reserved had come in.
  J (No mistakes)

Now write the numbers 19–22 on your paper. Read the underlined sentences. Then choose the answer that best combines them into one sentence. Write the letter for that answer.

19 Matthew read a book.

Nicole took a nap.

   A Matthew and Nicole read a book and took a nap.

   B Matthew read a book, and Nicole took a nap.

   C The book, Matthew read it, and Nicole took a nap.

   D Read a book and took a nap, Matthew and Nicole did.

20 Rita likes the idea.

Lewis likes the idea.

   F Lewis likes and Rita likes the idea.

   G The idea Rita likes is the idea Lewis likes.

   H Rita and Lewis like the idea.

   J They like the idea, Rita and Lewis.

21 The boys washed the dishes.

The boys dried the dishes.

   A The boys washed and dried the dishes.

   B The dishes which the boys washed they dried.

   C Washed and dried by the boys the dishes were.

   D The dishes were washed by and dried by the boys.

22 The actors will bow.

The audience will clap.

   F The actors and the audience will bow and clap.

   G Clap for the bowing actors, the audience will.

   H The actors will bow, and the audience will clap.

   J Bow the actors will, and the audience will clap.

(pages 98–99)

1 What Are Verbs?

- A verb is a word that shows action.
- The verb is the main word in the predicate.

Remember

● Write the verb in each sentence.

Example: The band | marches down the street.   *marches*

1. We | watch it go by.
2. Many children | follow the drum major.
3. A tall boy | carries the flag.
4. The flag | waves in the wind.
5. Two clowns | dance.
6. Hannah | beats the drum.

▲ Write the verb in each sentence.

Example: My family works in the yard.   *works*

7. Mom cuts the grass.
8. Rasheed trims the bushes.
9. I rake the leaves into a pile.
10. Tonya plants some vegetables.
11. My sisters paint the old fence.
12. Dad waters the daffodils and the tulips.

■ Think of a verb that makes sense in each sentence. Then write the sentences.

Example: Nick _____ to the mailbox.   *Nick walks to the mailbox.*

13. He _____ a letter to his pen pal, Eric.
14. Eric _____ in Toronto, Canada.
15. Once Nick _____ Eric.
16. He _____ to Canada in an airplane.
17. The boys _____ a hockey game.
18. They _____ Lake St. Louis.

(pages 100–101)

2 Verbs in the Present

- Add -s to a verb in the present when the noun in the subject is singular.
- Do not add -s to a verb in the present when the noun in the subject is plural.

Remember

● Choose the correct present time of the verb in each pair of sentences below. Write the correct sentences.

Example: Your body <u>works</u> hard. *Your body works hard.*
Your body <u>work</u> hard.

1. Your ears <u>hears</u>.
   Your ears <u>hear</u>.
2. Your brain <u>think</u>.
   Your brain <u>thinks</u>.

3. Your eyes <u>see</u>.
   Your eyes <u>sees</u>.
4. Your heart <u>pump</u> blood.
   Your heart <u>pumps</u> blood.

▲ Write each sentence. Choose the correct verb in ( ).
Example: Children (need, needs) good food.
Children need good food.

5. Your body (use, uses) food in many ways.
6. Bananas (give, gives) us energy.
7. Beans (make, makes) the body stronger.
8. Nicole (pack, packs) a cheese sandwich for lunch.

■ Write the correct present time of each verb in ( ). Then write whether the subject is singular or plural.

Example: Mr. Lee _____ about hearts. (talk) *talks singular*

9. Hearts _____ blood. (pump)
10. Tubes _____ to and from the heart. (lead)
11. The lungs _____ blood. (get)
12. The brain _____ blood too. (need)

(pages 102–103)

3 More Verbs in the Present

- Add -es to a verb in the present that ends with s, sh, ch, or x, when it is used with a singular noun.
- If a verb ends with a consonant and y, change the y to i before adding -es.

● Write the verb in each pair that is spelled correctly.

Example: carryes
   carries *carries*

1. mixs 3. pushs 5. fixes 7. hurryes
 mixes   pushes   fixs   hurries
2. teaches 4. marries 6. cries 8. catchs
 teachs   marrys   cryes   catches

▲ Write each sentence. Choose the correct verb in ( ).

Example: Spiders (catch, catches) bugs. *Spiders catch bugs.*

9. A spider (push, pushes) a silk thread into the air.
10. Strong winds (carry, carries) the silk to a tree.
11. The spider (stretches, stretch) silk to make a web.
12. Bugs (flies, fly) into the web.
13. Then the spider (rush, rushes) to its meal.

■ Write the correct present time of each verb in ( ). Then write *singular* if the subject is singular. Write *plural* if the subject is plural.

Example: Scientists _____ dolphins. (study) *study plural*

14. A mother dolphin _____ her baby. (touch)
15. The mother _____ it to the top of the water. (push)
16. The baby _____ for a breath of air. (rush)
17. Other dolphins _____ through the water. (hurry)
18. Many people _____ the dolphins. (watch)

(pages 104–105)

4 Verbs in the Past

- A verb in the past time shows that an action has already happened.
- Add *-ed* to most verbs to show past time.

Remember

● Write the word in each pair that shows past time.

Example: jump

       jumped   *jumped*

1. splashed
   splash
2. watched
   watches
3. packed
   packs
4. laughed
   laugh
5. pitched
   pitches
6. barks
   barked
7. rush
   rushed
8. crosses
   crossed

▲ Change the verb in ( ) to show past time. Write each sentence.

Example: Long ago people _____ in groups. (travel)
      Long ago people traveled in groups.

9. Hunters _____ wild animals for food. (hunt)
10. Early people _____ berries and nuts. (gather)
11. Then people _____ new ways of doing things. (learn)
12. They _____ with simple tools. (work)
13. Men and women _____ seeds. (plant)

■ Change the verb in each sentence to show past time. Write the sentences.

Example: I learn about Christopher Columbus.
      I learned about Christopher Columbus.

14. Columbus talks to the Queen of Spain.
15. He asks for three ships.
16. His ships sail across the Atlantic Ocean.
17. The sailors reach land in 1492.
18. They land off the coast of North America!

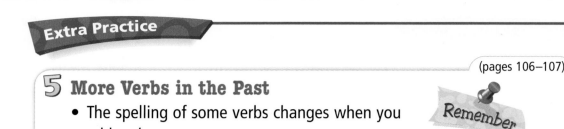

(pages 106–107)

5 More Verbs in the Past

- The spelling of some verbs changes when you add -ed.

Remember

● Write the past time for each verb below. Drop or add letters as needed.

Example: copy + ed = *copied*

1. dry + ed =
2. hike + ed =
3. hop + ed =
4. tag + ed =

5. sneeze + ed =
6. hope + ed =
7. marry + ed =
8. trot + ed =

9. pin + ed =
10. hurry + ed =
11. decide + ed =
12. grab + ed =

▲ Write each verb below to show past time.

Example: drip *dripped*

13. taste
14. worry
15. drag
16. bounce

17. nod
18. skate
19. try
20. carry

21. shop
22. bake
23. step
24. cry

■ Change the verb in each sentence below to show past time. Write the sentences.

Example: George Washington Carver lives on a farm.
George Washington Carver lived on a farm.

25. He loves plants.
26. Some people name him the "plant doctor."
27. Carver chops wood for money.
28. He saves money for school.
29. Carver studies all about plant life.
30. He raises many kinds of plants.
31. Carver tries many experiments with peanuts.
32. George Washington Carver cares about his work.

(pages 108–109)

⑥ Verbs in the Future

- A verb in the future time shows an action that is going to happen.

Remember

● Write *present* if the underlined verb shows present time. Write *past* if the verb shows past time. Write *future* if the verb shows future time.

Example: Winter <u>will arrive</u> soon. *future*

1. The pond in the park <u>will freeze</u>.
2. Gabriel <u>visits</u> the pond.
3. The first snow <u>fell</u> yesterday.
4. More snow <u>will make</u> good sledding.
5. One hill in the park <u>is</u> long and steep.

▲ Change the verb in ( ) to show future time. Write each sentence.

Example: The frozen pond _____ in spring. (thaw)
The frozen pond will thaw in spring.

6. The ice _____ into pieces. (break)
7. Slowly the pieces _____ away. (melt)
8. Then the geese and swans _____. (return)
9. Children _____ off their shoes and socks. (take)
10. They _____ in the pond. (wade)

■ Change the verb in each sentence below to show future time. Write the sentences.

Example: Spring passes quickly into summer.
Spring will pass quickly into summer.

11. The days grew hot and sticky.
12. Children put on their bathing suits.
13. They ran into the pond.
14. Later they dried off in the sun.
15. A cool breeze ripples the pond.

(pages 112–113)

7 The Special Verb *be*

- The verb *be* has special forms.
- *Am, is,* and *are* show present time.
- *Was* and *were* show past time.

Remember

● Write each sentence. Choose the correct verb in ( ).

Example: It (is, are) time for school.   *It is time for school.*

1. I (am, is) on the bus with my friends.
2. The bus (is, are) late.
3. We (is, are) late for school.
4. My teacher (was, were) worried.
5. The other students (was, were) already busy.

▲ Each sentence shows present time. Change the underlined verb to show past time. Write the new verbs.

Example: Two letters <u>are</u> in the mail.   *Two letters were in the mail.*

6. One letter <u>is</u> from Lisa.
7. It <u>is</u> very interesting.
8. Her family <u>is</u> in Texas for two weeks.
9. Her brothers <u>are</u> in a contest.
10. Sam and Alex <u>are</u> both winners.

■ Use *am, is, are, was,* or *were* to complete each sentence correctly. Write the sentences.

Example: We _____ at the library now.   *We are at the library now.*

11. The library _____ a busy place now.
12. The librarians _____ always very helpful.
13. Yesterday we _____ in the reading room.
14. The reading room _____ quiet then.
15. Three children _____ studying at our table.

(pages 114–115)

8 Helping Verbs

Remember

- *Has* and *have* are helping verbs.
- Use *has* with a singular noun in the subject and with *he, she,* or *it.*
- Use *have* with a plural noun in the subject and with *I, you, we,* or *they.*

● Write each sentence. Choose the correct verb in ( ).

Example: The frog (has, have) hopped onto a rock.
The frog has hopped onto a rock.

1. Lions (has, have) roared in the jungle.
2. The squirrels (has, have) cracked some nuts.
3. A bird (has, have) flapped its wings.
4. A horse (has, have) trotted down the street.

▲ Complete each sentence correctly with *has* or *have.* Write the sentences.

Example: I _____ read about animals.   *I have read about animals.*

5. Animals _____ protected themselves well.
6. A skunk _____ sprayed its enemies.
7. Prairie dogs _____ dug holes in the ground.
8. An insect _____ turned brown like a twig.

■ Rewrite each sentence by adding the helping verb *has* or *have* to the main verb.

Example: Army ants lived in large groups.
Army ants have lived in large groups.

9. The groups moved from place to place.
10. They traveled only at night.
11. The queen settled down in one spot.
12. Many ants hatched from her eggs.

(pages 116–117)

⑨ **Irregular Verbs**

- The verbs *go, see, do, run,* and *come* have special spellings to show past time.

Remember

● Choose the verb in ( ) to complete each sentence correctly. Write the sentences.

Example: Carrie has (came, come) to Missouri.
Carrie has come to Missouri.

1. She (saw, seen) her grandfather one day.
2. They (went, gone) to a ball game.
3. The pitcher (ran, run) after a ball.
4. The batter had (ran, run) to third base.
5. Both teams have (did, done) their best.

▲ Write the correct past time of each verb in ( ).

Example: A flower show has _____ to town. (come) *come*

6. Today we _____ to the show. (go)
7. Aubrey had _____ with us. (come)
8. We have _____ Japanese trees at the show. (see)
9. Dave _____ to the roses first. (run)
10. He _____ dozens of beautiful yellow roses. (see)

■ Use the correct past time of the verbs in the box to complete each sentence. You can use a verb more than once. Write the sentences.

Example: Officer Hill has _____ to my school.
Officer Hill has come to my school.

go
run
see
come
do

11. He _____ with a film about safety.
12. Lori's class had already _____ the film.
13. They saw a car that _____ through a red light.
14. One child _____ to the hospital in a police car.
15. Officer Hill _____ a good job at our school.

(pages 118–119)

10 More Irregular Verbs

Remember

- The verbs *give*, *write*, *eat*, *take*, and *grow* have special spellings to show past time.

● Choose the verb in ( ) to complete each sentence correctly. Write the sentences.

Example: I (wrote, written) about Edward Villella.
I wrote about Edward Villella.

1. Edward Villella (took, taken) dance lessons.
2. He had (took, taken) acting lessons too.
3. He (grew, grown) up to be a famous ballet dancer.
4. Edward (gave, given) many performances.
5. Reporters have (wrote, written) about his life.

▲ Write the correct past time of each verb in ( ).

Example: Derek _____ a trip to the West. (take)   *took*

6. His family _____ picnic lunches along the way. (eat)
7. Derek _____ me a letter from California. (write)
8. He _____ me a cactus from Arizona. (give)
9. It had _____ in a cactus garden. (grow)
10. I have _____ it some water. (give)

■ Use the correct past time of the verbs in the box to complete each sentence. Write the sentences.

Example: Pat has _____ about Amelia Earhart.
Pat has written about Amelia Earhart.

11. Amelia _____ excited about her flight alone.
12. Her flight across the Atlantic _____ over fifteen hours.
13. She _____ very little food during her flight.
14. President Hoover had _____ her a medal.
15. Many people have _____ about her trip.

| take |
| write |
| give |
| eat |
| grow |

(pages 120–121)

11 Contractions with *not*

Remember

• A contraction is a shortened form of two words joined together. Use an apostrophe in place of the missing letter or letters.

● Write the contraction in each sentence.

Example: Dad doesn't have his car keys.   *doesn't*

1. They aren't in his pocket.
2. Dad isn't happy at all.
3. He can't drive the car.
4. Mom hasn't seen the keys.

5. I don't see them anywhere.
6. Couldn't they be in the car?
7. We haven't looked there.
8. Shouldn't we have an extra set?

▲ Write the contractions for the words below.

Example: did not   *didn't*

9. were not
10. could not
11. have not
12. are not
13. had not

14. cannot
15. should not
16. does not
17. will not
18. is not

■ Write each sentence. Replace a word or words in each sentence with a contraction.

Example: Cocoa was not home.   *Cocoa wasn't home.*

19. I did not hear her bell.
20. She cannot have gone too far.
21. We have not fed her yet.
22. The kittens are not with her.
23. Cocoa would not hide in a tree!
24. She could not be in the garage.
25. We were not worried about Cocoa.
26. The cat will not be gone for long.

Rough wooden bow
Sea and sky of blue—
Cotton-ball clouds
Drift drowsily overhead.

Adjectives and Adverbs

1 What Are Adjectives?

One-Minute Warm-Up

One student chooses an object in the classroom and says three words to describe it. For example, *The object I am thinking of is large, green, and smooth. What is it?* (the chalkboard) Whoever guesses correctly chooses the next object, and the game continues.

- **Words that describe, or tell about, nouns are called adjectives.** Adjectives make sentences more interesting. They give details that make your meaning clearer.

  Loud sirens woke me up.   (What kind of sirens?)

  The old barn was on fire.   (What kind of barn?)

- The adjectives in the sentences above tell *what kind*. Notice that an adjective usually comes before the noun it describes.

Try It Out

Speak Up What is the adjective that describes each underlined noun?

1. Trucks rushed to the smoky <u>fire</u>.
2. A black <u>dog</u> barked at the trucks.
3. A tall <u>man</u> watched the fire.
4. The empty <u>building</u> burned quickly.
5. Firefighters sprayed water from hoses on the angry <u>flames</u>.
6. Thick <u>smoke</u> came out of the windows.
7. Soon the tired <u>firefighters</u> were done.

Write the adjective that describes each underlined noun.

Example: Leaves fell from the bushy <u>trees</u>.   *bushy*

8. Alonzo raked the leaves into a huge <u>pile</u>.
9. A yellow <u>butterfly</u> flew onto the leaves.
10. A frisky <u>kitten</u> ran after the butterfly.
11. The dry <u>leaves</u> blew everywhere.
12. Alonzo packed the leaves into brown <u>bags</u>.
13. He put the bags into the old <u>truck</u>.
14. Then Alonzo heard a squeaky <u>noise</u>.
15. The nosy <u>kitten</u> had jumped into the truck.

16–22. This ad has seven adjectives that tell *what kind*. Write the ad. Underline the adjectives.

Example: Max has green eyes.   *Max has <u>green</u> eyes.*

FREE KITTEN

   Would you like a free pet? A cuddly kitten needs a home. Max has gray fur. His tail has a white tip. His funny tricks will delight you. Will you give Max a happy home? Please call 555-8002 for a wonderful pet.

Writing Wrap-Up

WRITING • THINKING • LISTENING • SPEAKING

DESCRIBING

Write an Ad

   Write an ad for an animal that needs a home. Use adjectives to describe the animal. Draw a picture of it on the back of your paper, leaving out the animal's name. With a small group, take turns reading your ads and naming the adjectives. Then put all the pictures on a table. Who can guess which picture goes with each ad?

2 More Adjectives

Read the sentence below. Find the adjective that tells *what kind*. Can you find the other adjective?

Gabby curled her short hair with two fingers.

—from *Gabby Growing Up*, by Amy Hest

- You have learned that adjectives can tell *what kind*. Adjectives such as *one*, *ten*, *many*, and *several* tell *how many*.

  Two families traveled to New York.

  They passed many towns along the way.

- An adjective that tells *how many* comes before the noun it describes.

Try It Out

Speak Up What is the adjective that describes each underlined noun?

1. The trip took five <u>hours</u>.
2. They spent seven <u>days</u> in New York.
3. New York City has several <u>museums</u>.
4. One <u>museum</u> has stuffed wild animals that look real.
5. The three <u>brothers</u> took a ferry ride.
6. They took ten <u>pictures</u> of the Statue of Liberty.
7. Some <u>people</u> climbed the stairs inside the statue.
8. A few <u>children</u> ran up the stairs.

Write the adjective that describes each underlined noun.

Example: One <u>day</u> the families went to the Bronx Zoo.   *One*

9. The zoo has many <u>animals</u>.
10. It took several <u>hours</u> to see everything.
11. Two <u>bears</u> waded in a pool.
12. A trainer fed some <u>lions</u>.
13. Four <u>elephants</u> drank water.
14. Three <u>goats</u> walked up to the fence.
15. We saw some <u>tigers</u> sleeping on a rock.
16. A few <u>monkeys</u> made faces at us.

17–24. These directions have eight adjectives that tell *how many*. Write the directions. Underline the adjectives.

Example: You will go past one school.   *You will go past <u>one</u> school.*

Directions to Midland Zoo
  The drive to the zoo takes ten minutes from your house. Go down Lee Street for five miles. Turn left onto River Road. Drive past three banks. Then you will see several stores. Turn right after the stores. Drive for a few blocks. Look for two statues of zebras. The entrance to the zoo is behind the statues. Most people can park in the lot. There is enough space for ninety cars.

Writing Wrap-Up   WRITING • THINKING • LISTENING • SPEAKING

EXPLAINING

Write Directions
  Choose an object in the classroom. Write directions to the object. Include adjectives that tell *what kind* and *how many*. Read the directions to a partner. Have your partner follow the directions to the object. Were your directions clear?

Writing with Adjectives

Elaborating Sentences Good writers create pictures in the reader's mind. You can do this when you write, too, by adding adjectives that tell *what kind* and *how many*.

> The ocean was near our hotel. We swam for hours.

> The shining blue ocean was near our hotel. We swam for three long hours.

Apply It

1–8. Add two adjectives to each sentence in the scrapbook. Use the pictures to help you. Write the new sentences.

Surf, Sun, Sand!

The waves raced along the shore.

Alana and I built a castle with towers.

A dog woke me up.

I made a necklace of shells for Grandma.

Combining Sentences You can make your writing smooth and clear if you combine some sentences. Try moving adjectives to combine sentences.

The two choppy sentences below are both about a Ferris wheel. You can combine them by moving the adjective *huge* to the first sentence. Take out *It was*.

I rode on a Ferris wheel. It was huge.

I rode on a huge Ferris wheel.

> Check to see that your new sentences make sense.

Apply It

9–12. Revise these paragraphs from a journal. Combine each pair of underlined sentences.

Revising

Sunday, July 11

Today we went to a beach. It was rocky. Nick let me use his goggles. I saw two jellyfish in the water. They were ugly.

Later we went to an amusement park. I rode on a roller coaster. It was scary. Then we went into the fun house. The slide was my favorite part. It was bumpy. I also liked the crazy mirrors. We laughed hard because we looked so silly!

3 Using *a*, *an*, and *the*

What is wrong with this silly tongue twister? How can you fix it?

Alex Alligator ate a acorn, a apple, a apron, and a airplane!

The words *a, an,* and *the* are special adjectives called articles. Follow the rules below when you use articles.

- Use *a* and *an* with singular nouns. Use *a* before words that begin with a consonant sound. Use *an* before words that begin with a vowel sound.

  Jess stands in **a** long line.

  Our plane leaves in **an** hour.

- Use *the* before both singular and plural nouns.

  I wait at **the** gate.   Jess buys **the** tickets.

Try It Out

Speak Up Which article in ( ) may be used before each word below?

1. (the, an) pen
2. (a, an) fat cat
3. (a, an) egg
4. (a, an) old farm
5. (a, an) heavy jacket
6. (the, an) frisky animals
7. (a, an) owl
8. (the, an) bumpy road
9. (a, an) apple
10. (a, an) kite
11. (a, an) red hat
12. (a, an) airplane
13. (the, an) funny joke
14. (an, a) huge garden
15. (the, an) purple flowers
16. (a, an) angry bull

Write each sentence. Choose the correct article in ( ).

Example: Buddy is (a, an) unusual dog. *Buddy is an unusual dog.*

17. He is (a, an) aid to hearing-impaired children like Tim.
18. He understands (the, a) hand signals that Tim uses.
19. Buddy alerts Tim to (the, an) important sounds.
20. Tim starts to cross (a, an) street.
21. Buddy hears (a, an) car.
22. (The, An) smart dog steps in front of Tim.

23–28. This part of a letter has six incorrect articles. Write the letter correctly.

Example: Pixie watched from the shade of a oak tree.
Pixie watched from the shade of an oak tree.

Proofreading

Dear Grandma,

My dog Pixie is an hero. One day I was picking all a ripe apples from a apple tree. All of a best apples were up high. I reached for two big ones. Suddenly I heard a crack! A broken tree limb knocked me to the ground. Pixie knew it was a emergency. She gave an loud bark and ran to get Dad.

Writing Wrap-Up   WRITING • THINKING • LISTENING • SPEAKING

INFORMING

Write Safety Tips

Write a list of tips that can help prevent accidents. Use the words *a, an,* and *the* in your sentences. With a small group, take turns reading your tips aloud. Make a final list of the best tips for the class.

4 Comparing with Adjectives

One-Minute Warm-Up

THE PLANETS
By GAIL GIBBONS

Read the sentence below. Find the adjective that tells *how many*. Then find the adjective that is the opposite of the word *largest*.

> Mercury is the second smallest planet of the nine planets and is made up of rock and metal.

—from *The Planets,* by Gail Gibbons

Adjectives describe nouns. They can also show how people, places, or things are alike or different. Study the two rules below for comparing with adjectives.

- Add *-er* to most adjectives to compare *two* persons, places, or things.

    Mars is a smaller planet than Jupiter.

- Add *-est* to most adjectives to compare *more than two* persons, places, or things.

    Pluto is the smallest planet of all.

Try It Out

Speak Up Which adjective form in ( ) will complete each sentence correctly?

1. Venus has a (shorter, shortest) year than Jupiter.
2. Jupiter is a (colder, coldest) planet than Venus is.
3. Mercury is (nearer, nearest) of all to the Sun.
4. Uranus is (warmer, warmest) than Neptune.
5. Saturn is the (warmer, warmest) of the three.
6. Earth is (nearer, nearest) the Sun than Mars is.

Write each sentence. Choose the correct form of the adjective in ( ).

Example: The planet (nearer, nearest) to Earth is Venus.
The planet nearest to Earth is Venus.

7. A year on Earth is (shorter, shortest) than a year on Mars.
8. The planet with the (longer, longest) year is Pluto.
9. Mars is (cooler, coolest) than Earth.
10. Mercury is a (smaller, smallest) planet than Mars is.
11. Pluto is the (smaller, smallest) of the three.

12–16. This list of facts about Jupiter has five incorrect adjectives with *-er* and *-est*. Write the facts correctly.

Example: A day on Jupiter is shortest than a day on Earth.
A day on Jupiter is shorter than a day on Earth.

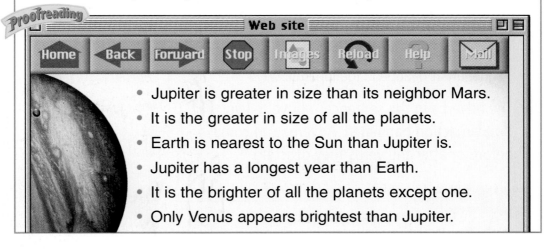

Proofreading

Web site

Home | Back | Forward | Stop | Images | Reload | Help | Mail

- Jupiter is greater in size than its neighbor Mars.
- It is the greater in size of all the planets.
- Earth is nearest to the Sun than Jupiter is.
- Jupiter has a longest year than Earth.
- It is the brighter of all the planets except one.
- Only Venus appears brightest than Jupiter.

Writing Wrap-Up   WRITING • THINKING • LISTENING • SPEAKING

COMPARING / CONTRASTING

Write Facts

Make a poster comparing facts about Earth and Jupiter. Use adjectives that end with *-er* and *-est* in your sentences. Then compare your poster with a partner's.

5 What Are Adverbs?

Read the sentences below. Which word describes how you should walk on Mother Earth?

At night around the campfire, Grandpa tells his tales.

* * *

"Walk softly on Mother Earth," he says.

—from *Red Bird,* by Barbara Mitchell

- You have learned that adjectives describe nouns. **Words that describe verbs are called adverbs.**

  Kim walked up to the horse bravely. (walked how?)

  She carefully sat on the horse. (sat how?)

  The horse stood quietly. (stood how?)

  Suddenly it galloped. (galloped how?)

- The adverbs in the sentences above tell you *how* an action happened. Adverbs can come before or after the verbs they describe.

 Tip

Most adverbs that tell *how* end in *-ly.*

Try It Out

Speak Up Which word in each sentence is an adverb?

1. Kim's horse ran swiftly.
2. Suddenly they came to a fence.
3. The horse jumped the fence nicely.
4. It landed safely on its feet.
5. Kim happily patted the horse's neck.

Write each sentence. Underline the adverb that tells *how*.

Example: Mr. Tanaka and Omi talked eagerly about horses.
Mr. Tanaka and Omi talked eagerly about horses.

6. They drove quickly to the stable.
7. Daisy munched hungrily on hay.
8. Calmly Omi put the saddle on Daisy.
9. Daisy poked Omi gently with her nose.
10. The horse easily carried Omi on her back.
11. Daisy held her head proudly.
12. Gracefully she trotted across the field.

13–20. This part of a story has eight adverbs that tell *how*. Write the story. Underline the adverbs.

Example: Tyler raced noisily down the stairs.
Tyler raced noisily down the stairs.

The sun shone brightly the morning of Tyler's birthday. He rubbed his eyes sleepily. Slowly he crawled out of bed. Suddenly he heard a whistle. Tyler ran excitedly to the window. His parents waved cheerfully from the yard. A horse stood quietly beside them. It happily nibbled at the grass.

Writing Wrap-Up WRITING • THINKING • LISTENING • SPEAKING

NARRATING

Write a Story About Yourself

Write a story about something special that happened to you. Tell why it was special. Use adverbs to tell how it made you feel. Then read your story to a partner. Have your partner name the adverbs.

6 Other Kinds of Adverbs

Read the sentence below. Which word tells when people look at manatees?

Today people look at manatees and wonder how anyone could think they were mermaids.

—from *Manatees*, by Emilie U. Lepthien

Adverbs tell *how* an action happens. They can also tell *when* and *where* an action happens.

When: Yesterday my family drove to Florida.

Where: We arrived there at night.

Adverbs That Tell *when*		Adverbs That Tell *where*	
always	soon	ahead	here
first	then	around	nearby
later	today	away	out
next	tomorrow	everywhere	there
often	yesterday	far	upstairs

Try It Out

Speak Up What is the adverb in each sentence? Does each adverb tell *where* or *when*?

1. Dad always takes a map on trips.
2. The map was not upstairs.
3. He walked all around.
4. He searched everywhere for it.
5. Then he checked the garage.
6. Tomorrow Dad will get a new map.

Write each sentence and underline the adverb. Then write *when* or *where* after each one.

Example: We soon found the hotel.   *We soon found the hotel.* *when*

7. We went upstairs and unpacked our suitcases.
8. Next, we took a bus tour.
9. We visited the famous Monkey Jungle first.
10. Many baby monkeys played there.
11. Their mothers stayed nearby and slept.
12. I stopped often and took pictures.

13–18. This schedule has six adverbs that tell *when* or *where.* Write the schedule. Underline the adverbs.

Example: We arrived in Brazil yesterday.
  We arrived in Brazil yesterday.

- Today we will tour the city of Rio de Janeiro.
- We will rent a car and drive around.
- First, we will explore the National Museum of Fine Arts.
- We will visit other interesting museums nearby.
- Then we will eat lunch at a hotel near Copacabana Beach.
- We will see tropical plants tomorrow at the Botanical Garden.

Writing Wrap-Up WRITING • THINKING • LISTENING • SPEAKING

INFORMING

Write a Schedule

A relative from another country is coming to visit you. Write a schedule of four or five things you will see and do during the visit. Use adverbs from the chart on page 154. Find a partner and discuss your schedules. Did your partner list similar things to see and do?

Writing with Adverbs

Elaborating Sentences You know that adverbs tell *how, when,* and *where* something happens. You can tell more in your sentences by adding adverbs.

We talked about our trip.   We talked **excitedly** about our trip.

We packed our suitcases.   We **carefully** packed our suitcases.

Often you can choose where to place an adverb in a sentence.

Soon we will be flying.   We will be flying **soon**.

We **soon** will be flying.   We will **soon** be flying.

Apply It

1–6. Revise this part of a personal narrative by adding an adverb to each sentence. Choose adverbs from the box or think of your own. Write the new paragraph.

eagerly	wildly	quickly	really	truly
slowly	suddenly	smoothly	early	then
soon	finally	first	carefully	later

Revising

Plane Ride

Look! I'm Flying!

   We boarded the plane. The jet engines started. The plane raced along the runway and rose into the air. My heart was beating, and my stomach filled with butterflies. I relaxed when the flight became smooth. I loved the ride!

Combining Sentences Short, choppy sentences can be combined to make your writing smoother. Combine two sentences by moving an adverb.

We will visit the market.
We will visit it later.   } We will visit the market later.

I love a smooth sentence!

Apply It

7–10. Revise this travel brochure. Combine each pair of choppy sentences.

Revising

Outdoor Market

People sell products at a big market. They sell them outside. You can smell delicious foods. You can smell them everywhere.

Shoppers look at the products. They look at them carefully.

Shoppers try to get a fair price. They always want a fair price.

Using *to*, *two*, and *too*

One-Minute Warm-Up

Something is wrong with this e-mail message. Fix the message by switching two words.

> ☐ ═══ e-mail ═══ ☐
>
> Please bring to notebooks two the meeting.

The words *to*, *two*, and *too* sound exactly alike, but they are spelled differently and have different meanings. The clues in a sentence can help you decide which word to use. Study the following chart to learn what each word means.

Word	Meaning	Example
to	in the direction of	I went **to** school.
two	a number (2)	I ate **two** plums.
too	also more than enough	I ate pears **too**. I ate **too** much.

Try It Out

Speak Up Would you use *to*, *two*, or *too* to complete each sentence?

1. Mom took me _____ her office.
2. She took my best friend _____.
3. Her office is _____ blocks from our house.
4. There were _____ many stairs to climb.
5. We walked _____ the elevators.
6. We rode up _____ floors.
7. Later, Mom will take us _____ a restaurant for lunch.

Complete each sentence with *to, two,* or *too.* Write the sentences.

Example: We went _____ the park.   *We went to the park.*

8. Shana and I invited our parents along _____.
9. _____ park rangers greeted us.
10. They pointed _____ a long trail.
11. The trail led _____ a beautiful lake.
12. We hiked for _____ hours.
13. It was not _____ hard for us.
14. We reached the lake at _____ o'clock.

15–20. This e-mail invitation has six mistakes in using *to, two,* and *too.* Write the invitation correctly.

Example: Bring a towel too the park.   *Bring a towel to the park.*

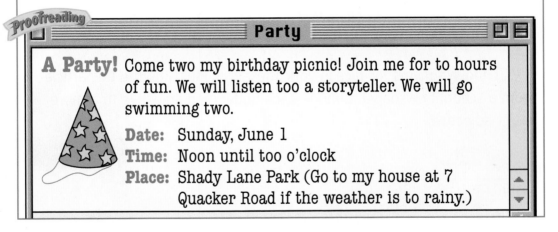

Proofreading

Party

A Party! Come two my birthday picnic! Join me for to hours of fun. We will listen too a storyteller. We will go swimming two.

Date: Sunday, June 1
Time: Noon until too o'clock
Place: Shady Lane Park (Go to my house at 7 Quacker Road if the weather is to rainy.)

Writing Wrap-Up   WRITING • THINKING • LISTENING • SPEAKING

CREATING

Write a Reply

You have received an invitation to a friend's birthday picnic. Write a reply telling why you cannot go. Use the words *to, two,* and *too* at least once. Read your reply to a partner. Have your partner spell each *to, two,* and *too* that you used. Do they match the words you wrote?

Using Exact Adjectives

Adjectives add details about people, places, and things. When you write, use exact adjectives so the reader can picture what you are saying.

Less exact adjective: The boy is feeding his big dog.

More exact adjective: The boy is feeding his enormous dog.

Apply It

1–5. Find synonyms for *nice* in your Thesaurus Plus. Rewrite this article from a school newspaper. Change each underlined adjective to a more exact adjective.

Revising

Washington School News

The Firefighter

A firefighter came to talk to the class. She said hello to everyone, which was very <u>nice</u> of her. She even brought every student a red key chain with the number of the fire department on it. How <u>nice</u> that was! It was <u>nice</u> to listen to her speak because she had such a <u>nice</u> voice. What a <u>nice</u> time we had!

Enrichment

Adjectives!

Shape Poems

Write a poem, using the form below.

noun—
adjective, adjective, adjective *(describes the noun)*—
verb
adverb, adverb, adverb *(tells how, when, or where)*.

Cut out the shape of the noun in your poem. Copy the poem onto the shape.

Clouds —
Dark, gray, rainy —
Move
Quickly away today.

Toy Catalog

Bike

Jump Rope

Paint Set

$3.98
bright colors
handy case

Make a catalog for a toy company. Draw pictures of three toys. Use a separate sheet of paper for each toy. Include the name of the item and its price. Add labels that describe its special features. Use an adjective in each label. Then staple the pages of your catalog together.

Challenge Draw an item that moves or has moving parts for your catalog, such as a bike or a robot. Use adverbs in some of your labels.

Example: The arms move up and down.

1 **What Are Adjectives?** *(p. 142)* Write each sentence. Underline the adjective that tells *what kind.*

1. Kim read a story about a young girl.
2. The girl was carried away by a strong wind.
3. The wind carried her to a new land.
4. A woodsman, a lion, and a kind scarecrow helped her.

2 **More Adjectives** *(p. 144)* Write each sentence. Underline the adjective that tells *how many.*

5. Some people collect paintings by Norman Rockwell.
6. My mother has two pictures in the den.
7. A museum in Massachusetts has several paintings.
8. Rockwell painted many covers for magazines.

3 **Using *a, an,* and *the*** *(p. 148)* Choose the article in ( ) that goes with each word. Write the article.

9. (a, an) fork   11. (an, the) squirrel
10. (a, an) aunt   12. (a, an) old house

4 **Comparing with Adjectives** *(p. 150)* Write the correct form of the adjective in ( ) to complete each sentence.

13 The lion tamer is _____ than the clown. (tall)
14. The man on stilts is the _____ of all. (tall)
15. The white horse is _____ than the gray horse. (fast)
16. The brown horse is the _____ of the three horses. (fast)

5 **What Are Adverbs?** *(p. 152)* Write each sentence. Underline the adverb that tells *how.*

17. The lights shone brightly in my neighbor's yard.
18. Quietly I peeked into the yard.
19. Some people were singing loudly.
20. They happily invited me to join them.

 See www.eduplace.com/kids/hme/ for an online quiz.

6 Other Kinds of Adverbs *(p. 154)* Write each sentence. Underline the adverb that tells *when* or *where.*

21. Mr. Marullo often washes his car.
22. I watch nearby.
23. The water sprays everywhere.
24. Mr. Marullo always gets wet.

7 Using *to*, *two*, and *too* *(p. 158)* Complete each sentence with *to*, *two*, or *too.* Write the sentences.

25. _____ children in our class want to be animal doctors.
26. They went _____ an animal hospital.
27. They saw _____ sick animals.
28. The children visited a dog kennel _____ .

Mixed Review 29–34. This page from a bird book has two incorrect articles, two incorrect adjectives with *-er* and *-est*, and two mistakes in using *to*, *two*, and *too.* Write the page correctly.

Proofreading Checklist
Are these words used correctly?
✔ the articles *a*, *an*, and *the*
✔ adjectives with *-er* and *-est*
✔ *to*, *two*, and *too*

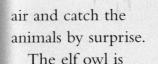

    People think owls are smartest than other birds. This is not true. Their big eyes just make them look wise. A owl is a excellent hunter, though. It sees well at night. Its hearing is good two. Owls listen to the sounds small animals make. They fly silently through the air and catch the animals by surprise.

elf owl

    The elf owl is the smaller of all the owls. The greatest of all in size is the great gray owl. Some owls have to tufts of feathers on their heads. These feathers are often called "horns."

✓ Test Practice

Write the numbers 1–6 on a sheet of paper. Read each group of sentences. Choose the sentence that is written correctly. Write the letter for that answer.

1 A Let's make an pitcher of grape juice.

B Here is a spoon for stirring.

C There is a empty glass for you to use.

D I would like a ice cube.

2 F August was the warmer month of the year.

G Of all the months, February has the fewer days.

H October was coolest than September.

J Is November shorter than December?

3 A Brett and Tricia went to the library.

B Brett found to books about paper airplanes.

C Tricia borrowed a book and a magazine two.

D She will return them in too weeks.

4 F Brandon is working slowly.

G His work is neat than mine.

H Holly has finish several pages in an hour.

J This is the harder page of all.

5 A Moon Lake is smallest than Deer Lake.

B The deepest part of the lake is right here.

C The ducks are loudest than the geese.

D Of all the beaches, this one is the cleanly.

6 F Bring this shopping list two the store.

G Please buy to gallons of milk.

H Get bread and bananas too.

J Carry the bags too the car.

Now write the numbers 7–10 on your paper. Read the passage all the way through once. Then look at the underlined parts. Decide if they need to be changed or if they are fine as they are. Choose the best answer from the choices given. Write the letter of that answer.

Mr. Sanchez lives next door to us. He is the kindest person in our

7 A a kindest
   B the more kinder
   C the most kindest
   D (No changes)

neighborhood. He remembers all his neighbors birthdays. He helps

8 F neighbors'
   G neighbor's
   H neighbors's
   J (No changes)

the neighbors with their heavy chores too. Last week Mr. Sanchez got very sick. My mother quickly

9 A quickest
   B quicker
   C more quicker
   D (No changes)

called all the neighbors. They visited him they cheered him up. Soon Mr. Sanchez felt much better.

10 F visited him and cheered
   G visited him, they cheered
   H visited him, cheered
   J (No changes)

Unit 1: The Sentence

Four Kinds of Sentences *(pp. 36, 38)* Write each sentence correctly.

1. do you have a dog
2. ashley has a collie
3. watch its tail
4. it moves so quickly

Subjects and Predicates in Sentences *(pp. 40, 42)* Write each group of words that is a sentence. Draw a line between the subject and the predicate. If the group of words is not a sentence, write *not a sentence*.

5. Luis builds model cars.
6. His sister Nicole.
7. The weather is rainy.
8. They play together.
9. Can hear the rain.

Run-on Sentences *(p. 44)* Correct each run-on sentence by writing two sentences.

10. My first bike was a tricycle a tricycle has three wheels.
11. Now I have a new bike it goes faster.
12. Bikes used to have wooden wheels they looked funny.
13. Once I saw a race the bike riders were in teams.
14. The race lasted six days it was held inside a building.

Unit 2: Nouns

Common and Proper Nouns *(pp. 60, 62)*
Write each noun. Then write *common* or *proper*.

15. My uncle lives in Texas.
16. Uncle Jack owns a ranch.
17. His family raises cattle.
18. Matt took a trip there.
19. Jennifer sent pictures.
20. Dallas looks great!

 See www.eduplace.com/kids/hme/ for a tricky usage or spelling question.

Nouns in the Subject *(p. 64)* Write the noun in the subject of each sentence.

21. Exercise is important.
22. The heart works hard.
23. Weak muscles become strong.
24. My aunt Val jogs.
25. Grandpa swims often.
26. Holly listens to an exercise tape.

Singular and Plural Nouns
(pp. 68, 70, 71, 72) Write the plural form of each noun.

27. vegetable
28. patch
29. goose
30. city
31. box
32. mouse

Possessive Nouns *(pp. 74, 76)* Write the possessive form of each noun.

33. swimmer
34. woman
35. families
36. children
37. Alex
38. monkey

Unit 3: Verbs

What Are Verbs? *(p. 98)* Write each verb.

39. Mr. Page plows the field.
40. Mrs. Page repairs the tractor.
41. Pat puts the crops on the truck.
42. It takes a long time.
43. They work hard.

Verbs in the Present *(pp. 100, 102)*
Choose the correct verb. Write the sentences.

44. I (watch, watches) the harbor.
45. Two boats (sails, sail) toward me.
46. They (toss, tosses) in the waves.
47. Dad (steers, steer) one boat.
48. Mom (carry, carries) the life jackets.

Verbs in the Past *(pp. 104, 106)* Write the past time of each verb.

49. hum
50. bury
51. rake
52. spy
53. chop
54. lift

Verbs in the Future *(p. 108)* Write the future time of each verb.

55. build
56. hurry
57. watch
58. leap
59. play
60. read

Helping Verbs *(p. 114)* Complete each sentence with *has* or *have*. Write each sentence.

61. Ana _____ started a coin collection.
62. She _____ collected coins from different countries.
63. My grandparents _____ discovered a great coin shop.
64. They _____ surprised Ana with a Japanese coin.

The Verb *be* and Irregular Verbs *(pp. 112, 116, 118)* Write each sentence. Use the correct verb in ( ).

65. Hakeem had (ate, eaten) something bad.
66. We (was, were) upset.
67. He (is, are) much better today.
68. He (went, gone) back to school.

Contractions with *not* *(p. 120)* Write the contraction for each word or words.

69. will not
70. is not
71. cannot
72. had not
73. were not
74. should not

Unit 4: Adjectives and Adverbs

What Are Adjectives? *(pp. 142, 144)* Write the adjective in each sentence. Do not write *a, an,* or *the.*

75. Some people are fixing a road.
76. They wear warm jackets and hats.
77. A woman runs a heavy machine.
78. The machine moves huge piles of dirt.
79. Sometimes I can hear the loud drill.

Using *a, an, the* and *to, too, two* *(pp. 148, 158)* Write each sentence. Choose the correct word.

80. Marta has taken (too, two) riding lessons.
81. Each lesson lasted (a, an) hour.
82. Today she rode (to, too) (the, a) old barn.
83. Her riding teacher went (to, too).
84. Marta brought (a, an) sweater with her.

Comparing with Adjectives *(p. 150)* Write each sentence. Use the correct form of the adjective in ( ).

85. Yesterday was _____ than today. (damp)
86. Today is the _____ day of the week. (bright)
87. The nights are _____ than the days. (cool)
88. Tuesday was _____ than Wednesday. (bright)
89. Winter nights are _____ of all. (cold)

What Are Adverbs? *(pp. 152, 154)* Write each adverb.

90. Yesterday Sam was painting his room.
91. The telephone rang loudly.
92. Sam ran upstairs and answered it.
93. Sam's curious puppy carelessly bumped the can of paint.
94. The paint spilled everywhere!

(pages 142–143)

1 What Are Adjectives?

- An adjective is a word that describes a noun.
- Some adjectives tell *what kind.*

Remember

● Write the adjective that describes the underlined noun.

Example: Josh got a new <u>bike</u> yesterday.   *new*

1. He rode it down a bumpy <u>street</u>.
2. Daniel heard the loud <u>horn</u>.
3. They rode to the sandy <u>beach</u> together.
4. The boys jumped into the cool <u>water</u>.
5. Josh forgot to bring his purple <u>towel</u>.

▲ Write each sentence. Underline the adjective that tells *what kind.*

Example: Gina and I carried the heavy suitcases.
Gina and I carried the <u>heavy</u> suitcases.

6. We put them into the brown car.
7. Soon we saw the busy airport.
8. Noisy airplanes were landing everywhere.
9. We handed a young man the tickets.
10. The plane took off with a loud roar.

■ Write each sentence. Use a different adjective to describe each underlined noun.

Example: The <u>bus</u> went by.   *The old bus went by.*

11. It stopped at the <u>park</u>.
12. My <u>sister</u> and I got off the bus.
13. We wore <u>hats</u> and light jackets.
14. A <u>baby</u> was sleeping in a carriage.
15. A man walked a <u>dog</u> along the sidewalk.
16. Some women fed the <u>squirrels</u>.

(pages 144–145)

2 More Adjectives

- Some adjectives tell *how many.*

Remember

● Complete each sentence with an adjective that tells *how many.* Write the sentences. Use the words in the box.

Example: Tony and Alex explored _____ caves.
Tony and Alex explored two caves.

| some |
| two |
| several |
| three |
| many |
| eight |

1. Alex took _____ flashlights with him.
2. Tony packed _____ sandwiches.
3. The boys climbed over _____ rocks.
4. Tony saw _____ footprints.
5. Then _____ birds flew into the cave.

▲ Write each sentence. Underline the adjective that tells *how many.*

Example: The movie about deserts took two hours.
The movie about deserts took <u>two</u> hours.

6. One desert is called the Sahara.
7. Did you notice the five camels?
8. They can go for many months without water.
9. Deserts may not get rain for several years.
10. A few deserts do have water holes.

■ Write each sentence with an adjective that tells *how many.* Underline the noun each adjective describes.

Example: _____ people took a trip to Africa.
Several <u>people</u> took a trip to Africa.

11. The group watched _____ animals in the jungle.
12. Roberto saw _____ elephants.
13. Samantha surprised _____ monkeys.
14. _____ hippos swam in the water with their babies.

(pages 148–149)

3 Using *a*, *an*, and *the*

- *A*, *an*, and *the* are special adjectives called articles.
- Use *a* before a word that begins with a consonant sound. Use *an* before a word that begins with a vowel sound.

Remember

● Choose the correct group of words in each pair. Write the correct group.

Example: a ox
an ox *an ox*

1. an peach
   a peach
2. an elm tree
   a elm tree

3. an old dog
   a old dog
4. an quiet deer
   a quiet deer

5. a eagle
   an eagle
6. an uncle
   a uncle

▲ Write each sentence. Use the correct article.

Example: Walt Disney was (a, an) artist. *Walt Disney was an artist.*

7. He wanted (a, an) animal for his cartoons.
8. He remembered (a, an) pet mouse named Mortimer.
9. Mortimer was (a, an) interesting mouse.
10. Disney drew (a, an) cartoon mouse named Mickey.
11. (An, The) first Mickey Mouse film opened in 1928.

■ Complete each sentence with *a, an,* or *the.* Write the sentences. Be sure that your answers make sense.

Example: Why is Sally Ride _____ famous person?
Why is Sally Ride a famous person?

12. Sally Ride is _____ astronaut.
13. She was _____ first American woman in space.
14. In 1983 Sally took _____ exciting trip.
15. She flew on one of _____ space shuttles.
16. Sally quickly became _____ celebrity.

(pages 150–151)

4 Comparing with Adjectives

Remember

- Add *-er* to most adjectives to compare two persons, places, or things.
- Add *-est* to most adjectives to compare more than two persons, places, or things.

● Make three columns on your paper. In the first column, copy the adjectives. In the middle column, write the adjectives with *-er*. In the third column, write the adjectives with *-est*.

Example: loud

Adjective	*With* -er	*With* -est
loud	louder	loudest

1. new
2. soft
3. tall
4. old
5. fast
6. short
7. young
8. smooth

▲ Write each sentence. Use the correct form of the adjective in ( ).

Example: A zebra is (taller, tallest) than a tiger.
A zebra is taller than a tiger.

9. A giraffe is the (taller, tallest) of the three.
10. The hummingbird is the (smaller, smallest) of all birds.
11. A blue jay has a (longer, longest) life than a robin.
12. A lion is a (faster, fastest) runner than a goat.

■ Write each sentence. Use the correct form of the adjective in ( ). Then underline the adjectives that compare more than two nouns.

Example: The sailboat is the _____ boat of all. (long)
The sailboat is the longest boat of all.

13. The canoe is _____ than the rowboat. (long)
14. My fishing pole is _____ than yours. (new)
15. Colin's fishing pole is the _____ of all. (new)
16. This fish is the _____ of the three. (short)

(pages 152–153)

5 What Are Adverbs?

- A word that describes a verb is an adverb.
- Adverbs that tell *how* usually end in *-ly*.

Remember

● Write the sentences. Complete each one with an adverb that tells *how*. Use a different adverb in each sentence. Use the words in the box.

Example: Birds fly _____.   *Birds fly swiftly*.

1. Baby chicks hatch _____.
2. A robin builds its nest _____.
3. Woodpeckers drill _____ into trees.
4. _____ an owl takes flight.
5. Sea gulls glide _____ through the air.

swiftly
Silently
noisily
easily
slowly
carefully

▲ Write each sentence. Underline the adverb.

Example: Cranes fly smoothly.   *Cranes fly smoothly*.

6. Whooping cranes usually lay two eggs a year.
7. Normally one chick lives.
8. Scientists eagerly help the birds.
9. Gently they place one egg in another nest.
10. Another bird hatches the egg successfully.

■ Write the sentences. Complete each one with a different adverb that tells *how*.

Example: _____ Taylor hurried to the field day.
Eagerly Taylor hurried to the field day.

11. She _____ waited for the sack race to begin.
12. The whistle blew _____.
13. Three children _____ took the lead.
14. The crowd yelled _____.
15. _____ Taylor was winning the race!

(pages 154–155)

6 Other Kinds of Adverbs

- Adverbs can tell *when* and *where* an action happens.

Remember

● Write the adverb. The word in ( ) tells you what kind of adverb it is.

Example: Dad drives a bus everywhere. (where) *everywhere*

1. He leaves for his job early. (when)
2. Today people climbed onto the empty bus. (when)
3. They can always get seats. (when)
4. Dad pulls away from the bus stop. (where)
5. The bus travels far. (where)
6. Tomorrow Dad will take me with him. (when)

▲ Write each sentence. Underline the adverb.

Example: The Wright Brothers often talked about planes.
The Wright Brothers <u>often</u> talked about planes.

7. They soon built one.
8. Then the brothers tested the airplane.
9. The airplane flew around for a short time.
10. Today airplanes travel great distances.
11. They can fly everywhere.

■ Write the sentences with adverbs from the box. Underline the verbs.

Example: _____ I rode in a helicopter.
Today I <u>rode</u> in a helicopter.

12. We _____ stayed in our seats.
13. _____ the pilot changed direction.
14. He turned the helicopter _____.
15. _____ we passed a huge cloud.
16. I have asked him for a ride _____.

| Then |
| around |
| Once |
| again |
| always |
| Today |

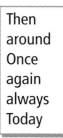

(pages 158–159)

7 Using *to*, *two*, and *too*

Remember

- *To*, *two*, and *too* sound alike but have different meanings.
- *To* means "in the direction of."
- *Two* is a number.
- *Too* means "also" or "more than enough."

● Write each sentence. Use the correct word in ( ).

Example: Emily and Wing went (to, two) the pet shop.
Emily and Wing went to the pet shop.

1. Wing bought (too, two) fish.
2. He bought some food for them (too, to).
3. Emily walked over (to, two) the puppies.
4. She watched (two, too) brown ones.
5. The children stayed at the store (to, too) long.

▲ Write each sentence with *to*, *two*, or *too*.

Example: Grandma went _____ college.   *Grandma went to college.*

6. She took _____ courses.
7. One course was _____ crowded.
8. Grandma used _____ kinds of computers in class.
9. Grandma took me _____ a class.

■ Write *correct* if the underlined word is correct. If it is not, write the sentence correctly.

Example: A ship sailed <u>too</u> an island.   *A ship sailed to an island.*

10. The trip takes <u>two</u> hours.
11. A sailor moved <u>too</u> the controls.
12. The captain was at the controls <u>to</u>.
13. She turned the wheel <u>to</u> the right.
14. The boat got <u>two</u> the island exactly on time.

The Statue of Liberty stands majestically on Liberty Island in New York Harbor. The people of France gave the statue to the United States as a gift in 1884.

Capitalization and Punctuation

1 Correct Sentences

One-Minute Warm-Up

Each student receives a card with an end mark on it. Everyone stands as a volunteer says a sentence. Those who have cards with the end mark for that sentence should hold up their cards. Anyone who has the correct end mark but fails to hold it up sits down. Students left standing after several rounds are the winners.

Every sentence begins with a capital letter and ends with an end mark. Study these rules.

- End a statement with a period.

   I will do my science report on the computer.

- End a question with a question mark.

   What will you write about?

HELP

? Tip

Always check your writing for run-on sentences.

- End a command with a period.

   Print the report out now.

- End an exclamation with an exclamation point.

   The printer works so fast!

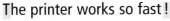

Try It Out

Speak Up How would you write each sentence correctly?

1. look at these computer games
2. this game is terrific
3. may I try another game on your computer
4. the first level is easy
5. watch me get through the maze

Write each sentence correctly.

Example: what is the Internet   *What is the Internet?*

6. the Internet is a network of computers
7. thousands of smaller networks are connected to the Internet
8. it has information on everything
9. how can I connect my computer to the Internet
10. get a modem
11. modems connect computers to the Internet through telephone lines

12–18. This interview has three missing capital letters and four missing or incorrect end marks. Write the interview correctly.

Example: Reporter: tell us how old you are?
   Reporter: Tell us how old you are.

Proofreading

Oscar Falls Victim to Third-Grade Whiz!

Reporter: you just beat the world's smartest computer at checkers. What does that feel like.
Tamika: It feels wonderful
Reporter: nobody ever beats Oscar. How did you do it? tell us your secret?
Tamika: I cannot tell you in front of Oscar He might beat me next time.

Writing Wrap-Up   WRITING • THINKING • LISTENING • SPEAKING

PERSUADING

Write a Letter

You want to try the new computer game Recess All Day. Write a letter convincing your teacher that this game would be good for the class. Use the four kinds of sentences. Read your letter to a partner. Make your voice show the sentence types you used. Did you give good reasons?

Writing Good Sentences

Writing Different Types of Sentences You know that sentences can be statements, questions, commands, or exclamations. Make your writing lively by using all four types of sentences.

The first paragraph below has only statements. You can see how exclamations, questions, and commands make the second paragraph more interesting.

> Learning new words takes time. There is a sure way to succeed. You can try the Mem R. Ize computer game.

> Learning new words takes time! Is there a sure way to succeed? Try the Mem R. Ize computer game.

Apply It

1–6. Rewrite this part of a bulletin-board notice. Change each underlined statement to another type of sentence. The word in ( ) tells you the type of sentence to write.

Revising

Join the Club

Computer software costs a lot. (exclamation) Not everyone can buy all the new programs. (question) We can think about this. (command) It would be great to have an after–school computer club. We could play computer games and learn new skills.

You can help me start a computer club. (question) You can talk to your family and teachers about it. (command) I think they will like the idea of learning together. We would have fun too. (exclamation)

Combining Sentences You know that the words *and, or,* and *but* can be used to join complete sentences. You can also use *because, before, after, when,* and *while.*

I memorized the names of all fifty states. I practiced on a computer map.
I memorized the names of all fifty states after I practiced on a computer map.

My brother and I do our homework. We play computer games.
My brother and I do our homework before we play computer games.

Apply It

7–10. Rewrite each cartoon caption. Join the two sentences with the word in ( ).

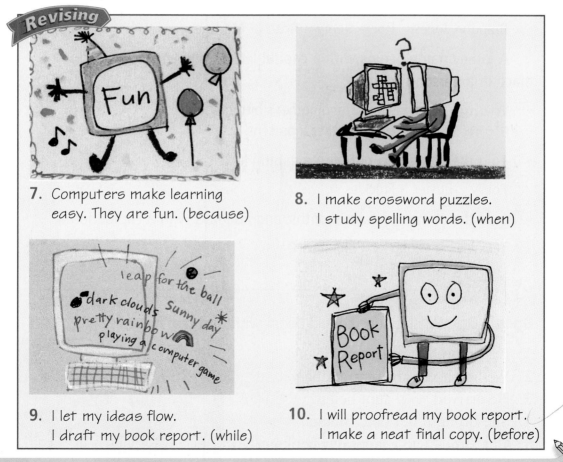

Revising

7. Computers make learning easy. They are fun. (because)

8. I make crossword puzzles. I study spelling words. (when)

9. I let my ideas flow. I draft my book report. (while)

10. I will proofread my book report. I make a neat final copy. (before)

2 Capitalizing Proper Nouns

Read the sentence below. How many nouns can you find? Which are common nouns? Which are proper nouns?

When Pepita walked into her yard after school, she found Lobo sleeping on the front porch.

—from *Pepita Talks Twice/Pepita habla dos veces,*
by Ofelia Dumas Lachtman

There are many kinds of proper nouns. Always begin a proper noun with a capital letter.

• Begin the name of a particular person with a capital letter.

Brandon Jones   Uncle Henry   Rosa L. Martinez

A family name begins with a capital letter only when it is used in place of a person's name.

Wrong: Today is my Grandmother's birthday.
Right: I gave Grandmother a present.

• Begin the name of a pet with a capital letter.

Pokey   Buster   Freckles

• Begin the names of days, months, and holidays with a capital letter.

Tuesday   February   Columbus Day

Try It Out

Speak Up Which nouns should begin with a capital letter?

1. Last monday we had company.
2. We had a visit from grandpa.
3. He arrived with aunt helen.
4. She brought her dog, muggs.
5. Our family had a labor day cookout.

Correct each sentence.

Example: I showed mom my guest list.   *I showed Mom my guest list.*

6. I was born on flag day.
7. I hope aunt julie can come to my birthday party.
8. My aunt visits us every june.
9. I addressed her invitation to julia r. simon.
10. Did duke chew some of the invitations?
11. On sunday he chewed the one for my grandpa.
12. I invited grandpa by telephone yesterday.

13–20. This part of a journal entry has eight missing or incorrect capital letters. Write the journal entry correctly.

Example: My sister emma helped my Uncle with the cooking.
           My sister Emma helped my uncle with the cooking.

Proofreading

On sunday we had a picnic to celebrate memorial day. As usual, uncle Pete kept us laughing. He pretended to be a famous chef named Frank n. Burger. Grandpa Travis and I sprayed each other with a garden hose. Later, my dog, poppy, stole the show. She snatched a piece of chicken from my Uncle and dropped it in front of mom.

Writing Wrap-Up   WRITING • THINKING • LISTENING • SPEAKING

EXPLAINING

Write an Explanation

Write a paragraph about your favorite holiday. Explain why it is your favorite. Include the name of the holiday, the month in which it occurs, and the names of the people you see that day. Then read your paragraph to a partner. Compare the holidays you wrote about.

Mechanics

3 Capitalizing Other Nouns

One-Minute Warm-Up

Read the sentence below. Which proper nouns name people? Which proper noun names a place?

> Now Halmoni was taking Yunmi for a visit to Korea to meet all her aunts and uncles and cousins.
>
> —from *Yunmi and Halmoni's Trip,* by Sook Nyul Choi

- The name of a particular place is a proper noun. Particular places include streets, cities and towns, states, countries, schools, parks, rivers, and lakes. Names of particular places begin with capital letters.

Park Street	Clarke Elementary School
New York City	Whitehall Park
Texas	Red River
Canada	Lake Erie

- Begin each important word in a proper noun with a capital letter. Do not begin *of* with a capital letter.

United States of America   Cape of Good Hope

Try It Out

Speak Up Which nouns should begin with a capital letter?

1. Antonio Diaz lives on pine street.
2. His house is near franklin park.
3. He will travel to new hampshire next month.
4. His cousin Rita lives in a town called east meadow.
5. Someday Antonio wants to visit the gulf of mexico.

Gulf of Mexico

Correct each sentence.

Example: I am a citizen of the united states of america.
I am a citizen of the United States of America.

6. I live in florida.
7. My town is called fort lauderdale.
8. My house is on whitehall drive.
9. We swim at hollywood beach.
10. My sisters go to dillard high school.
11. Our neighbors used to live in egypt.
12. They lived in a city called giza.
13. They sailed on the nile river.

The Nile

14–20. This part of an online travel guide to Phoenix, Arizona, has seven missing or incorrect capital letters. Write the information correctly.

Example: You can go boating on canyon lake.
You can go boating on Canyon Lake.

Proofreading

Travel Guide

The sun shines in Phoenix three hundred days a year. You can swim in apache lake on the salt River. There is biking and fishing at Papago park. When it does rain, you can visit the Phoenix Museum Of History or shop at a big mall on cactus road.

Writing Wrap-Up

WRITING • THINKING • LISTENING • SPEAKING

CREATING

Write Riddles

Write some riddles that describe places in your city or town. Use proper nouns in your riddles. For example, you might write *What has books, begins with the letter* b, *and can be found on Bleeker Street?* *(Answer: Baker Library)* Have a partner guess the answers to your riddles and say what word or words begin with a capital letter.

4 Abbreviations

One-Minute Warm-Up

Read the sentence below. Find the person's name that begins with a title. What punctuation mark comes at the end of the title?

In the car pool Mrs. Gibson let Becky have a seat by the window.

—from *Alexander and the Terrible, Horrible, No Good, Very Bad Day*, by Judith Viorst

- **An abbreviation is a short way to write a word.** Most abbreviations begin with capital letters and end with periods.

Days of the Week	
Sunday	Sun.
Monday	Mon.
Tuesday	Tues.
Wednesday	Wed.
Thursday	Thurs.
Friday	Fri.
Saturday	Sat.

Months of the Year			
January	Jan.	July	——
February	Feb.	August	Aug.
March	Mar.	September	Sept.
April	Apr.	October	Oct.
May	——	November	Nov.
June	——	December	Dec.

- **Titles are special words used with people's names.** Abbreviations are used for most titles. The title *Miss* does not have an abbreviation.

Dr.　Mr.　Miss　Mrs.　Ms.

Try It Out

Speak Up How would you write each name and abbreviation correctly?

1. fri
2. nov
3. mr Peter Adams
4. miss Rosa Santos
5. oct
6. dr Pat Johnson

A visit to the dentist

Write the correct abbreviation for each day and month.

Example: Thursday *Thurs.*

7. Monday
8. April
9. December
10. March

11. Saturday
12. Wednesday
13. September
14. Sunday

15. February
16. October
17. Tuesday
18. January

19–24. This schedule has six incorrect abbreviations. Write the schedule correctly.

Example: tues., aug. 7: mr Will Fixit talks about home repairs.
Tues., Aug. 7: Mr. Will Fixit talks about home repairs.

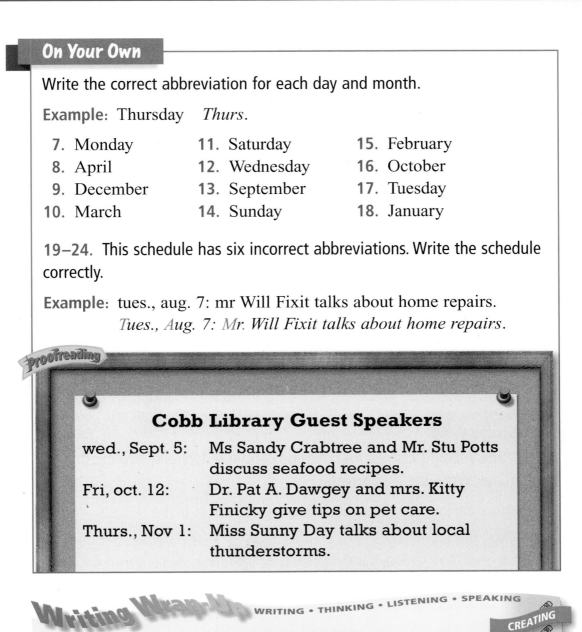

Cobb Library Guest Speakers

wed., Sept. 5: Ms Sandy Crabtree and Mr. Stu Potts discuss seafood recipes.

Fri, oct. 12: Dr. Pat A. Dawgey and mrs. Kitty Finicky give tips on pet care.

Thurs., Nov 1: Miss Sunny Day talks about local thunderstorms.

WRITING • THINKING • LISTENING • SPEAKING

CREATING

Write a Schedule

Make up funny names that match a person's job. For example, *Mr. Weedy* could be a gardener and *Ms. Piper* a plumber. Then write a schedule of guest speakers for Career Day at school. Use abbreviations for days, months, and people's titles. Read your schedule to a small group. Have them spell the abbreviations you used.

5 Book Titles

Look at the picture. What do you think this book might be about? Make up an interesting title for the book.

Begin the first, last, and each important word in a book title with a capital letter. Always underline a book title.

Tim has the book <u>The Lost and Found</u>.   My sister read <u>Rain Forest Babies</u>.

Try It Out

Speak Up How would you write these titles?

1. trapped by the ice
2. the birthday swap
3. two days in may
4. miss rumphius

On Your Own

5–10. This reading list has four missing capital letters and two missing underlines. Write the list correctly.

Example: carlos and the squash plant   *Carlos and the Squash Plant*

Proofreading

<u>Chicken Sunday</u>	The Talking cloth	Henry and Ribsy
Freckle juice	The ballad of Mulan	Nights of the pufflings

Writing Wrap-Up

WRITING • THINKING • LISTENING • SPEAKING

SUMMARIZING

Write Book Summaries

Write the titles of books you like on index cards. Write a few sentences about each book. Work with a partner to make sure your book titles are written correctly. Keep your cards in a class box.

6 Introductory Words

One-Minute Warm-Up

Read each sentence. Which one is correct? Why?

Yes painting is my hobby.

No, I don't think I have a messy hobby.

A comma shows a pause. Use a comma after *yes, no, well,* and order words when they begin a sentence. Some order words are *first, second, next,* and *finally*. Do not use a comma after *then*.

Yes, I love to finger-paint.   First, I need paper.

Try It Out

Speak Up Where are commas needed?

1. Well is the door wet?
2. No it's not painted yet.
3. First the paint spilled.
4. Then I fell.

On Your Own

5–8. This script has four missing or incorrect commas. Correct the script.

Example: Kim: Well can I help paint?   *Kim: Well, can I help paint?*

Proofreading

Tim: Yes I guess so. First, get a brush.
Kim: Then, what do I do?
Tim: Next you dip it. No you dip it, not drip it!

Writing Wrap-Up   WRITING • THINKING • LISTENING • SPEAKING

EXPLAINING

Write Instructions

Write a paragraph that tells a friend how to do something, such as tie shoelaces or make a bed. Use order words. Read your instructions to a partner. Have your partner follow them. Were your instructions clear?

7 Commas in a Series

One-Minute Warm-Up

Read the sentence aloud. When do you pause? Why?

She put the bag of marbles, the harmonica, and the seashell comb on her bedside table.

—from *Birthday Blizzard,* by Bonnie Pryor

A comma tells a reader where to pause. A comma also helps to make the meaning of a sentence clear.

When you list three or more words together in a sentence, the list is called a series. Use commas to separate the words in a series.

Lisa Anne and Jason have birthdays in May.
Lisa, Anne, and Jason have birthdays in May.

In the first sentence above, it is not clear how many children have birthdays. In the second one, you can tell that three different children have birthdays. The commas help to make the meaning of the sentence clear.

Wrong: Mike asked for sneakers toys and a puppy.
Right: Mike asked for sneakers, toys, and a puppy.

Try It Out

Speak Up Where are commas needed in each sentence?

1. Carlos Brian and Nicole came to my party.
2. The room was filled with balloons streamers and signs.
3. We had sandwiches juice and cookies.
4. There are more parties in June July and August.
5. One party will have music races and prizes.
6. The prizes will include ribbons toys and books.

Write each sentence. Put commas where they are needed.

Example: I visited Grandma on Friday Saturday and Sunday.
I visited Grandma on Friday, Saturday, and Sunday.

7. Mom Dad and Jon met me there.
8. Uncle Jack Matt and Emily came over on Sunday.
9. I went with Jon Emily and Matt to the park.
10. Emily took a ball bats and gloves with her.
11. Jon searched for rabbits birds and squirrels.
12. Grandma made noodles fish and salad for dinner.
13. Then we explored boxes trunks and suitcases in Grandma's attic.

14–18. This list has five missing commas. Write the list correctly.

Example: The hatbox holds yarn lace and ribbon.
The hatbox holds yarn, lace, and ribbon.

Proofreading

Treasures in the Attic

- The red suitcase holds dresses hats, and shoes.
- Books, magazines and newspapers are in the large boxes.
- Letters from Grandpa, Marie and Phil are in the blue shoebox.
- A few large jars are filled with rocks, shells, and marbles.
- Toys games and dolls are in the trunk.

Writing Wrap-Up

WRITING • THINKING • LISTENING • SPEAKING

INFORMING

Write a List

Help a new student find things in your classroom. Write sentences listing the things that are kept in cabinets, closets, and drawers. Use a series of three or more things in each sentence. Read your sentences to a partner. Work together to check that you used commas correctly.

Writing Good Sentences

Combining Sentences to Make a Series Good writers combine short, choppy sentences into longer, smoother sentences. Each of the three choppy sentences below has a noun that tells what the children made. Putting those nouns in a series makes one smooth sentence.

The children made cards.
The children made gifts.
The children made decorations.

} The children made cards, gifts, and decorations.

Remember to add *and* after the last comma.

Apply It

1–4. Rewrite the poem on the birthday card. Combine each underlined group of sentences into one new sentence.

Revising

Happy Birthday, Grandma!

Grandma is as sweet as honey.
She is smart. She is kind. She is funny.

She is the world's best grandmother.
Flowers love her. Animals love her. Children love her.

I like to be with her all day.
We love to talk. We laugh. We play.

She is the best person I know of.
She gives me treats. She gives me hugs. She gives me love.

You have learned how to make smoother sentences by joining single words in a series. You can also join groups of words in a series.

We played games.
We drew pictures.
We read stories.

We played games, drew pictures, and read stories.

Big sandwiches were on the table.
Tossed salads were on the table.
Two cakes were on the table.

Big sandwiches, tossed salads, and two cakes were on the table.

Apply It

5–8. Rewrite this e-mail message. Combine each set of underlined sentences into one new sentence.

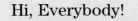

e-mail

Hi, Everybody!

Grandma and I went to the new aquarium. We saw floating jellyfish. We saw giant turtles. We saw cute baby sharks. Then we went to see moray eels. We had lunch. We went shopping. We bought T-shirts.

On Saturday Grandma and I had a party. My four cousins came. The Abbott twins came. My little brother came. Everyone stayed all day! We played dodge ball. We ate six pizzas. We watched a video.

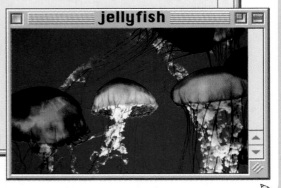

jellyfish

8 Quotation Marks

Read the sentences below. How can you tell that someone is talking?

One day Mrs. Wells comes by. "This is right where my grandmother's bedroom used to be," she says. "That's why I planted my flowers there."

—from *City Green,* by DyAnne DiSalvo-Ryan

- You have read stories in which people talk, or have a conversation, with each other. **Quotation marks (" ") show you the exact words that each person says.**

- When you write a conversation, be sure to put quotation marks at the beginning and the end of the exact words someone says.

    Nick said, "Look at my terrarium!"

    Ming asked, "What is a terrarium?"

Try It Out

Speak Up Where do quotation marks belong in each sentence?

1. Nick said, A terrarium is a garden in a bottle.
2. Ming asked, How did you put it together?
3. Nick said, I put soil in the bottle and added plants.
4. Ming asked, How do the plants get water?
5. Nick answered, I spray water from a bottle.
6. Ming exclaimed, Your terrarium is great!
7. Nick asked, Would you like me to help you make one?

Write each sentence. Add quotation marks.

Example: Tara said, I like to read fables and folktales.
Tara said, "I like to read fables and folktales."

8. Serena asked, Have you read any tales about Paul Bunyan?
9. Tara asked, Who is Paul Bunyan?
10. Serena replied, Paul Bunyan was a lumberjack.
11. Tara asked, What does a lumberjack do?
12. Serena explained, A lumberjack cuts down trees.
13. Serena added, Paul Bunyan had a huge blue ox named Babe.

14–20. This part of a fable has seven missing quotation marks. Write the fable correctly.

Example: The lion exclaimed, You woke me up!
The lion exclaimed, "You woke me up!"

Proofreading

The lion said, You will make a tasty snack."
The mouse exclaimed, "Please do not eat me!
The mouse added, "Let me go and I will help you one day."
The lion asked, How could one so small help a great beast like me?
The mouse replied, Even little creatures can be good friends."
The lion said, You are too small to eat anyway.

Writing Wrap-Up   WRITING • THINKING • LISTENING • SPEAKING

NARRATING

Write a Conversation

Imagine that you have become your favorite story character for a day. Write a conversation between you and someone else. Use quotation marks to show what each of you says. Then read your conversation to a partner. Does your partner recognize your character?

9 More About Quotation Marks

Read this sentence. What two marks can you switch to make the sentence correct?

Dad said? "Would you like to fly a kite,"

You have learned that quotation marks set off someone's exact words. Follow these rules when you write a conversation.

- Use a comma to separate the speaker's exact words from the rest of the sentence.

  Bethany said, "Look at my new kite."

- Begin the first word inside the quotation marks with a capital letter.

  Kareem asked, "Will it fly?"

- Put the end mark inside the quotation marks.

  Derek replied, "I will hold the string."
  Bethany asked, "Is the wind strong enough?"

Try It Out

Speak Up Where does a comma, a capital letter, and an end mark belong in each sentence?

1. Bethany said "let's start running"
2. Kareem said "run down the hill"
3. Bethany asked "will the kite get caught in a tree"
4. Derek answered "now you are fine"
5. Kareem cried "the kite is in the air"
6. Bethany asked "should I let out more string"
7. Derek said "let's see how high it will go"

Write each sentence correctly. Add a comma, a capital letter, an end mark, or quotation marks to each sentence.

Example: Elena asked, "What will we make in art class"
Elena asked, "What will we make in art class?"

8. Mrs. Porter said, "today we will make pottery.
9. Caleb asked, How do you make pottery"
10. Mrs. Porter asked "Have you ever played with clay?
11. Curtis exclaimed, I love playing with clay"
12. Curtis added "I made a dish for my mother"

13–18. This article from a school newspaper has two missing quotation marks, one missing comma, one missing end mark, and two missing capital letters. Write the article correctly.

Example: Lorenzo said, "each mask is different.
Lorenzo said, "Each mask is different."

Proofreading

Colorful Masks Delight Students

Students agree that the masks are the most interesting things to see at the school art show. I asked Lorenzo Sanchez, "what are the masks made of"
Lorenzo explained, "The masks are made of clay."
He added, "We used glazes to make them shiny.
Katie Shulman exclaimed "they took forever to dry!

Writing Wrap-Up WRITING • THINKING • LISTENING • SPEAKING

INFORMING

Write a Survey

Take a survey of three or four classmates. Ask them what their favorite thing to do is. Write each person's exact words. Remember to use quotation marks. Then read the survey to a small group. What activity was the most popular?

Enrichment

Capitalization!
Punctuation!

Character Quotations

Think about a character from a book you have read recently. For example, it might be Robert D. Ballard from his book *Finding the Titanic*. What could the character say to make your classmates want to read the book? Think of one good sentence and write it down. Use quotation marks correctly. Share your paper with your classmates.

> **Example:** Robert Ballard exclaimed, "I found the <u>Titanic</u> on the bottom of the ocean!"

Challenge Write a newspaper column that offers tips about books children should or should not read. Make up quotations from children who have read the books.

Special Days Book

Make a booklet of days to remember. Fold seven sheets of paper together and staple the fold. On the cover, write *Special Days*. Write the name of a month at the top of each page. Divide each month by days of the week. Write in holidays, birthdays, and any other special dates.

1 Correct Sentences *(p. 178)* Write each sentence correctly.

1. are masks made of wood or rubber
2. they can be made of many things
3. look at this mask
4. it looks so scary
5. would you like to make a mask

2 Capitalizing Proper Nouns *(p. 182)* Write each sentence correctly.

6. Every year I go to uncle larry's ranch.
7. This year I am going on labor day.
8. That holiday always falls on a monday.
9. We will take grandpa to a horse show.
10. My uncle is riding his horse sparky.
11. First prize last year went to sally j. hayes.

3 Capitalizing Other Proper Nouns *(p. 184)* Write each sentence correctly.

12. Have you ever been to idaho?
13. My friend lives in the city of pocatello.
14. She was born in canada.
15. Now she goes to madison elementary school.
16. We hike in caribou national forest.
17. Picnics in ross park are always fun!

4 Abbreviations *(p. 186)* Write the abbreviation for each day and month correctly. Write each name correctly.

18. December
19. mr phil johnson
20. Wednesday
21. dr alan chin
22. miss marta garcia
23. February
24. ms hilda goodman
25. mrs kim wong

5 **Book Titles** *(p. 188)* Write these book titles correctly.

26. the old man and his door
27. one day in the desert
28. seven candles for kwanzaa
29. dancing rainbows
30. little house in the big woods
31. the three javelinas

6 **Introductory Words** *(p. 189)* Write each sentence. Put a comma where it is needed.

32. Yes Ed's snowman is big.
33. First he made the snowman's body.
34. Next he made the head.
35. Then he made a face.
36. Finally Ed took a picture.
37. No the sun didn't melt the snowman.
38. Well he won the contest.

7 **Commas in a Series** *(p. 190)* Write each sentence. Put commas where they are needed.

39. Miss Todd Mrs. Chu and Mr. Stone are salespeople.
40. They sell clothes jewelry and shoes.
41. The rings pins and watches cost a lot.
42. Does Miss Todd work on Monday Tuesday and Thursday?
43. Sarah Patrick and Robin went shopping.
44. Patrick bought shirts slacks and socks.
45. Did you see the kittens puppies and fish at the pet shop?

8 **Quotation Marks** *(p. 194)* Write each sentence. Add quotation marks.

46. Dad asked, Will you win the sack race?
47. Tim answered, I can run faster than Michael.
48. Dad asked, How old is Michael?
49. Tim said, He is three years older than I am.
50. Dad exclaimed, You must be pretty fast!

51. Tim said, I came in second last year.
52. Tim added, Everyone gets a prize.

9 **More About Quotation Marks** *(p. 196)* Write each sentence. Add a comma, a capital letter, an end mark, or quotation marks to make it correct.

53. Abigail asked, "Would you like to go to Funland"
54. Jamie replied "I will ask my parents."
55. Abigail said, "some of the rides are scary."
56. Abigail added, My favorite part is the fun house.
57. Billy said "The strange mirrors make me laugh."
58. Abigail said, I like the bumper cars too.
59. Jamie asked, "will your brother go on any of the rides?"
60. Abigail answered, His favorite part is the food!
61. Billy exclaimed, "I love cotton candy"

Mixed Review 62–68. This story beginning has three missing or incorrect capital letters, two missing commas, and two missing quotation marks. Write the story correctly.

Proofreading Checklist

Did you use these correctly?
✔ capital letters
✔ commas
✔ quotation marks

Fearless Francine

One saturday Francine Dupree was sitting on a bench in sunset Park. She was reading an exciting new book called <u>Ruth To the Rescue</u>. Ruth was a girl detective. She found missing dogs cats, and snakes. Francine finished the book and looked up. A nice neighbor named Mr. Jordan was walking by. He looked very upset.

Francine asked, What is the matter?
The neighbor replied, "Well my snake has disappeared!"

✓ Test Practice

Write the numbers 1–8 on a sheet of paper. Choose the best way to write the underlined part of each sentence. Write the letter for that answer. If there is no mistake, write the letter for the last answer.

1 Bring this to <u>mr Lane</u>.

  A Mr Lane

  B mr. Lane

  C Mr. Lane

  D (No mistakes)

2 How many blocks are we from the <u>Garden theater</u>.

  F Garden theater?

  G Garden Theater?

  H garden theater.

  J (No mistakes)

3 I go to the <u>Barton School</u>.

  A barton school

  B barton School

  C Barton school

  D (No mistakes)

4 Ken was born <u>dec 5</u>, 1992.

  F dec. 5

  G Dec 5

  H Dec. 5

  J (No mistakes)

5 Have you read a book called <u>Dinosaur dreams</u>.

  A Dinosaur Dreams?

  B Dinosaur dreams?

  C Dinosaur Dreams.

  D (No mistakes)

6 <u>Yes aunt Mary</u> will visit us.

  F Yes, aunt Mary

  G Yes, Aunt Mary

  H Yes Aunt Mary

  J (No mistakes)

7 <u>Jars bottles and cans</u> go there.

  A Jars bottles, and, cans

  B Jars, bottles and, cans

  C Jars, bottles, and cans

  D (No mistakes)

8 Tami <u>said I just lost a tooth</u>.

  F said, "I just lost a tooth."

  G said "I just lost a tooth."

  H said, I just lost a tooth."

  J (No mistakes)

Now write the numbers 9–14 on your paper. Read the passage and look at the numbered, underlined parts. Choose the correct way to write each underlined part. If the part is already correct, choose the last answer, "Correct as it is." Write the letter for the answer you choose.

Last spring ms Davis took an unusual trip. She rode across
               (9)
the united states of america. She did not drive a car. She traveled
            (10)
by bus train and taxi. Her trip began in oregon on mar 21. She spent
     (11)   (12)
a week in the rocky Mountains and visited six cities. In April she
              (13)
arrived in Maine. She got off the bus and said, "I'm here at last."
                                               (14)

9 A ms. Davis
   B Ms Davis
   C Ms. Davis
   D Correct as it is

10 F United States of America
   G United states of America
   H United States Of America
   J Correct as it is

11 A bus, train and, taxi
   B bus train, and taxi
   C bus, train, and taxi
   D Correct as it is

12 F oregon on Mar 21.
   G Oregon on Mar. 21.
   H Oregon on mar. 21
   J Correct as it is

13 A rocky mountains
   B Rocky mountains
   C Rocky Mountains
   D Correct as it is

14 F said, I'm here at last."
   G said "I'm here at last."
   H said, "I'm here at last.
   J Correct as it is

(pages 178–179)

1 Correct Sentences

- Begin every sentence with a capital letter.
- End a statement or a command with a period.
- End a question with a question mark.
- End an exclamation with an exclamation point.

● Each sentence below is missing a capital letter or an end mark. Write each sentence correctly.

Example: Do you want a computer   *Do you want a computer?*

1. i can't wait to get one!
2. Can a computer think
3. computers play games.
4. Wow, this computer sings

▲ Write each sentence correctly.

Example: a robot is a machine   *A robot is a machine.*

5. it has a computer for a brain
6. how are robots different from other computers
7. many robots have arms or hands
8. tell me what robots can do
9. robots can do simple jobs around the house
10. they never get tired

■ Each sentence has the wrong end mark. Write each sentence correctly. Then write *statement, question, exclamation,* or *command* next to each sentence.

Example: will robots be used in the future!
   Will robots be used in the future?   question

11. robots could help fight fires?
12. can computers save lives.
13. computers can help doctors save lives!
14. look at this new computer?
15. it is so tiny?

(pages 182–183)

2 Capitalizing Proper Nouns

- Begin the name of a particular person, pet, day, month, or holiday with a capital letter.

Remember

● Write the proper noun that is correct in each pair.

Example: nicole Sanchez

Nicole Sanchez   *Nicole Sanchez*

1. Chirpy
   chirpy
2. aunt sue
   Aunt Sue
3. Memorial day
   Memorial Day
4. Anne
   anne
5. sunday
   Sunday
6. lester t. Dodge
   Lester T. Dodge

▲ Write each sentence correctly.

Example: I am ted a. squire.   *I am Ted A. Squire.*

7. I was named after uncle theodore.
8. My favorite holiday is thanksgiving.
9. The holiday comes in november.
10. I visit grandfather on that day.
11. Once he invited rona c. forbes to dinner.
12. She surprised me with a kitten named rags.

■ Write each sentence. Add a proper noun for the word in ( ).

Example: Every _____ I go on vacation. (month)
Every July I go on vacation.

13. I usually spend my vacation with _____. (person)
14. This year _____ came with me. (pet)
15. On _____ I went to a parade. (holiday)
16. I saw my friend _____ there. (person)
17. One _____ night I had a party. (day)
18. I invited _____ and _____. (people)

(pages 184–185)

3 Capitalizing Other Nouns

- Begin the name of a particular place with a capital letter.
- Begin each important word in a proper noun with a capital letter.

Remember

● Write the correct proper noun in each pair.

Example: dade city
    Dade City   *Dade City*

1. Africa
   africa

2. bear Lake
   Bear Lake

3. Jackson Park
   jackson park

4. smithtown
   Smithtown

5. California
   california

6. gulf of Mexico
   Gulf of Mexico

▲ Write each sentence correctly.

Example: In 1896 utah became a state.   *In 1896 Utah became a state.*

7. It is part of the united states of america.
8. The green river flows through the state.
9. Its largest city is salt lake city.
10. One of its lakes is lake powell.
11. I visited zion national park once.
12. Peter goes to the brigham young school.

■ Write a sentence to answer each question.

Example: What park do you go to?   *I go to Rose Park.*

13. What street do you live on?
14. What town or city does your best friend live in?
15. What country would you like to visit?
16. What is the name of your school?
17. What lake or river would you like to swim in?
18. What state would you like to live in when you grow up?

(pages 186–187)

4 Abbreviations

Remember

- An abbreviation is a short way of writing a word.
- Most abbreviations begin with capital letters and end with periods.

● Write the correct abbreviation in each pair.

Example: Thurs. *Thurs.*
Thurs

1. Oct.
   oct.
2. Mr.
   mr.
3. feb
   Feb.

4. Nov
   Nov.
5. Tues.
   Tues
6. Dr.
   Dr

7. Apr.
   apr.
8. mrs.
   Mrs.
9. Sun
   Sun.

10. Jan.
    jan.
11. wed
    Wed.
12. Dec.
    dec

▲ Write each abbreviation and name correctly.

Example: dr lawrence stone *Dr. Lawrence Stone*

13. mar
14. mrs Carla gomez
15. dr roger wang

16. aug
17. miss Megan Shaw
18. sat

19. mr paul wilson
20. ms mary Rossi
21. sept

■ Write the answer to each question. Use the abbreviations that you have learned.

Example: Which day starts the school week? *Mon.*

22. Which month comes after March?
23. Which day ends the school week?
24. In which month is Valentine's Day?
25. Which day comes after Tuesday?
26. What is your teacher's name?
27. In which month is your favorite holiday?
28. Which day comes before Sunday?

| FEBRUARY | | | | | | |
S	M	T	W	T	F	S
	1	2	3	4	5	6
7	8	9	10	11	12	13
14	15	16	17	18	19	20
21	22	23	24	25	26	27
28						

(page 188)

5 Book Titles

- Begin the first, last, and each important word in a book title with a capital letter. Underline the title.

Remember

● Copy these sentences. Underline the book titles.

Example: I read the book Miss Nelson Is Missing.
I read the book <u>Miss Nelson Is Missing</u>.

1. The Trumpet of the Swan is about a swan named Louis.
2. I read Seal Surfer.
3. Dogzilla is the funny story of a bad dog and some brave mice.
4. Would you like to read Two Days in May?
5. Who wrote the book How to Eat Fried Worms?

▲ Write each book title correctly.

Example: arrow to the sun *<u>Arrow to the Sun</u>*

6. the skirt
7. the adventures of sparrow boy
8. raising dragons
9. a toad for tuesday
10. the waterfall
11. the most wonderful egg in the world

■ Write each sentence correctly.

Example: Robin read help! I'm a Prisoner in the library.
Robin read <u>Help! I'm a Prisoner in the Library</u>.

12. Who wrote the book a wrinkle in time?
13. two bad ants was fun to read.
14. I enjoyed tracks in the wild.
15. My favorite book is alice ramsey's grand adventure.
16. Have you read poppa's new pants?
17. My teacher read us the magic school bus in the solar system.
18. Our school library has james and the giant peach.

(page 189)

⑥ Introductory Words

- Use commas after *yes, no, well,* and order words at the beginning of a sentence. Do not use a comma after *then.*

Remember

● Write the sentence that is correct in each pair.

Example: Well what time is it?
Well, what time is it?   *Well, what time is it?*

1. Yes, I'm in a hurry.
   Yes I'm in a hurry.
2. Well I've plenty to do.
   Well, I've plenty to do.

3. First, I'll get dressed.
   First I'll get dressed.
4. Then, I'll go to school.
   Then I'll go to school.

▲ Write these sentences correctly.

Example: Yes the television is broken.   *Yes, the television is broken.*

5. No you cannot fix it.
6. Well we should call a repair shop.
7. First get the telephone book.
8. Second look up the telephone number.
9. Next call the repair shop.
10. Finally wait for the repairperson.

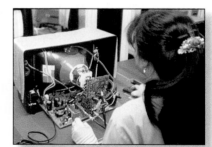

■ Add a word from the box to each sentence. Write each sentence correctly.

Example: _____ it is fun to bake bread.   *Yes, it is fun to bake bread.*

| First | No | Second | Yes | Finally | Then | Well |

11. _____ I did not add the flour.
12. _____ how long should it bake?
13. _____ place the bread in a pan.
14. _____ put the pan in the oven.
15. _____ check the time.
16. _____ remove the bread carefully.

(pages 190–191)

7 Commas in a Series

- A series is a list of three or more words.
- Use commas to separate words in a series.

Remember

● Write each sentence. Underline the words in a series.

Example: Kim, Eric, and Carey are on baseball teams.
Kim, Eric, and Carey are on baseball teams.

1. The games are on Sunday, Monday, and Tuesday.
2. Girls, boys, and coaches meet at the field.
3. The ball sails over Ina, Luis, and Henry.
4. Kim runs to first base, second base, and third base.

▲ Write each sentence correctly.

Example: Amy Kurt and Carlos visited the library.
Amy, Kurt, and Carlos visited the library.

5. Amy found a book about stars planets and comets.
6. Mercury Venus and Mars are on the cover.
7. Carlos chose books about apes wolves and bears.
8. Kurt saw Mrs. Taylor Sam and Sal.
9. Sal wrote a report on seals whales and sharks.

■ Write each sentence correctly. Write *correct* for ones that need no commas.

Example: Dale Hideo and Mallory went shopping.
Dale, Hideo, and Mallory went shopping.

10. They looked at games toys and clothes.
11. Hideo bought a card and gloves for his mother.
12. He tried on shoes coats and belts.
13. Mallory saw a puppy and rabbits in the pet store.
14. Cats fish and snakes are Dale's favorite pets.

(pages 194–195)

8 Quotation Marks

- Use quotation marks (" ") at the beginning and end of a person's exact words.

Remember

● Write each sentence. Underline the speaker's words.

> **Example:** Chris said, "The basketball contest is starting."
> *Chris said, "The basketball contest is starting."*

1. Greg asked, "What kind of contest is it?"
2. Chris answered, "It's called Around the World."
3. Chris added, "Players take turns shooting from different spots on the court."
4. Greg said, "I would like to try that!"

▲ Write each sentence. Add quotation marks.

> **Example:** Nakisha said, I just finished a great book.
> *Nakisha said, "I just finished a great book."*

5. Jason asked, What kind of book is it?
6. Nakisha replied, It's a mystery book.
7. Jason asked, May I borrow your book?
8. Nakisha said, I will bring it to school tomorrow.
9. Jason said, Maybe I can use it for my next book report.

■ In each sentence below, quotation marks are in the wrong place. Write each sentence correctly.

> **Example:** "Kyle asked, How does a blind person read?"
> *Kyle asked, "How does a blind person read?"*

10. "Abby said, A blind person can use Braille."
11. "Kyle asked, "What is Braille?
12. "Abby said," It's an alphabet made of raised dots.
13. "Kyle" asked, Where can you find books with Braille?
14. Abby "said, The library has books written in Braille."

(pages 196–197)

⑨ More About Quotation Marks

- Use a comma to separate the speaker's exact words from the rest of the sentence.
- Begin a quotation with a capital letter.
- Put the end mark before the last quotation mark.

Remember

● Write each sentence correctly. Add a comma where it is needed.

Example: Brett asked "Do sharks have teeth?"
Brett asked, "Do sharks have teeth?"

1. Tina said "A shark has several rows of teeth."
2. Brett asked "What do sharks eat?"
3. Tina replied "Sharks eat meat and fish."
4. Ryan exclaimed "Some sharks are forty feet long!"

▲ Write each sentence correctly. Add a comma, a capital letter, an end mark, or quotation marks.

Example: Andy asked, "what is a squid?" *Andy asked, "What is a squid?"*

5. Vanessa said, "it is a sea animal."
6. Nicole asked, "What does a squid look like "
7. Ming said "It has a soft body and ten arms."
8. Andy asked, "What does a squid eat "
9. Vanessa replied "It eats small fish."

■ Write each sentence correctly. Add a comma, a capital letter, an end mark, and quotation marks.

Example: Liza said look at this picture *Liza said, "Look at this picture."*

10. Jamal explained it is a fish called an electric eel
11. Kara asked where does the eel live
12. Jamal said some eels live in South America
13. Liza asked why is it called an electric eel
14. Jade replied it gives an electric shock to its enemies

Pronouns

Yoo-hoo! Look at us.

We are up here.

Take our picture.

1 Subject Pronouns

Read the sentences below. What word in the second sentence takes the place of *The rain*?

The rain falls faster and harder. It blows against the windows and doors.

—from *Flash, Crash, Rumble, and Roll*, by Franklyn M. Branley

- **A pronoun is a word that can take the place of one or more nouns in a sentence.**

Nouns	Pronouns
Kayla heard the wind.	She heard the wind.
The wind was howling.	It was howling.
The children stayed home.	They stayed home.

- The pronouns above are subjects. **The pronouns *I, you, he, she, it, we,* and *they* are subject pronouns.** Pronouns can be singular or plural. Study the chart below.

Subject Pronouns				
Singular	I	you	he	she	it
Plural	we	you	they		

Try It Out

Speak Up Find the subject pronouns.

1. Last night we had a big storm.
2. I heard loud thunder.
3. It woke everyone up.
4. He saw a flash of lightning.
5. Are you sure the rain has stopped?

Write a subject pronoun to replace the underlined word or words.

Example: Rafael and I went camping.   *We*

6. The campers sat around the fire.
7. The fire felt warm.
8. Rafael played the guitar.
9. Jeff and I sang a song.
10. What song did your sister sing?
11. The song was about a boat at sea.
12. Should you and I go camping sometime?

13–18. Write this poem. Use a subject pronoun in place of the underlined word or words.

Example: The clouds make pictures in the sky.
They make pictures in the sky.

A Summer Day

Kelly fishes in the lake.
Josh gathers stones with his brother Jake.
You and I play hide-and-seek.
A mouse scurries by with a little squeak.
Kim and Casey put worms in a jar.
This day is the best by far!

Writing Wrap-Up

WRITING • THINKING • LISTENING • SPEAKING

CREATING

Write a Poem

Write a poem about something you and a friend like to do outdoors. Use as many subject pronouns as you can. Then find a partner and read your poems to each other. Name the subject pronouns you each used.

2 Pronouns and Verbs

One-Minute Warm-Up

What's wrong with this cheer? How can you fix it?

I screams, you screams, we all screams for ice cream!

Make up your own version of this cheer. Have your classmates join in.

You know that a pronoun can be the subject of a sentence. Remember that verbs in the present have two forms. The correct form of the verb to use depends on the subject pronoun.

- Add -s or -es to a verb in the present when the subject is *he, she,* or *it.*

  She **fixes** dinner.   He **sets** the table.

- Do not add -s or -es to a verb in the present when the subject is *I, you, we,* or *they.*

  I **fix** dinner.   We **set** the table.

Try It Out

Speak Up Choose the correct verb form to complete each sentence.

1. They (like, likes) eggs for breakfast.
2. You (buys, buy) twelve eggs.
3. I (cracks, crack) six eggs in half.
4. She (adds, add) some milk.
5. We (mix, mixes) the eggs in a bowl.
6. He (get, gets) the frying pan.
7. You (pour, pours) the eggs into the pan.

Write each sentence. Choose the correct verb form in ( ).

Example: We (sees, see) some balloons. *We see some balloons.*

8. They (float, floats) over the trees.
9. You (jumps, jump) for the silver balloon.
10. I (takes, take) the balloon with the red string.
11. She (reaches, reach) for the biggest balloon.
12. It (break, breaks) with a pop.
13. He (find, finds) a message inside the balloon.
14. It (tells, tell) about children in another town.

15–20. This bulletin-board message has six incorrect verb forms. Write the message correctly.

Example: She teach me about France. *She teaches me about France.*

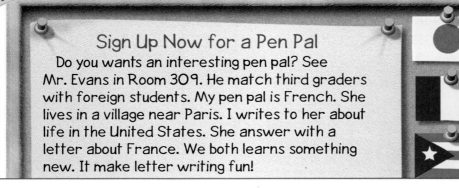

Proofreading

Sign Up Now for a Pen Pal
Do you wants an interesting pen pal? See
Mr. Evans in Room 309. He match third graders
with foreign students. My pen pal is French. She
lives in a village near Paris. I writes to her about
life in the United States. She answer with a
letter about France. We both learns something
new. It make letter writing fun!

Writing Wrap-Up WRITING • THINKING • LISTENING • SPEAKING

EXPRESSING

Write a Message

Write a message to Mr. Evans. Ask him to match you up with a pen pal. Write three sentences about yourself, your family, and your hobbies. Use subject pronouns. Then read your message to a partner. Work together to make sure that you used the correct verb forms.

3 Object Pronouns

me you
him her it
us them

Complete the sentence below with a noun. The noun can name one or more persons or things.

I painted a picture of _____.

Then have a classmate replace your noun with a pronoun from the easel.

- A subject pronoun can be the subject of a sentence. **The pronouns *me, you, him, her, it, us,* and *them* are called object pronouns**. Object pronouns follow action verbs and words like *to, for, at, of,* and *with*.

Nouns
Nina painted with <u>Louis</u>.
Ben and I met <u>Nina and Louis</u>.
Ben brought a <u>brush</u>.

Pronouns
Nina painted with him.
Ben and I met them.
Ben brought it.

- The pronouns *it* and *you* are both subject pronouns and object pronouns. Study the chart below.

Object Pronouns					
Singular	me	you	him	her	it
Plural	us	you	them		

Try It Out

Speak Up Find the object pronouns.

1. Mrs. Russell told us about the school play.
2. Lisa tried out for it.
3. Mrs. Russell gave a part to me.
4. Ernesto painted the stage for her.
5. Mira watched them.
6. Aunt Ruth made a costume for you.

Change the underlined word or words in each sentence to a pronoun. Write the new sentences.

Example: Rob came with <u>Dad and me</u>.   *Rob came with us.*

7. I invited <u>Rob</u> to the game.
8. You went with <u>Hannah</u>.
9. Rob sat with <u>Kyle and me</u>.
10. Did you hear <u>the two bands</u>?
11. Ana wore <u>a funny hat</u>.
12. The hat kept <u>Ana</u> warm.

13–18. Write this part of an e-mail. Use an object pronoun in place of the underlined word or words.

Example: I passed the ball to <u>Cheryl</u>.   *I passed the ball to her.*

---

e-mail

You've Got Mail!

Hi, Aunt Sue! Let me tell you about our last game. The score was tied with one minute left. Brandon passed the ball to Jill. I stole <u>the ball</u> from her. Nobody on my team was free to take a shot. The other team was guarding <u>our team</u> really well. Suddenly Dan ran toward the basket. I faked a pass to <u>Dan</u>. The other players fell for <u>the trick</u>. I fooled <u>the other players</u> and took the last shot myself. We won! Our coach, Mr. Ames, was so proud. We owe <u>Mr. Ames</u> the victory, though. He is the best!

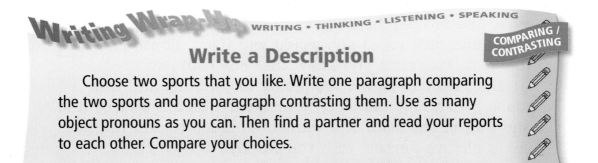

Writing Wrap-Up   WRITING • THINKING • LISTENING • SPEAKING

COMPARING / CONTRASTING

Write a Description

Choose two sports that you like. Write one paragraph comparing the two sports and one paragraph contrasting them. Use as many object pronouns as you can. Then find a partner and read your reports to each other. Compare your choices.

Writing with Pronouns

Writing Clearly with Pronouns Be careful not to repeat a pronoun too many times. Your sentences may become boring and choppy. The reader may forget whom or what you are talking about. Count the number of times the pronoun *it* is used in the following paragraph.

> This race was important to Eric. It would be difficult, but it would test his skill. It could make him a hero. It was Eric's chance to win his first trophy.

The same paragraph is clearer when one of the pronouns is changed to a noun.

> This race was important to Eric. It would be difficult, but it would test his skill. This race could make him a hero. It was Eric's chance to win his first trophy.

You can also choose a different noun to take the place of a pronoun. This will make your writing more interesting.

> This event could make him a hero.

Apply It

1–5. Revise this part of a story. Replace each underlined pronoun with a noun.

Revising

> Marie and the other runners lined up for the race. She felt her heart pounding. She was ready to start, and she hoped she would win. Last month she had lost. This time she knew that she could do it.
>
> The race started. It was going to be close, and that made it exciting. Marie shot forward. She felt strong, and she was in the lead. She wanted so much to win it! She could picture herself with the trophy.

Combining Sentences You know how to combine sentences using a comma and the word *and*. If both parts of the sentence have the same noun as the subject, sometimes you can replace one of the nouns with a pronoun. This will save you from writing the same noun twice in the same sentence.

Reggie snatched the ball.
Reggie leaped for the basket. } Reggie snatched the ball, and he leaped for the basket.

Apply It

6–10. Rewrite each yearbook caption by combining the two sentences. Change the underlined words to pronouns. Write the new sentences.

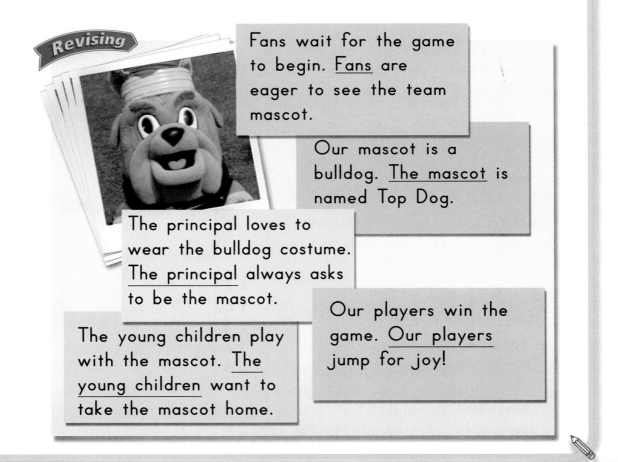

Revising

Fans wait for the game to begin. <u>Fans</u> are eager to see the team mascot.

Our mascot is a bulldog. <u>The mascot</u> is named Top Dog.

The principal loves to wear the bulldog costume. <u>The principal</u> always asks to be the mascot.

Our players win the game. <u>Our players</u> jump for joy!

The young children play with the mascot. <u>The young children</u> want to take the mascot home.

4 Using *I* and *me*

What is wrong with this message? How can you fix it?

> Mom,
> I and Dad will be back in an hour.
> Alana

- You often use the pronouns *I* and *me* when you speak and write. Use the pronoun *I* only as the subject of a sentence. Use the pronoun *me* only as an object pronoun.

  Subject Pronoun   **Object Pronoun**

  I left a message for Nate.   Nate called me right back.

- When you talk about another person and yourself, it is polite to name yourself last. Always capitalize the word *I*.

  Nate and I helped Mom.   She gave Nate and me some money.

Try It Out

Speak Up Choose the correct word or words in ( ) to complete each sentence.

1. (Nate and I, Nate and me) bought model airplanes.
2. Dad helped (I, me).
3. He gave (Nate and me, me and Nate) some paint.
4. (I, Me) painted my airplane blue.
5. Mom brought sandwiches to (Nate and I, Nate and me).
6. (Me and Nate, Nate and I) finished our airplanes after lunch.

Write each sentence. Use the correct word or words in ( ).

Example: (Abby and I, I and Abby) went to the store.

Abby and I went to the store.

7. Mom gave (I, me) the grocery list.
8. (I, Me) left the list in the car.
9. Darcie brought the list to (Abby and I, Abby and me).
10. (Darcie and I, Darcie and me) stood in line.
11. Darcie bought (Abby and me, me and Abby) magazines.
12. (Mom and I, Mom and me) put the bags in the car.
13. (Me and Abby, Abby and I) unpacked the groceries.

14–18. This story has five mistakes in using *I* and *me*. Write the story correctly.

Example: Me and Dad love breakfast. *Dad and I love breakfast.*

Proofreading

A Special Day

Today Dad got a surprise from Mom and I. Mom woke me up early. Then me and Mom went quietly to the kitchen. I helped Mom make breakfast. Mom and me tiptoed upstairs with the tray of food and the newspaper. The food smelled great! Dad opened one eye and grinned. He gave Mom and I a big hug. Later me and Dad read the comics together.

Writing Wrap-Up   WRITING • THINKING • LISTENING • SPEAKING

NARRATING

Write a Story About Yourself

Write about a time when you and a friend or relative did something nice for someone. Use *I* and *me* in your sentences. Read your story to a partner. Together, make sure you used *I* and *me* correctly.

5 Possessive Pronouns

Read the sentences below. What word shows ownership?

Nathan motioned for Gainey to talk through the receiver. Mr. Gainey put the cone to his mouth.

—from *Radio Boy*, by Sharon Phillips Denslow

A noun that shows ownership is a possessive noun. Some pronouns can take the place of possessive nouns. **A pronoun that shows ownership is called a possessive pronoun.**

Nouns

Ashley's radio is broken.
She took it to Al's shop.
Ashley has the twins' radio.

Pronouns

Her radio is broken.
She took it to his shop.
Ashley has their radio.

Study the chart below.

Possessive Pronouns						
my	your	her	his	its	our	their

Try It Out

Speak Up Find the possessive pronoun in each of the following sentences.

1. My class watches a video about two gorillas.
2. Their names are Koko and Michael.
3. Koko wants to hold her kitten, Smoky.

Koko signs to her trainer.

Which possessive pronoun would you use in place of the underlined words?

4. Koko's best friend is Michael.
5. Michael paints a picture on Michael's paper.
6. The gorillas play games with the gorillas' trainer.

Write the sentences. Underline the possessive pronoun in each sentence.

Example: Koko plays with her kitten. *Koko plays with <u>her</u> kitten.*

7. Koko puts it on her lap.
8. She brushes its fur.
9. I can't believe my eyes!
10. Gorillas love their pets too!

11. Michael signs to his trainer.
12. He gives his trainer a hug.
13. Our class was amazed by Koko and Michael.

14–18. Write this part of a speech. Use a possessive pronoun in place of the underlined word or words.

Example: Koko knows the <u>sign's</u> meaning.
Koko knows its meaning.

Koko and Michael have shown that gorillas can use <u>gorillas'</u> hands to communicate, or "talk." Koko talks about her kitten. She tells the trainers, "I love <u>Koko's</u> kitten." Koko has a special computer. <u>The computer's</u> buttons have pictures on them. Koko uses <u>Koko's</u> computer to answer questions.

Michael talks too. He tells how he and <u>Michael's</u> mother were chased by hunters. People should make sure gorillas in the wild are protected.

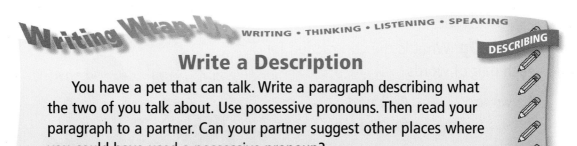

Writing Wrap-Up WRITING • THINKING • LISTENING • SPEAKING

DESCRIBING

Write a Description

You have a pet that can talk. Write a paragraph describing what the two of you talk about. Use possessive pronouns. Then read your paragraph to a partner. Can your partner suggest other places where you could have used a possessive pronoun?

6 Contractions

One-Minute Warm-Up

Use Ready Rags!

This ad is too long. What other contractions can you use to make it shorter?

It's time for spring cleaning. You will clean better with Ready Rags. They are soil spoilers!

You know that a contraction is a word made by putting two words together. An apostrophe replaces the letter or letters that are left out. Many contractions are made by joining a pronoun and a verb.

Two Words
We have cleaned the attic.

Contraction
We've cleaned the attic.

Common Contractions with Pronouns			
I am	I'm	it will	it'll
he is	he's	we will	we'll
she is	she's	they will	they'll
it is	it's	he has	he's
you are	you're	she has	she's
we are	we're	it has	it's
they are	they're	I have	I've
I will	I'll	you have	you've
you will	you'll	we have	we've
he will	he'll	they have	they've
she will	she'll		

Try It Out

Speak Up What is the contraction for each pair of words?

1. we are
2. she will
3. it has
4. I will
5. he is
6. you have

I'll help you.

Write the contractions for the underlined words.

Example: <u>We will</u> clean the whole house.   *We'll*

7. <u>It is</u> such a big job.
8. <u>It will</u> take a long time.
9. <u>We are</u> a good cleanup team.
10. What a mess <u>they have</u> made!
11. <u>She has</u> left her clothes on the floor.
12. <u>You are</u> a hard worker.
13. When we finish, <u>I am</u> going to take a nap.

14–18. These rhymes have five incorrect contractions. Write the rhymes correctly.

Example: Its never too soon to clean your room.
   It's never too soon to clean your room.

Proofreading

Rhyme Time

- A boy looks keen when hes clean.
- A girl is mighty when she's tidy.
- Rooms look sweeter when theyr'e neater.
- If you leave a mess, Il'l like you less!
- Well have more fun if our work is done.
- Things do not stray when youve' put them away.

Writing Wrap-Up WRITING • THINKING • LISTENING • SPEAKING

CREATING

Write Silly Rhymes

Make up silly rhymes about cleaning your room or doing other chores around the house. Use a contraction in each one. Read your rhymes to a small group. Have them clap when they hear a contraction. Then ask for a volunteer to spell the contraction.

7 Using *there*, *their*, and *they're*

GREAT!

What two words should you switch to make the sentence correct?

Their having a sale on they're dinosaur books.

The words *there*, *their*, and *they're* sound alike but have different spellings and meanings. Remember that the clues in a sentence can help you decide which words to use.

HELP
? Tip

If you are not sure which word to use, look it up in a dictionary.

Word	Meaning	Example
there	at or in that place	They work **there**.
their	belonging to them	It's **their** store.
they're	they are (contraction)	**They're** at work.

Try It Out

Speak Up Would you use *there*, *their*, or *they're* to complete each sentence?

1. Mr. and Mrs. Foster have great books in _____ bookstore.
2. I went _____ today.
3. I saw my two favorite books _____.
4. _____ in the mystery section.
5. Isn't _____ bookstore a great place?
6. I will go _____ again soon.

On Your Own

Write the sentences. Complete each one with *there*, *their*, or *they're*.

Example: Carrie and Alex begin _____ paper route early.
Carrie and Alex begin their paper route early.

7. _____ earning money for new bicycles.
8. They pick up _____ newspapers at the corner.
9. The delivery truck meets them _____.
10. They deliver newspapers in _____ neighborhood.
11. They know most of the people who live _____.
12. _____ route starts at my house.
13. _____ always on time.

14–18. This ad has five mistakes in using *there*, *their*, and *they're*. Write the ad correctly.

Example: Their the greatest bikes!
They're the greatest bikes!

Proofreading

> Swifties are known for they're smooth ride. They're strong and light. There frames never rust. Their tires never get flat. If you want to get someplace quickly, you will get their faster on a Swifty bicycle. There on sale this week at the Bike Barn. While you are their, pick up a Swifty bike helmet too.

Writing Wrap-Up

WRITING • THINKING • LISTENING • SPEAKING

DESCRIBING

Write an Ad

Write an ad for a new product, such as sneakers, backpacks, or soccer balls. What makes them special? Use *there*, *their*, or *they're* in each sentence. Then read your ad to a partner. Is your ad lively and convincing? Work together to make sure you used *there*, *their*, and *they're* correctly.

Homophones

Homophones are words that sound alike but have different spellings and different meanings. *There, their,* and *they're* are homophones. When you write, make sure you use the correct homophones. The chart below shows some homophones and their meanings.

Homophone	Meaning
your	belonging to you
you're	you are
its	belonging to it
it's	it is
here	at a place
hear	to take in sounds through the ears

Apply It

1–6. Rewrite this e-mail. Use the correct homophones. The chart will help you.

Revising

e-mail

To: Nathan

Subject: Good News

    Your not going to believe this. Yesterday we got a kitten! Its so cute. The family next door has a cat that had babies. Yesterday they put a sign in their front yard that said Kittens for Sale. We got there early to pick the best one. It looks like you're cat, but it's paws are white. Last night I could here it meowing. I hope it doesn't fight with your dog. I wish you were hear!

Enrichment

Pronouns!

Yard Sale

You and your friends are having a yard sale. Write an advertisement announcing the sale. When and where will it be held? What will be for sale? Use pronouns in your ad. Underline each one.

Yard Sale Today!

We are cleaning out our garage.

I am selling my fish tank.

Time Machine

Pretend that a time machine takes you to another time and place. You meet and talk with someone in this new setting. Decide on your new time and place. Then draw a cartoon strip about your experience. Write the conversation in speech balloons. Use the pronouns *I* and *me*.

Challenge See how many of these pronouns you can use at least once in your cartoon: *I, he, she, it, we, they, me, you, him, her, us, them.*

1 **Subject Pronouns** *(p. 214)* Write a pronoun to replace the underlined word or words in each sentence.

1. <u>Jon</u> sings a song to the crowd.
2. <u>Mia</u> plays along on the piano.
3. <u>The children</u> take a bow.
4. <u>The concert</u> is over too soon.
5. <u>Mom and I</u> clap loudly.
6. <u>The students</u> clear the stage.

2 **Pronouns and Verbs** *(p. 216)* Choose the correct verb form to complete each sentence. Write the sentences.

7. You (wash, washes) the fish tank.
8. She (fill, fills) the tank with water.
9. They (place, places) the fish in the tank.
10. He (reach, reaches) for the food.
11. I (feed, feeds) the fish.

3 **Object Pronouns** *(p. 218)* Write a pronoun to replace the underlined word or words in each sentence.

12. Tasha went to the pet store with <u>Mike and me</u>.
13. The pet store owner fed <u>the cats and fish</u>.
14. He handed a tiny kitten to <u>Tasha</u>.
15. He handed a spotted rabbit to <u>Mike</u>.
16. Mike bought the rabbit for <u>Tasha and me</u>.

4 **Using *I* and *me*** *(p. 222)* Write each sentence, using the correct word or words in ( ).

17. Dad gave (I, me) a map.
18. (Mario and I, Mario and me) went on a hike.
19. (I and Jim, Jim and I) fished all afternoon.
20. Then it rained on (Jim and I, Jim and me).
21. Jim gave (I, me) a rain hat.

5 **Possessive Pronouns** *(p. 224)* Write the sentences. Underline the possessive pronoun in each sentence.

22. My mother made different sandwiches for everyone.
23. You ate your sandwich very slowly.
24. Molly had a strange look on her face.

See www.eduplace.com/kids/hme/ for an online quiz.

25. Matt gave his sandwich to Megan.
26. Mom had mixed up our sandwiches!

6 **Contractions** *(p. 226)* Write the contraction for each pair of words.

27. I will
29. they have
31. I am
28. we are
30. it is
32. he has

7 **Using *there*, *their*, and *they're*** *(p. 228)* Complete each sentence with *there*, *their*, or *they're*. Write the sentences.

33. Mr. Kaplan and Cindy are on _____ boat.
34. _____ sailing to Westport.
35. I am meeting them _____.
36. On Saturday _____ having a picnic on the beach.
37. _____ boat is entered in a race on Sunday.

Mixed Review 38–44. This note has two incorrect verb forms, two mistakes in using *I* and *me*, one missing apostrophe, and two mistakes in using *there*, *their*, and *they're*. Write the letter correctly.

Proofreading Checklist
Are these words written correctly?
✔ verb forms
✔ *I* and *me*
✔ contractions
✔ *there*, *their*, and *they're*

Proofreading ——— **STEPHEN** ———

Dear Aunt Jenny,

Thank you for the paint set. Maria and me love it! We uses it every day. I get the easels. She mix the paints. Then we paint pictures. Mom and Dad hung our pictures in there office. They're sure Maria and I will be famous artists!

Me and Maria are going to art school this summer. We'll learn more about painting their. Ill send you my best picture!

Love,
Stephen

Test Practice

Write the numbers 1–8 on a sheet of paper. Choose the best way to write the underlined part of each sentence. Write the letter for that answer. If there is no mistake, write the letter for the last answer.

1 A dog chased <u>Joan and I</u>.

   A Me and Joan

   B I and Joan

   C Joan and me

   D (No mistakes)

2 <u>We'll</u> be on vacation soon.

   F Will

   G We

   H We're

   J (No mistakes)

3 Carlos put the letter in <u>he</u> pocket.

   A him

   B his

   C he's

   D (No mistakes)

4 Mr. Lee is <u>they're</u> teacher.

   F their

   G there

   H they

   J (No mistakes)

5 <u>Tia and me</u> like that band.

   A Me and Tia

   B I and Tia

   C Tia and I

   D (No mistakes)

6 We <u>stay</u> at Grandma's farm every summer.

   F stays

   G staying

   H has stayed

   J (No mistakes)

7 I think <u>their</u> going to win!

   A they

   B they're

   C there

   D (No mistakes)

8 Go now or <u>you're</u> be late!

   F you'll

   G you

   H you've

   J (No mistakes)

Now write the numbers 9–14 on your paper. Look at each underlined part of the paragraph. Find the correct way to write the underlined part in each numbered line. Write the letter of that answer. If the part is already correct, write the letter for the last answer, "Correct as it is."

(9)   Wild rabbits live all over the world. In <u>north america</u>,
(10) wild rabbits make <u>their</u> homes in prairies, fields, and marshes.
(11) <u>A adult rabbit is</u> about a foot long and may weigh five pounds.
(12) Enemies of wild rabbits include <u>hawks dogs and foxs</u>. To
(13) avoid danger, a <u>rabbit uses its</u> sharp sense of hearing. A wild
(14) <u>rabbits's</u> keen sense of smell also helps it escape from enemies.

9 **A** North america

  B north America

  C North America

  D Correct as it is

10 **F** they're

  G there

  H them

  J Correct as it is

11 **A** A adult rabbits are

  B An adult rabbit is

  C An adult rabbit are

  D Correct as it is

12 **F** Hawks, dogs and, foxes

  G Hawks, dogs and foxs

  H hawks, dogs, and foxes

  J Correct as it is

13 **A** rabbits use its

  B rabbit uses their

  C rabbit use its

  D Correct as it is

14 **F** rabbit's

  G rabbits

  H rabbits'

  J Correct as it is

Now write the numbers 15–20 on your paper. Look at each underlined part of the paragraph. Find the correct way to write the underlined part in each numbered line. Write the letter of that answer. If the part is already correct, write the letter for the last answer, "Correct as it is."

(15)   Kevin and Kurtis Monroe are twins. They <u>were</u> born

(16) on <u>oct</u> 27, 1991. The brothers are alike in many ways. Height

(17) is not one of them. Kevin is <u>too inchs</u> taller than Kurtis. Kevin

(18) used to tease <u>his</u> brother about being short. Kurtis just smiled.

(19) Then he said, <u>I was born first.</u> Kevin doesn't tease Kurtis

(20) much anymore. <u>Their</u> really best friends.

15 A are
   B was
   C is
   D Correct as it is

16 F Oct
   G oct.
   H Oct.
   J Correct as it is

17 A two inches
   B to inchs
   C too inches
   D Correct as it is

18 F he's
   G him
   H their
   J Correct as it is

19 A "I was born first.
   B "I was born first."
   C I was born first"
   D Correct as it is

20 F They's are
   G They're
   H There
   J Correct as it is

Unit 1: The Sentence

Subjects and Predicates in Sentences *(pp. 40, 42)* Write each sentence. Draw a line between the subject and the predicate.

1. Kate wrote a social studies report.
2. Her teacher read it to the class.
3. It was about George Washington.
4. George Washington was born in 1732.
5. He became the first President of the United States.

Unit 2: Nouns

Common and Proper Nouns *(pp. 60, 62)* Write each noun. Then write *common* or *proper* after each one.

6. August was a busy month.
7. Ben Wright and Carmen Rivera had parties.
8. My family spent a week in New Hampshire.
9. Our town held a fair.
10. Grandma flew in from San Francisco.
11. Uncle Dave held a clambake at the beach.

Singular and Plural Nouns *(pp. 68, 70, 71, 72)* Write the plural form of each noun.

12. porch
13. princess
14. tooth
15. penny
16. goose
17. desk

Possessive Nouns *(pp. 74, 76)* Write each word group, using the possessive form of the underlined noun.

18. a <u>girl</u> kite
19. <u>boys</u> bikes
20. <u>Spencer</u> lunch
21. <u>men</u> belts
22. <u>babies</u> rattles
23. <u>painter</u> ladder

See www.eduplace.com/kids/hme/ for a
tricky usage or spelling question.

Cumulative Review   **237**

Unit 3: Verbs

Verbs in the Present, Past, and Future *(pp. 100, 102, 104, 106, 108)*
Write the verbs. Label each one *present, past,* or *future.*

24. Kyle loves all kinds of animals.
25. One day Mom surprised Kyle with a puppy.
26. The puppy chases our kittens under the bed.
27. Once, the puppy buried a bone in our neighbor's yard.
28. I will get the puppy a new collar soon.

The Special Verb *be,* **Helping Verbs, and Irregular Verbs**
(pp. 112, 114, 116, 118) Write each sentence correctly.

29. The newspaper has (came, come).
30. A girl (has, have) delivered it.
31. It (was, were) on the front porch.
32. The children (took, taken) the newspaper indoors.
33. The rain (has, have) soaked the front page.

Unit 4: Adjectives and Adverbs

Adjectives *(pp. 142, 144)* Write the adjectives.

34. Kim and two friends took the ferry to Shelter Island.
35. They looked at the beautiful water along the way.
36. The children rented some bicycles.
37. They rode the bikes around the small island.
38. The tired children slept on the ferry home.

Adverbs *(pp. 152, 154)* Write each adverb.

39. Brett always attends the Thanksgiving
    Day parade.
40. Usually Dad goes with him.
41. Brett races ahead with other children.
42. They soon find a good spot.
43. Suddenly the floats appear.

Unit 5: Capitalization and Punctuation

Four Kinds of Sentences and Proper Nouns

(pp. 178, 182, 184) Write each sentence correctly.

44. Have you fished in Lake White
    this summer
45. Is it near bellmore high school?
46. ask Aunt Ruth for directions to the lake.
47. My friend eric greenberg caught ten
    fish in two hours!
48. Come with me on Sunday

Abbreviations and Book Titles *(pp. 186, 188)* Write each abbreviation, name, and book title correctly.

49. sept
50. fri
51. mrs lee duffy
52. dr fred kent
53. kitoto the mighty
54. the empress and the silkworm

Commas *(pp. 189, 190)* Write each sentence. Put commas where they are needed.

55. Mark Jasmine and Seth went on a treasure hunt.
56. Well Jasmine found the red pencil.
57. Seth found the seashell a comb and the soap.
58. Mark found the chalk the button and the pine cone.
59. Yes Mark won first prize.

Quotation Marks *(pp. 194, 196)* Write each sentence. Add capital letters, commas, end marks, and quotation marks where needed.

60. Grandpa asked, Did you go to the library?
61. Amanda answered "I found a book about rainbows."
62. Grandpa asked, "Do you see the rainbow in the sky"
63. Amanda exclaimed, it is so beautiful!
64. Grandpa said, "I saw seven colors in the rainbow"

Unit 6: Pronouns

Subject and Object Pronouns *(pp. 214, 218)* Write a pronoun to replace the underlined words.

65. <u>Stacey and Brian</u> went to the Grand Canyon.
66. The children rode with <u>Aunt Gert and Uncle Leroy</u>.
67. <u>Aunt Gert</u> drove the car.
68. Brian explored <u>the canyon</u> on a donkey.

Pronouns and Verbs *(p. 216)* Write each sentence, using the correct present form of the verb in ( ).

69. I (paint) my room.
70. He (move) the bed.
71. You (hang) a poster.
72. They (finish) the job.

Possessive Pronouns *(p. 224)*
Write the sentences. Underline the possessive pronoun in each sentence.

73. My mother has a job.
74. Her office is busy.
75. Our car did not start.
76. Mom rode with your aunt.

Contractions *(p. 226)* Write the contractions.

77. it is   79. I am   81. you are
78. he has   80. it will   82. she is

Using *I, me, there, their,* and *they're* *(pp. 222, 228)* Write each sentence correctly.

83. Dad and (I, me) chop wood for the fireplace.
84. Ed helps Dad and (I, me).
85. Dad and Ed wear (there, their) hats.
86. (I, Me) bring the wood into the den.

(pages 214–215)

1 Subject Pronouns

Remember

- A pronoun takes the place of one or more nouns.
- The pronouns *I, you, he, she, it, we,* and *they* are subject pronouns. Pronouns can be singular or plural.

● Write each sentence. Underline the pronoun.

Example: I looked at the stars.   *I looked at the stars.*

1. They seemed far away.
2. I found the Big Dipper.
3. Where is it?
4. He looked for the moon.
5. She pointed to the sky.
6. Did you see the moon?
7. We saw the full moon.
8. It was high overhead.

▲ Write a pronoun to replace the underlined word or words.

Example: Many people are on the beach.   *They*

9. The sun feels very hot.
10. Brandon collects shells.
11. Maria goes swimming.
12. Tina and Maria sit under an umbrella.
13. Grandma gives us sandwiches.
14. The beach is lots of fun.

■ Change the underlined word or words in each sentence to a subject pronoun. Write the sentences. Then write *plural* if the pronoun is plural.

Example: Uncle Joe and I walked to the library.
            We walked to the library.   plural

15. The library is five blocks away.
16. David was at the library.
17. David and I waved to each other.
18. Two children read quietly.
19. Mr. Putnam works at the library.
20. Uncle Joe took out three books.

(pages 216–217)

2 Pronouns and Verbs

- Use the form of the verb that goes with the subject pronoun. Add *-s* or *-es* to a verb in the present when the subject is *he, she,* or *it.*
- Do not add *-s* or *-es* to a verb in the present when the subject is *I, you, we,* or *they.*

Remember

● Write the correct sentence in each pair.

Example: We plays a game.
We play a game. *We play a game.*

1. It seems easy.
   It seem easy.
2. I tells Billy the rules.
   I tell Billy the rules.

3. He move three spaces.
   He moves three spaces.
4. You takes a turn.
   You take a turn.

▲ Write each sentence, using the correct verb form.

Example: You (find, finds) a map. *You find a map.*

5. It (leads, lead) to a surprise.
6. We (follow, follows) the directions.
7. We (rush, rushes) over the hill.
8. I (help, helps) with the search.
9. We (sees, see) three tiny kittens by the barn.

■ Write each sentence. Use the correct form of the verb in ( ).

Example: She _____ lettuce. (buy) *She buys lettuce.*

10. He _____ an orange. (eat)
11. I _____ for the cereal. (search)
12. She _____ for the milk. (reach)
13. You _____ five pounds of potatoes. (want)
14. He _____ in line. (stand)
15. They _____ for the groceries. (pay)

(pages 218–219)

3 Object Pronouns

Remember

- The pronouns *me, you, him, her, it, us,* and *them* are object pronouns.
- *It* and *you* are both subject and object pronouns.

● Write *singular* if the underlined pronoun is singular. Write *plural* if the underlined pronoun is plural.

Example: Mrs. Robbins taught <u>us</u> about old coins.   *plural*

1. Everyone listened to <u>her</u>.
2. Mrs. Robbins handed two silver dollars to <u>me</u>.
3. The government made <u>them</u>.
4. Sam brought in some coins for <u>us</u>.
5. The dates on <u>them</u> were very old.

▲ Write each sentence. Change the underlined word or words to a pronoun.

Example: We collect <u>seashells</u>.   *We collect them.*

6. Emilio found a shell for <u>Krista</u>.
7. Krista washed <u>the shell</u> in the sink.
8. She showed the shell to <u>Troy</u>.
9. Troy gave a book about shells to <u>the boys</u>.
10. I found a picture of <u>the shell</u>.

■ Write each sentence, using a subject or an object pronoun. Use a different pronoun in each sentence.

Example: Sarah started a stamp collection with _____.
   Sarah started a stamp collection with them.

11. _____ surprised Sarah with an airplane stamp.
12. Peter saved a bird stamp for _____.
13. I gave a Mexican stamp to _____.
14. Today _____ went to Mr. Tello's store.
15. He had some old stamps for _____.

(pages 222–223)

4 Using *I* and *me*

- Use *I* as the subject of a sentence. Use *me* as an object pronoun. Always capitalize the word *I*.
- Name yourself last when you talk about another person and yourself.

Remember

● Write the correct sentence in each pair.

Example: Ed and I made masks.   *Ed and I made masks.*
Ed and me made masks.

1. Me drew the shape.
   I drew the shape.
2. Ed asked I for glue.
   Ed asked me for glue.
3. I used the scissors.
   Me used the scissors.

4. Mom helped me and Ed.
   Mom helped Ed and me.
5. I and Ed worked hard.
   Ed and I worked hard.
6. My mask fit me.
   My mask fit I.

▲ Write each sentence, using the correct word or words.

Example: (Alana and I, Alana and me) built a robot.
Alana and I built a robot.

7. The grocer gave (me, I) some large boxes.
8. (Me, I) put the boxes together.
9. (Alana and I, Alana and me) added arms and legs.
10. Mark handed (I, me) the paint.
11. (I and Robin, Robin and I) painted two eyes.

■ Write each sentence correctly with *I* or *me*.

Example: _____ and Al own model cars.   *Al and I own model cars.*

12. _____ and Al raced the cars.
13. Everyone watched _____ and Al.
14. The green car belonged to _____.
15. _____ was the winner of the race!

(pages 224–225)

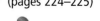

5 Possessive Pronouns

Remember

- A possessive pronoun shows ownership.
- The pronouns *my, your, her, his, its, our,* and *their* are possessive pronouns.

● Write each sentence. Underline the possessive pronoun.

Example: Is that your kite?   *Is that your kite?*

1. My kite is colorful.
2. Has Amanda seen our new train?
3. Its wheels are big and shiny.
4. Where are your puzzles?
5. Robert put his puzzles on the shelf.

▲ Change each underlined word or words to a possessive pronoun. Write the new groups of words.

Example: Pedro's and my dog   *our dog*

6. Dad's car
7. Mrs. Green's book
8. the giraffe's food
9. the girls' games
10. Lisa's sandwich
11. Rob's and my bike
12. the puppet's face
13. the man's coat
14. Allison and Pete's paint
15. Tony's and my horse

■ Complete each sentence with a possessive pronoun that goes with the underlined word or words. Write the sentences.

Example: Matt and Cristina looked out _____ window.
            Matt and Cristina looked out their window.

16. The big tree had lost _____ leaves.
17. Luis and I waited inside for _____ ride.
18. Elena buttoned _____ raincoat.
19. I looked for _____ warm socks.
20. You wore _____ rain hat.

(pages 226–227)

6 Contractions

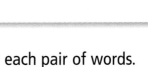
Remember

- A contraction can be made by joining a pronoun and a verb. Use an apostrophe in place of the letter or letters that are left out.

● Write the word in ( ) that is a contraction for each pair of words.

Example: I will (Ill, I'll) *I'll*

1. he has (he's, hes)
2. it is (its, it's)
3. we have (weve, we've)
4. she will (she'll, shel)

5. you have (youve, you've)
6. they will (they'll, theyll)
7. you are (your, you're)
8. I am (Im, I'm)

▲ Write the contraction for each pair of words below.

Example: she is *she's*

9. they will
10. we are
11. I am
12. he will

13. I have
14. they are
15. he has
16. we have

17. it is
18. you will
19. she has
20. we will

■ Write each sentence. Replace two words in each sentence with a contraction.

Example: We are practicing outdoors.
   We're practicing outdoors.

21. She is my music teacher.
22. First, they will play the violins.
23. He has already learned the new song.
24. She will tap out the beat for us.
25. It is lively outside.
26. I am excited.
27. Tomorrow we will play for our school.
28. I have invited my family.

(pages 228–229)

7 Using *there*, *their*, and *they're*

Remember

- Use *there* to mean "at or in that place."
- Use *their* to mean "belonging to them."
- Use *they're* to make the contraction for *they are.*
- Use sentence clues to decide which word to use.

● Write each sentence. Use the correct word in ( ).

Example: (They're, There) all at the movies. *They're all at the movies.*

1. My friends go (there, their) every Sunday.
2. They are with (they're, their) parents.
3. (There, They're) seeing a funny movie.
4. (There, Their) favorite actors are in it.
5. I might go (they're, there) with them next Sunday.

▲ Complete each sentence with *there, their,* or *they're.* Write the sentences.

Example: Lin and Dan invited _____ friends on a picnic.
Lin and Dan invited their friends on a picnic.

6. _____ bringing plenty of food.
7. It will not take long to walk _____.
8. The children will eat _____ lunches quickly.
9. They will swim in the lake _____.

■ Write each sentence. Write *correct* if the underlined word is correct.
If the underlined word is not correct, replace it with *there, their,* or *they're.*

Example: My grandparents are busy in <u>there</u> store.
My grandparents are busy in their store.

10. <u>Their</u> getting ready for a big sale.
11. The store is near <u>their</u> home.
12. I go <u>they're</u> to shop.
13. Do you want to shop <u>there</u> now?
14. <u>There</u> prices are low.

2

Writing, Listening, Speaking, and Viewing

What You Will Find in This Part:

Narrating and Entertaining

What You Will Find in This Section:

Listening to a Narrative

A **narrative** is a story. It can be true or made up. Listening to a story is different from listening to a report. When someone tells you a story, you usually listen for enjoyment. Here are some ideas to help you be a good listener.

Guidelines for Listening to a Story
▶ Listen for the main idea. What is the narrative about?
▶ Find out who the most important people in the narrative are.
▶ Listen for the setting. Where and when does the narrative takes place?
▶ Find out what happens. What are the main events in the narrative?

Try It Out Listen as your teacher reads aloud from *In My Momma's Kitchen,* by Jerdine Nolen. This part of the story is about something funny that happened with the author's cat, Janie. Listen for details that answer the questions below.

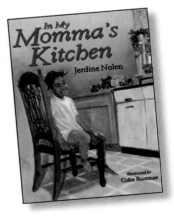

- Who are the important people or animals in the narrative?
- Where does the story take place?
- What are the main events?

 See www.eduplace.com/kids/ for information about Jerdine Nolen.

Writing a Narrative Paragraph

A **paragraph** is a group of sentences that tell about one thing. The first line of a paragraph is **indented**. This means that there is a space before the first word. A paragraph has a topic and a main idea. The **topic** is what the paragraph is about. The **main idea** is what the writer wants to say about the topic. All the sentences tell about the main idea.

A paragraph that tells a story is a **narrative paragraph.** The story can be true or made up. What is the topic of the narrative paragraph below? What is the main idea?

Indent ——
Lead sentence ——
Supporting sentences ——
Closing sentence ——

I practiced for two weeks before I learned to ride a bike. Mom or Dad would hold the bike from behind while I pedaled. We went out every day. I got better and better. I still didn't think I was ready to ride alone. Yesterday my mom let go and didn't tell me. When I saw that I was alone, I was so happy. Now I can ride all by myself!

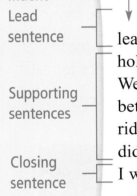

The topic is learning to ride a bike. The main idea is that it took the writer two weeks. Which sentence tells the topic and main idea?

The labels show the parts of a narrative paragraph.

- The **lead sentence** tells what the paragraph is about.
- The **supporting sentences** give details that tell what happens.
- The **closing sentence** ends the paragraph and finishes the story.

Think and Discuss In the paragraph above, what details does the writer give in the supporting sentences to tell what happened?

The Lead Sentence

The **lead sentence** is the first sentence in the paragraph. The lead sentence tells what the paragraph is about. It begins the story and may give a clue about the main idea.

Something about the main idea   What the paragraph is about

Example: I practiced for two weeks before I learned to ride a bike.

What might paragraphs with these lead sentences be about?

- When I came home from school yesterday, there was a skinny cat on the front porch.
- Mom is trying to teach me to cook, but I am a slow learner!

Try It Out Read the paragraphs below. They are missing the lead sentence. On your own or with a partner, write a lead sentence for each paragraph.

1. ___Lead sentence___. All my friends came. They brought me a lot of presents, and we played games. Then we had a cake with nine candles. I blew them all out. This was the best birthday I ever had.

2. ___Lead sentence___. I held my breath, and two seconds later I was under water. Then I swam to the surface. The sun hit my face. I looked up at the high dive and felt proud. I had finally jumped!

Supporting Sentences

Supporting sentences follow the lead sentence. They give details about the story. **Details** can answer the questions *Who? What? Where? When? Why?* and *How?* They help the reader see, hear, smell, taste, and feel what happened. In the bicycle paragraph on page 253, supporting sentences tell *who* helped the writer learn to ride. They also tell *when* the writer practiced and *how* she finally learned.

Who: <u>Mom or Dad</u> would hold the bike from behind while I pedaled.
When: We went out <u>every day</u>.
How: Yesterday <u>my mom let go and didn't tell me.</u>

Try It Out On your own or with a partner, choose one of the lead sentences below. List details about what you see, hear, smell, taste, and feel. Then write four supporting sentences.

1. Our picnic at the park had everything I love.
2. Our picnic at the park did not go as planned.

> **GRAMMAR TIP** *Use an exclamation point (!) to end a sentence that shows strong feeling.*

Keeping to the Main Idea Supporting sentences should tell only about the main idea. Do not tell about things that don't go with the story.

Think and Discuss Read the paragraph below. What is the main idea? Which sentence does not belong?

> Yesterday I slept too late, and everything went wrong after that. First, I ate breakfast too fast and spilled milk on my shirt. Then I had to change my shirt. As I ran to the bus stop, I stubbed my toe. I stubbed my toe at the pool last summer too. When I got to school, I remembered my lunch. It was still in the kitchen at home!

more ▶

Ordering Details The events in a narrative paragraph are usually told in the order they happened. **Time-clue words**, such as *first, next, then,* and *in the morning,* help connect events. What time-clue words do you see in the paragraph about sleeping late on page 255?

 See page 18 for more time-clue words.

Think and Discuss Read the paragraph below. Which two sentences are out of order? How would you fix the order?

    I loved riding the G-Force Spinner at the fair! The cage started spinning. First, we got into the cage and leaned against the wall. The spinning held us against the wall. Next, the floor dropped away, but we stayed stuck on the wall! By the end, I was ready to ride again!

The Closing Sentence

 A **closing sentence** ends the paragraph. This sentence can tell the end of the story. It can also tell how the writer felt or what the writer learned. In the birthday paragraph on page 254, the closing sentence tells how the writer felt.

Try It Out The paragraph below needs a closing sentence. On your own or with a partner, write two different closing sentences for it.

    Yesterday my mom and I tried to wash our dog, Shadow. Mom lifted Shadow into the tub. When she poured soapy water on him, he jumped out. Then he shook water and soap bubbles everywhere! Mom grabbed him and put him back in. He jumped out again. Finally, Mom said I had to get into the tub and hold Shadow while she scrubbed him. *Closing sentence*.

Write Your Own Narrative Paragraph

Now you can write your own narrative paragraph. Just tell a story about something that you did or saw. First, try to picture what happened. Then make a list of details. Put them in time order. Then tell your story to a partner. After that, you'll be ready to write!

Checklist for My Paragraph

✔ My **lead sentence** tells what my paragraph is about.

✔ My **supporting sentences** tell what happened in order. I used time-clue words to connect some sentences.

✔ My **details** give a clear picture of what happened.

✔ My **closing sentence** tells the end of the story, how I felt, or what I learned.

Looking Ahead

When you know how to write a narrative paragraph, writing a longer story is easy. The chart below shows how the parts of a narrative paragraph are like the parts of a longer story.

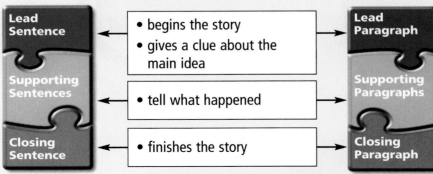

Narrative Paragraph   **Longer Narrative**

Lead Sentence	• begins the story • gives a clue about the main idea	Lead Paragraph
Supporting Sentences	• tell what happened	Supporting Paragraphs
Closing Sentence	• finishes the story	Closing Paragraph

Unit 7

Writing a Personal Narrative

I really surprised the class during show-and-tell time!

In this personal narrative, Patricia Polacco tells about an exciting experience she had horseback riding. Can you understand how she felt?

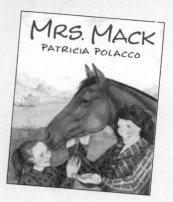

Mrs. Mack

from *Mrs. Mack*, by Patricia Polacco

It was a very sunny Friday when it happened. I arrived at the stables like always, but something seemed different. I knew that I was getting a new mount. Usually Donnie or Nancy would bring the new horse to me. But today Mrs. Mack went to get it.

 Go to www.eduplace.com/kids/ for information about Patricia Polacco.

more ▶
A Published Model **259**

As Donnie, Nancy, and I waited by the hitching post, I wondered which horse Mrs. Mack was going to bring. Maybe her horse, Apache! When I finally saw the look on Donnie's and Nancy's faces as they looked behind me, I knew it must be Apache. I could hear Mrs. Mack's voice talking softly to the horse.

But when I turned around, I saw it was not Apache. It was my Penny.

I couldn't breathe for a whole minute. Mrs. Mack handed me the reins, her eyes kind of watery-like. I drew up the reins and mounted without a word.

It felt as though time had stopped, the air wasn't moving. It seemed even the birds were watching.

"You made it, Hollywood," Donnie said softly as he smiled.

Nancy nodded and gave a thumbs-up.

I felt my heart connect with Penny's. Her body quivered. She waited for a signal from me to tell her what to do.

I touched her sides with my knees. Penny responded, almost jumping out from under me. I reined her in quickly. My heels were down, my tail tucked under, the reins light in my fingers—I remembered everything I'd been taught. It was second nature now.

"Take her in the corral for a few turns before you head out, Pat," Mrs. Mack called to me. She sat on the fence rails and watched Penny and me intently.

Penny seemed like part of me. She moved as I moved. Her thoughts were mine. We moved like dancers or ice skaters, together. I felt elegant and graceful on her. As I passed each

person at the fence, I caught their eyes. Even old Hap was there.

When I pulled up in front of Mrs. Mack, my mouth formed the words "Thank you. Thank you."

Mrs. Mack opened the gate and waved us toward the trail. We trotted through the gate, then we paused. Penny reared and I threw my hand over my head like a cowboy. My heart was singing.

Just then a leaf blew across the road in front of us. A single leaf! Penny stopped so suddenly that she leapt to the left. I lost my balance and fell from her back, hard to the ground.

I held on to the reins, and she dragged me for a few feet. I fought back the tears and the feeling of disappointment, and terror. When Penny finally stopped, I slowly stood up, dazed. My back hurt.

Everyone watched me. I started to lead Penny back to the stables when I heard Mrs. Mack shout, "No, Pat! Get back on that mare. Get on now!"

I couldn't. I was suddenly afraid of Penny. Afraid of her!

"Get back on, Pat," Mrs. Mack coaxed.

My tailbone hurt so much that I could hardly walk, but I knew that Mrs. Mack was right. I had to get back on her. My heart pounding in my ears, I came up beside Penny's neck.

"There, girl," I heard myself saying to her. I gathered up the reins, turned the stirrup, stepped into it, and flung myself back into the saddle. I leaned into Penny's withers. They shivered for a moment. I caught my breath. Then she leaned back into me and I knew she had forgiven my inexperience. She was willing to try again.

I sat straight in the saddle. Penny arched her neck and held her tail high. She reared slightly again, her hooves dancing, and we were under way. My breath caught when she stumbled on the ridge in the middle of the road. But after that her steps were sure and proud.

A touch from my knee and she broke into an elegant trot. Another, and she broke into a rocking canter. I found myself laughing out loud for the sheer pleasure of being on Penny's back.

Everyone around the corral started to clap. Even old Hap. As I cantered by him, I could see a grin. Donnie and Nancy cantered up to me. We exploded down the road together, the three of us!

Reading As a Writer

Think About the Personal Narrative

- Who is the *I* in the story?
- What are the important events in the story?
- Look at the last two paragraphs on page 262. What details help you see how Patricia Polacco felt when she and Penny started riding again?

Think About Writer's Craft

- In the first paragraph on page 259, the author says that "it happened," but she doesn't say what "it" was. Why not?

Think About the Pictures

- What two important story events do the pictures show? What details in each picture help you understand how Pat and Penny are feeling?

Responding

Write responses to these questions.

- **Personal Response** What part of the story did you like best? Why?
- **Critical Thinking** Why do you think the author wanted to tell this story?

What Makes a Great Personal Narrative?

A personal narrative is a true story about something that happened to the writer.

Remember to follow these guidelines when you write a personal narrative.

▶ Write a beginning that gets your audience curious.

▶ Use the pronoun *I.*

▶ Include only the events that are important to your story. Tell the events in order.

▶ Use details that tell what you saw, heard, or felt.

▶ Write in a way that sounds like you.

▶ Write an ending that tells how the story worked out or how you felt.

GRAMMAR CHECK

Be sure to write complete sentences. Begin each sentence with a capital letter, and use the correct end mark.

WORKING DRAFT

Daniel Estevez spent an interesting day helping his aunt with her job. He wrote this draft to share his experience with the rest of his family.

Daniel Estevez

Working Draft

My Visit to IBM

My aunt called me last April. She works for IBM in New York. She said, "We're having Kids Day at IBM. I think you'd have fun. Would you like to come?" My friend Sebastian lives in New York, and he was invited to Kids Day too.

> I like your beginning! You got me curious about Kids Day.

The day before Kids Day, my family and I went to New York. By the time we got to New York, it was dark. I woke up early the next morning. I wanted to get to IBM in time to have breakfast. At first, I couldn't find my toothbrush. I thought I had brought it, so I kept looking for it. Finally, I found it at the bottom of my suitcase.

After breakfast, Sebastian and I found out that we couldn't do the Kids Day activities. We were too young. My aunt took us to her office, and she found some other things for us to do.

> How did you feel when you couldn't do the Kids Day activities?

---

more

Working Draft

My aunt had a small office. She shared it with another person. She asked Sebastian and me to help her get some important packages mailed out. We had to make phone calls to make sure we had the right addresses.

We liked making phone calls, but I kept looking at the clock on my aunt's laptop computer and asking my aunt, "When's lunch?" Pretty soon my aunt started laughing every time either Sebastian or I asked her this question. After lunch, we helped get the packages ready to ship to people.

Finally, it was time to leave. That was my day at IBM.

> This part is important. Can you add more details?

> Your events are in perfect order. Nice work!

Reading As a Writer

- What did Sal like about Daniel's personal narrative? What questions did Sal have? What changes could Daniel make to answer Sal's questions?
- Look at the second paragraph on page 265. Which part is not important to the story?
- What other questions would you like to ask Daniel about his experience?

Daniel revised his personal narrative after discussing it with a classmate. Read Daniel's final paper to see the changes he made to improve his story.

My Day As a Grownup

by Daniel Estevez

My aunt called me last April. She works for IBM in New York. She said, "We're having Kids Day at IBM. I think you'd have fun. Would you like to come?" My friend Sebastian lives in New York, and he was invited to Kids Day too.

> You took out the part about your toothbrush. Good! It didn't keep to the topic.

The day before Kids Day, my family and I went to New York. By the time we got to New York, it was dark. I woke up early the next morning. I wanted to get to IBM in time to have breakfast.

After breakfast, Sebastian and I couldn't wait to start doing things at IBM. Then all of a sudden the whole day almost got wrecked. We found out that we couldn't do things with the other kids. We were too young for Kids Day. We felt really terrible, and we thought it wasn't fair at all! My aunt said, "Never mind." She took us to her office, and Sebastian and I got to do a lot of excellent things that the other kids didn't get to do.

> Now I can hear how you felt. Good job!

more

My aunt had a small office. She shared it with another person. She asked Sebastian and me to help her get some important packages mailed out. We had to make phone calls all over the world to make sure we had the right addresses. Sebastian and I worked together. Sebastian talked with the people who spoke English, and I talked with the people who spoke Spanish. I got to talk with people who live all over South America.

We liked making phone calls, but I kept looking at the clock on my aunt's laptop computer and asking my aunt, "When's lunch?" My stomach felt like an empty balloon. Pretty soon my aunt started laughing every time either Sebastian or I asked her that question. After lunch, we helped get the packages ready to ship to people.

> This comparison makes me feel hungry!

Finally, it was time to leave. For a day that started out in a way that didn't look too good, it turned out great. For a whole day we got to do stuff that grownups do. We got to talk with people all over the world, and we had good food too.

Reading As a Writer

- What changes did Daniel make to answer Sal's questions?
- Look at the first paragraph on this page. What new details did Daniel add?
- Compare the endings in Daniel's working draft and final copy. Why is the ending in the final copy better?

 See www.eduplace.com/kids/hme/ for more examples of student writing.

Write a Personal Narrative

▶ Start Thinking

📁 Make a writing folder for your personal narrative. Copy the questions in bold print, and put the paper in your folder. Write your answers as you think about and choose your topic.

- **Who will be my audience?** Will it be a friend? my class? a favorite family member?
- **What will be my purpose?** Do I want to make my audience laugh? to share a memory that is special or important to me?
- **How will I publish or share my personal narrative?** Will I act it out? make a tape recording? make a Big Book?

▶ Choose Your Story Idea

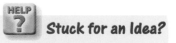

HELP ?   Stuck for an Idea?

Think about these.
- the day I got my pet
- my first bike ride
- a scary experience

See page 280 for more ideas.

❶ **List** three experiences you could write about.

❷ **Discuss** your ideas with a partner. Which ones does your partner like? Why? Is any idea too big? Daniel broke one big idea into smaller parts.

My Trip to New York

museum — IBM — zoo — ferry ride

❸ **Ask** yourself these questions about your ideas. Then circle the idea you will write about.

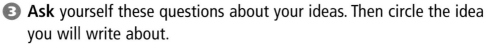

- Will I enjoy writing about this?
- Can I remember enough details?
- Will this interest my audience?

▶ Explore Your Story Idea

❶ **Think** of your experience as a group of photos in a photo album. Each photo shows an important event in your story.

- Draw your "photos." Write a few words about each one.

❷ **Choose** the photo that shows the most important part of your story, and circle it.

❸ **Write** details that your audience might need to know. Write the most details for the photo you circled. Use the Exploring Questions to help you.

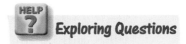

HELP ? **Exploring Questions**
- What did I do?
- What did I see? hear? touch? taste? smell?
- How did I feel?

Daniel drew these pictures and listed the events and details.

went to New York
woke up early
couldn't find toothbrush

couldn't do Kids Day activities
too young
went to my aunt's office

helped my aunt
got packages ready to mail
made phone calls
hungry for lunch

aunt invited me to IBM
lives in New York
has a poodle

HELP ? See page 14 for other ideas for exploring your topic.

Focus Skill

Organizing Your Narrative

Tell the events in the order they happened. Don't wait until the middle to say something that happened in the beginning. Your audience will get confused!

Keep to your topic. Take out events and details that are not needed to understand the important parts. Look at the detail below that Daniel crossed out.

I guess dogs aren't always important.

> aunt invited me to IBM
>
> lives in New York
>
> ~~has a poodle~~

Use time clues. Time clues help your audience understand when events happened. *First, before, later, soon,* and *after* are time clues.

....

Think and Discuss Look at Daniel's pictures on page 270.

- What could Daniel do to show the correct order of events?

▶ Plan Your Narrative

❶ Number your events in the order they happened. Cross out any events or details that don't belong in your story.

❷ Make a chart that shows your events in order. Add your details. Use this chart as a model.

Event 1	details
Event 2	details
Event 3	details

Focus Skill

Good Beginnings

The beginning of your story should be like the good smell of something in the oven. Make your audience hungry to find out what's cooking! Here are two different ways to begin.

Ask a question. A question makes your audience curious about your story.

Weak Beginning	Strong Beginning
My story is about the time I got lost when I was shopping with my mother.	Do you know what it's like to be lost for two hours in a huge, crowded shopping mall?

Set the scene. Picture your personal narrative as a play. The curtain has just gone up! Use details to show when and where the story begins.

Weak Beginning	Strong Beginning
My story is about the first time I went ice skating.	The morning was freezing, but the ice skating rink was shining brightly in the winter sun.

Try It Out

- With a partner, rewrite one of the weak beginnings to make it stronger. Then compare your beginning with your classmates'.

▶ Draft Your Beginning

① **Write** two different beginnings for your narrative. Ask a question in one, and set the scene in the other.

② **Choose** the beginning you like better.

HELP ? *Can't Get Started?*

For more ways to begin, open a few storybooks and read the first paragraph.

Focus Skill

Writing with Voice

You're the star of your personal narrative, so make it sound like you! When you write with voice, your audience can hear what you're like and how you feel. Writing without voice sounds boring and flat, like a robot talking.

Compare the weak and strong examples below. The strong example is from Patricia Polacco's story *Mrs. Mack*.

Weak Voice	Strong Voice
Penny was an easy horse to ride. She did whatever I wanted. I liked riding her.	Penny seemed like part of me. She moved as I moved. Her thoughts were mine. We moved like dancers or ice skaters, together.

Think and Discuss Compare the weak and strong examples above.

- Why does the weak voice sound flat?
- Which words in the second example show the writer's feelings?

▶ Draft Your Narrative

❶ **Write** the rest of your narrative. Skip every other line so you can make changes later. Don't stop to correct mistakes.

Tech Tip
Drafting on a computer can help you jot your ideas down quickly.

❷ **Use your chart** to help you. If you think of more events and details, add them to your story. Remember to use time clues.

❸ **Let your audience hear your voice.** Use words and details that show how you felt.

Focus Skill

Good Endings

In a good song, the last few notes tell you that the song is coming to an end. In a story, the ending should do the same job. Don't just come to a sudden stop and write "The End."

Tell how everything worked out. Compare these endings for a story about a lost cat.

Weak Ending	Strong Ending
We had almost given up. Then a lady called and said that she had found my cat.	I went to get Zorro right away. He looked so skinny and dirty! I hugged him until he purred. In a few days, he was my beautiful old cat again.

Share your thoughts and feelings about your experience. Did you end up feeling lucky? silly? proud? Did you learn something important? Compare these endings for a story about a music contest.

Weak Ending	Strong Ending
After all of the piano students had played, our teacher announced the winners. I won third prize.	At first, I was really upset that I didn't get first prize. Then I remembered that last year I didn't win anything! Suddenly, I felt great.

Think and Discuss

- Why are the strong endings better?
- Which sentences in Daniel's ending on page 268 tell how things worked out?

▶ ## Draft Your Ending

Write two endings for your narrative. Choose the ending you like better.

Evaluating Your Personal Narrative

▶ **Reread** your personal narrative. What do you need to do to make it better? Use this rubric to help you decide. Write the sentences that describe your narrative.

Rings the Bell!

- ☐ The beginning starts with a question or sets the scene.
- ☐ All of the events are important and in order.
- ☐ Details tell what I saw, heard, or felt.
- ☐ The ending tells how the story worked out or how I felt.
- ☐ My writing sounds like me.
- ☐ *There are almost no mistakes.*

Getting Stronger

- ☐ The beginning could be more interesting.
- ☐ Some sentences are not important to the story.
- ☐ More details are needed to describe what happened.
- ☐ My ending could tell more about how things worked out.
- ☐ A few parts of the story don't sound like me.
- ☐ *There are a few mistakes.*

Try Harder

- ☐ The beginning is boring.
- ☐ Many events are not important or are out of order.
- ☐ There are hardly any details.
- ☐ The story just stops.
- ☐ My writing doesn't sound like me.
- ☐ *There are a lot of mistakes.*

See www.eduplace.com/kids/hme/ to interact with this rubric.

► Revise Your Personal Narrative

1 **Revise** your narrative. Use the list of sentences you wrote from the rubric. Work on the parts that you described with sentences from "Getting Stronger" and "Try Harder."

HELP
? **Paragraph Tip**

If you have a very long paragraph with many events, group the events to make shorter paragraphs.

2 **Have a writing conference.**

When You're the Writer Read your personal narrative to a partner. Discuss any problems you're having. Take notes to remember what your partner says.

When You're the Listener Tell at least two things you like about the personal narrative. Ask questions about anything that is unclear.

What should I say?

The Writing Conference	
If you're thinking . . .	**You could say . . .**
The beginning isn't very interesting.	**Could you begin by asking a question or setting the scene?**
I wonder what this part has to do with the story?	**Is this part important? Can you leave it out?**
It's hard to picture what is going on here.	**Can you add more details so your audience can picture what happened?**
This doesn't sound like you.	**How did you feel when that happened?**
The story just stops at the end.	**How did everything work out?**

3 **Make more revisions** to your personal narrative. Use your conference notes and the Revising Strategies on the next page.

Revising Strategies

Elaborating: Word Choice You can paint a clear picture for your audience by using similes. A **simile** compares two different things by using the word *like* or *as.*

> My kite dipped and dived like a seagull.

> The sky was pink, gold, and purple, like a soap bubble.

> The lizard was as green and bumpy as a pickle.

▶ Find at least one place in your personal narrative where you can use a simile. 📖 See also page H11.

Elaborating: Details Add details to your sentences, or write more sentences.

Without Details	Elaborated with Details
A boy was watching us.	A little red-headed boy was watching us. He looked about six years old.

▶ Find at least two places in your personal narrative where you can add details.

Sentence Fluency Try writing sentences in different ways. Just keep the same meaning. Which way sounds most like you?

Two sentences	We heard a crash. We ran.
Combined with *and*	We heard a crash and ran. We heard a crash, and we ran.

▶ Write at least two sentences in your personal narrative a different way.

GRAMMAR LINK ▶ *See also pages 47 and 110.*

Proofread Your Personal Narrative

Proofread your personal narrative, using the Proofreading Checklist and the Grammar and Spelling Connections. Proofread for one skill at a time. Use a class dictionary to check spellings.

Proofreading Checklist

Did I
- ✔ indent all paragraphs?
- ✔ write complete sentences?
- ✔ begin every sentence with a capital letter?
- ✔ use correct end marks?
- ✔ correct any spelling errors?

📖 Use the Guide to Capitalization, Punctuation, and Usage on page H51.

Proofreading Marks

¶ Indent
∧ Add
⌇ Delete
≡ Capital letter
/ Small letter

HELP? **Proofreading Tip**

Place a ruler under each line as you read it.

Grammar and Spelling Connections

Correct Sentences Begin each sentence with a capital letter, and use the correct end mark.

Statement	We live on a noisy street.
Question	Did you ever ride a llama?
Command	Come with me.
Exclamation	That was a great shot!

GRAMMAR LINK ▶ *See also pages 36, 38, and 178.*

Spelling Short Vowels The short vowel sound in a word is usually spelled with just one letter: *a, e, i, o,* or *u.*

last   best   chip   pop   luck   📖 See the Spelling Guide on page H56.

▶ Publish Your Personal Narrative

❶ Make a neat final copy of your personal narrative. Be sure you formed your letters correctly and used good spacing. Check that you fixed all mistakes. If you used a computer, make all corrections. Then print out a final copy.

❷ Write a title that will make your audience curious, such as "A Miracle on the Soccer Field" rather than "The Soccer Game."

GRAMMAR TIP ▶ Begin the first, the last, and each important word in a title with a capital letter.

❸ Publish or share your narrative in a way your audience will enjoy.

Tips for Making a Big Book

- Use large paper. Make your words big and easy to read.
- Plan which part of your story you will put on each page. Leave plenty of room for pictures.
- Include the title and a picture on the cover. Staple the cover and pages together.

Ideas for Sharing

Write It
⭐ Make a Big Book for a younger child.

Say It
- Make a tape recording of your story. Add music or sound effects.

Show It
- Make a scrapbook with photos.
- Act out your story. See page 314 for tips.

▶ Reflect

Write about your writing experience. Use these questions to get started.

- What do you like best about your personal narrative?
- What did you learn that will help you next time?

- How does this paper compare with other papers you have written?

Writing Prompts

Use these prompts as ideas for a personal narrative or to practice for a test. Decide who your audience will be. Write your personal narrative in a way your audience will understand and enjoy.

1 Think about a special day that you spent with family or friends. What made it special? Did something funny, surprising, or exciting happen? Write about your experience.

2 Who is your best friend? Write about what happened when you met for the first time. What did you do? say? think?

3 Did you ever get lost? Where were you? How did you feel? What did you do? Write about what happened and how it turned out.

4 Think of a time when you felt very proud of yourself. Did you win something? help someone? learn a new skill? Write about what you did and how you felt.

Writing Across the Curriculum

5 FINE ART

The people in this painting are enjoying a day at the beach. Think about an experience you had outdoors. What makes the experience stand out in your mind? Write a personal narrative about what happened.

Superstock

On The Rocks
Anna Belle Lee Washington

Test Practice

This prompt to write a personal narrative is like ones you might find on a writing test. Read the prompt.

Think about a special day that you spent with family or friends. What made it special? Did something funny, surprising, or exciting happen? Write about your experience.

Here are some strategies to help you do a good job responding to a prompt like this.

Remember that a personal narrative is a true story about something that happened to the writer.

1 Look for clue words that tell what to write about. What are the clue words in the prompt above?

2 Choose a topic that fits the clue words. Write the clue words and your topic.

Clue Words	My Topic
a special day you spent with family or friends	I will write about the time my sister and I made pizza.

3 Plan your writing. Use a chart like this one.

Event 1	details
Event 2	details
Event 3	details

4 You will get a good score if you remember the description of what kind of personal narrative rings the bell in the rubric on page 275.

Writing a Friendly Letter

A **friendly letter** is a letter you write to someone you know. You can write about something that you have done or seen. You can write to ask how a friend or a relative is doing. Read this friendly letter.

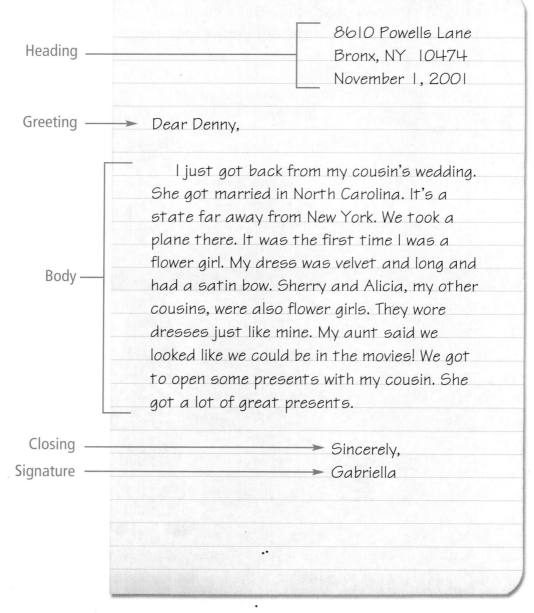

Heading

8610 Powells Lane
Bronx, NY 10474
November 1, 2001

Greeting

Dear Denny,

Body

I just got back from my cousin's wedding. She got married in North Carolina. It's a state far away from New York. We took a plane there. It was the first time I was a flower girl. My dress was velvet and long and had a satin bow. Sherry and Alicia, my other cousins, were also flower girls. They wore dresses just like mine. My aunt said we looked like we could be in the movies! We got to open some presents with my cousin. She got a lot of great presents.

Closing

Sincerely,

Signature

Gabriella

- The **heading** gives the writer's address and the date.
  What information is on each line?
- The **greeting** begins with *Dear* and gives the name of the person who gets the letter. Begin each word with a capital letter, and add a comma after the name. *Who will get Gabriella's letter?*
- The **body** is the main part of the letter.
  What did Gabriella write about?
- The **closing** ends the letter. Some closings are *Sincerely, Your cousin,* and *Love. What closing did Gabriella use?*
- The **signature** is the writer's name. *Where is the signature written?*

How to Write a Friendly Letter

1 **Choose** someone you want to write to.

2 **Make** a list of the things you want to say in your letter.

3 **Write** the letter. Be sure to include the five parts: the heading, the greeting, the body, the closing, and the signature.

4 **Proofread**. Use the Proofreading Checklist on page 278. Use a dictionary to check your spelling.

5 **Write** a neat final copy of your letter.

6 **Address** the envelope. Put a stamp on it. Mail your letter.

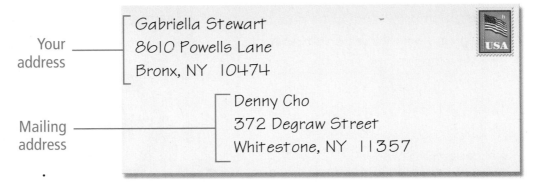

Your address

Gabriella Stewart
8610 Powells Lane
Bronx, NY 10474

Mailing address

Denny Cho
372 Degraw Street
Whitestone, NY 11357

Types of Friendly Letters

Invitation An invitation asks someone to come to an event, such as a party. The invitation tells the reason for the event. It also tells the date, time, and location. Read this invitation.

Dear Parents and Guardians,

You and your families are invited to the Palmdale Elementary School to see students' artwork.
The art show will be held Saturday, January 15, from 10 A.M. to 2:30 P.M. at the school.

We look forward to seeing you!

PALMDALE ELEMENTARY

Thank-you Letter A thank-you letter says thanks to someone. You can thank someone for a gift or for doing something special, such as helping you fix your bike.

Dear Marissa,

Thank you for fixing the chain on my bike. It kept falling off when I stopped. It doesn't do that anymore. I thought I had to get a new bike. Now I can ride it again without any trouble.

Your cousin,
Hector

Telling a Story About Yourself

When telling about something that happened to you, help your listeners picture what happened and feel how you felt. Follow these guides.

Guides for Telling a Story About Yourself

1. Begin in an interesting way. Tell the events in order and how the experience worked out.
2. Choose exact words that clearly describe the people, the action, and the setting.
3. Use your voice to show how each person talked or felt. Speak clearly.
4. Let your face show how you felt. Use your hands or body to show movements.
5. If you have pictures, show them as you talk.
6. Look at your audience. Speak loudly in a big room or more softly in a small space.

Apply It

Tell about something that happened to you or to a group of classmates. Follow the guides above.

Unit 8

Writing a Story

A loud boom in the distance made the two cubs stand still.

In this story, an old man and woman are having a problem with a billy goat. Read the story to find out what the problem is and how it turns out.

The Billy Goat and the Vegetable Garden

from *Señor Cat's Romance and Other Favorite Stories from Latin America,* retold by Lucía M. González

Once there was a very old woman and a very old man who lived on a farm. They shared a vegetable garden in which they grew tomatoes, lettuce, peppers, potatoes, beans, and plantains. They spent hours working in their garden and planning all the delicious dishes they were going to make with their vegetables.

One morning, a billy goat came into their garden and began eating up all the vegetables.

"Look!" cried the little old woman. "That billy goat is going to eat up everything in our garden. What shall we do?"

"Don't worry," said the little old man. "I can make him go away if I speak to him very, very nicely."

So he went down to the field where the billy goat was eating, and he patted it on its back. "*Buenos días,* Señor Billy Goat," he said. "Good morning. Please do not eat up our

Go to www.eduplace.com/kids/ for information about Lucía M. González.

more ▶

A Published Model   **287**

garden. You are so young and strong, and we are so old and weak. Surely you can find food somewhere else. Please go away."

But before the old man finished talking, the rude Señor Billy Goat's legs swung up in the air and his head bent low. Then he turned and charged at the old man with his horns!

"¡Ay, Mujer! ¡Mujer!" the old man cried out to his wife, running up the hill as fast as he could. "Open the door, please! The billy goat is after me!"

The little old man ran inside the house, shut the door, and began to cry.

"Do not cry," said his wife. "Perhaps a little tact and style is what he needs. I will go to him and make him go away." So she went down the hill to the field to have a talk with the billy goat herself.

Quietly, she tiptoed to where the billy goat was eating. Bowing low, she whispered, "Buenos días, Señor Billy Goat. A gracious good morning to you, kind sir, and I am sorry to disturb your breakfast.

This fine food you are eating must have taken some poor farmer a long, long time and much hard work to till the soil, and to plant the seeds, and to pull the weeds. But now, I have come to ask you—"

That was as far as she got, for the billy goat tired of her chatter and turned upon her. His legs swung up in the air, and his head was bent low, and he charged at her with his horns.

The old woman ran. Up the hill she went, crying, "*Ay*, Husband! Open the door, please! The billy goat is after me!" And she, too, tumbled inside the little house.

As soon as she was safely inside, they both began to cry. For they had been as polite and as tactful as anyone could ever be. But that mean-spirited billy goat still got the best of them. Then suddenly, something tickled the little old man's ear. He shook his head to get rid of it, and, as he did, down dropped a little red ant.

"I have come to help you," said the little ant. "I can make Señor Billy Goat go away from your garden."

"*You?*" cried the little old woman. "You are so small, what can you do? How can *you* help *us?*"

"Just watch me," said the ant. "You are being too nice to that bully. I can speak to him in the only language he understands."

And with that, the little ant crawled out of the house, through the field, and over to the billy goat. The goat didn't even see the little ant as he crawled up his hind leg, across his back, straight up to his ear—and stung him!

"¡*Ay!*" cried the billy goat.

more ▶

The little ant now crawled to the other ear and stung him. "¡Ay!" cried the billy goat again.

Then the little ant crawled up his back and down again—stinging him all over as he crawled along!

"¡Ay, ay, ay, ay, ay!" the billy goat cried. "I have stepped in an anthill! If I don't get out of this garden at once, these ants will eat me alive!"

Quickly, he jumped up into the air and ran out of the garden as fast as he could.

The little old man and the little old woman gave many thanks to that brave and clever little red ant for saving their vegetable garden, and they always made sure he had plenty to eat. They spent many hours that fall harvesting their beautiful ripe vegetables and talking about the delicious dishes they were going to prepare.

And what about the billy goat? Well, for all anyone knows, he hasn't gone near that vegetable garden to this very day!

Reading As a Writer

Think About the Story

- In the beginning of the story, what do you learn about the characters and setting? What problem do you learn about?
- How do the old man, the old woman, and the ant each try to solve the problem?
- At the end of the story, how does the problem work out?

Think About Writer's Craft

- Reread the fifth full paragraph on page 289. Why do you think the author put the words *you* and *us* in slanted type?

Think About the Pictures

- Compare the pictures on pages 288 and 290. Why do you think the goat is so large on page 288? Why is the ant so large on page 290?

Responding

Write responses to these questions.

- **Personal Response** If the old man and woman had come to you with their problem, what would you have told them to do?
- **Critical Thinking** Explain whether you think the ant was fair or unfair to the billy goat.

What Makes a Great Story?

A story is made up by an author. It tells how the characters try to solve a problem, and how it all turns out.

Remember to follow these guidelines when you write a story.

▶ Include a plot that has a beginning, a middle, and an end.

▶ Write an interesting beginning. Introduce the characters, the setting, and the problem.

▶ Show how the characters try to solve their problem in the middle.

▶ Show how the problem works out in the end.

▶ Tell only the important events, and tell them in an order that makes sense.

▶ Use details and dialogue to make the plot, characters, and setting interesting.

GRAMMAR CHECK

Use the right verb form to show past, present, and future time.

WORKING DRAFT

Emily Smith loves animals, especially dogs. She decided to write an exciting story about a dog who became a hero. She began with this draft of her story.

Emily Smith

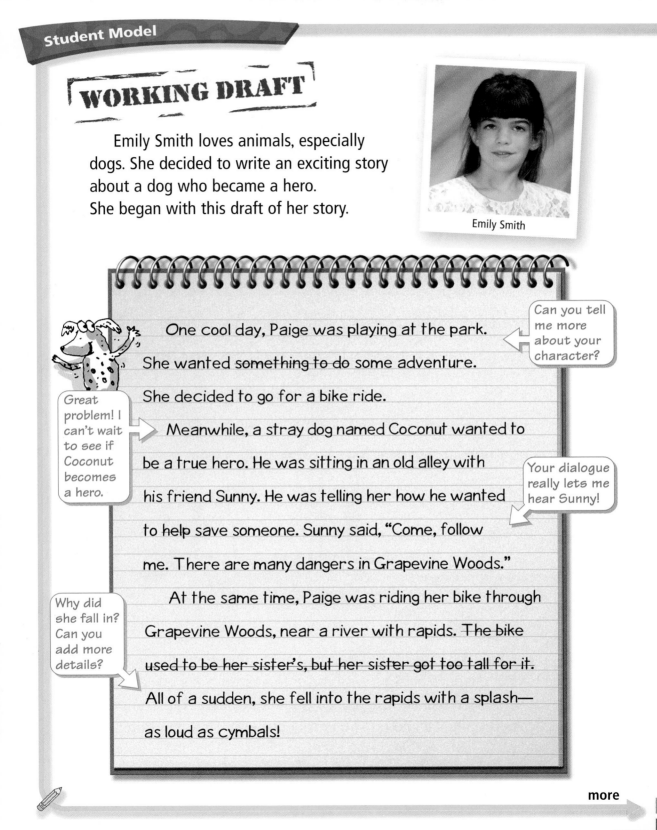

One cool day, Paige was playing at the park.

She wanted ~~something to do~~ some adventure.

She decided to go for a bike ride.

Meanwhile, a stray dog named Coconut wanted to be a true hero. He was sitting in an old alley with his friend Sunny. He was telling her how he wanted to ~~help~~ save someone. Sunny said, "Come, follow me. There are many dangers in Grapevine Woods."

At the same time, Paige was riding her bike through Grapevine Woods, near a river with rapids. ~~The bike used to be her sister's, but her sister got too tall for it.~~ All of a sudden, she fell into the rapids with a splash— as loud as cymbals!

Can you tell me more about your character?

Great problem! I can't wait to see if Coconut becomes a hero.

Your dialogue really lets me hear Sunny!

Why did she fall in? Can you add more details?

more

Sunny saw Paige's face peeking out of the water. She said, "Hey! Coconut! Here's your chance!" One time, Sunny saved a family by barking when she smelled smoke.

Coconut ran quickly to the water and dove in. He reached Paige, carried her on his back, and gently placed her on the grass. He could barely swim in the swishing water, but he could see Paige's tiny nose. He paddled as hard as he could to get to Paige.

When she woke up, she didn't know where she was. Coconut told her that she was safe.

Is this part in the right order?

Reading As a Writer

- What did Sal like about Emily's story? What questions did Sal have? What changes could Emily make to answer Sal's questions?
- Why did Emily cross out a sentence in the third paragraph on page 293? Which sentence should she cross out in the first paragraph on page 294?
- What questions would you like to ask Emily about her story?

FINAL COPY

Emily revised her story after discussing it with her classmates. Read her final paper to see the changes she made to improve her story.

The Hero
by Emily Smith

> I can picture Paige much better.

One cool day, Paige was playing at the park. She was six years old. She had brown eyes, and she had pretty golden hair. She was lonely, swinging there on the old tire swing, and she wanted some adventure. She decided to go for a bike ride.

Meanwhile, a stray German shepherd dog named Coconut wanted to be a true hero. He was sitting in an old alley with his friend Sunny, a golden retriever. He was telling her how he wanted to save someone. Sunny said, "Come, follow me. There are many dangers in Grapevine Woods."

> Nice details! Now I know more about the middle of your story.

At the same time, Paige was riding her bike through Grapevine Woods, near a river with fierce rapids. She saw a crow. She looked up, paying no attention to what was ahead of her. All of a sudden, she fell into the rapids with a splash— as loud as cymbals! She was knocked out!

Sunny saw Paige's face peeking out of the water. She said, "Hey! Coconut! Here's your chance!"

> You took out the part about Sunny saving a family because it didn't keep to the topic. Good!

more

Now the order makes sense.

Coconut ran quickly to the water and dove in. He could barely swim in the swishing water, but he could see Paige's tiny nose. He paddled as hard as he could to get to Paige. He reached Paige, carried her on his back, and gently placed her on the grass.

When she woke up, she said, "Where am I?"

"You're safe!" said Coconut.

Paige kneeled down, hugged Coconut, and said, "You are a hero!" Coconut smiled.

Just then some police cars and ambulances came. So did Paige's mom and dad. They looked as worried as beagles until they saw Paige safe and sound. Paige looked up, saw her mom and dad, and said, "This dog saved my life!"

From then on, Coconut was a member of the family. Every once in a while, Sunny came to visit. Everyone always remembered Coconut, the hero!

Reading As a Writer

- What changes did Emily make after thinking about Sal's questions?
- What details did Emily add to the ending of her story? Why?

  See www.eduplace.com/kids/hme/ for more examples of student writing.

Write a Story

▶ Start Thinking

📁 Make a writing folder for your story. Copy the questions in bold print, and put the paper in your folder. Write your answers as you think about and choose your topic.

- **Who will be my audience?** Will it be a younger class? my grandparents? the readers of a children's magazine?
- **What will be my purpose?** Do I want to write a funny story? an adventure story? a fairy tale?
- **How will I publish or share my story?** Will I publish it on my school's Internet site? make a book? read it to my class? act it out?

▶ Choose Your Story Idea

❶ **List** three ideas you could write about. Emily made character cards and setting cards. She picked a card from each group and thought of a story idea to go with them.

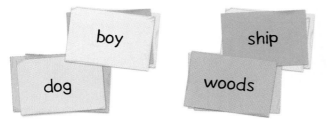

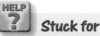

HELP ? **Stuck for an Idea?**

Use a story starter.
- Once upon a time there was a man who lived in the sea . . .
- Katie felt a wet nose on her face . . .
- Manuel ate a plum. Suddenly, he . . .

See page 308 for more ideas.

❷ **Discuss** your story ideas with a partner. Which idea does your partner like? Why? Which idea has a good beginning, middle, and end?

❸ **Ask** yourself these questions about each idea. Then circle the story idea that you will write about.

- Can I think of enough details for my story?
- Will I enjoy writing about this idea?

Focus Skill

Characters and Setting

The characters are the people and animals in your story. They can be daring heroes, funny creatures, or people like you. Use details to help your audience get to know your characters. Here are some kinds of details to think about.

What does this character look like? How old is the character? Does he or she have fuzzy hair? a pink baseball cap?

How does this character act or feel? Is the character friendly? silly? brave? grouchy?

What does this character like to do? Does he or she like to invent things? go in-line skating? explore new places?

Emily drew some pictures of her characters and wrote down details about each one. Here is an example.

Coconut
strong, brave
stray dog
wants to be a hero
gentle, likes children

GRAMMAR TIP Always begin the name of a character with a capital letter.

Try It Out

- With a partner, choose a character from "The Billy Goat and the Vegetable Garden." Draw a picture of the character. Then ask yourselves the questions in bold print above. Write down some details about the character that answer each question.

The setting tells where and when your story takes place. Here are some questions to think about.

When is this story happening? Is the time now or long ago? Is it morning? night? summer? winter?

What do the characters see and hear? Are they inside or outside? Do they see a cornfield? a messy room? cave walls? Do they hear horns honking? waves lapping?

Emily drew a picture of her setting and wrote down some details about it.

> **GRAMMAR TIP** The names of special places begin with capital letters.

Grapevine Woods
cool day
path
river
rapids

Try It Out

- Suppose a story takes place just outside your classroom in terrible weather. With your classmates, list some details that would help the audience picture the setting. Use the questions above for ideas.

▶ Explore Your Story Idea

❶ **List** the characters and setting for your story idea.

❷ **Draw** pictures of your characters and setting. Write some details about the pictures.

> **HELP?** See page 14 for other ideas about exploring your topic.

Focus Skill

Planning the Plot

Each story is different, but all stories are alike in some ways. Every story has a beginning, a middle, and an end, which make up the plot. Emily made a story map to plan the three parts of her story.

The beginning introduces the main characters, the setting, and a problem the characters have.

The middle shows how the characters try to deal with the problem.

The end shows how the problem works out.

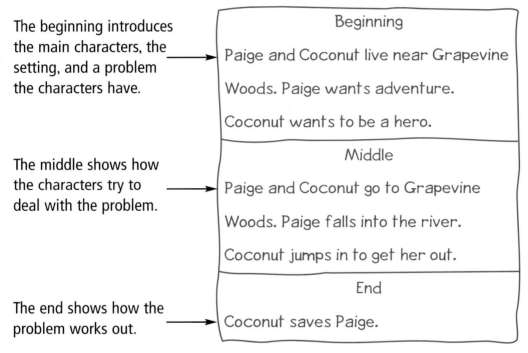

Beginning

Paige and Coconut live near Grapevine Woods. Paige wants adventure. Coconut wants to be a hero.

Middle

Paige and Coconut go to Grapevine Woods. Paige falls into the river. Coconut jumps in to get her out.

End

Coconut saves Paige.

Try It Out

● With your classmates, make a story map of "The Billy Goat and the Vegetable Garden" on page 287.

▶ Plan Your Story

Think about what will happen in the beginning, the middle, and the end of your story. Make a story map. Then use your story map to tell your story idea to a classmate.

HELP
? **Stuck in the Middle?**

If you don't have enough ideas for the middle of your story, try a new story idea.

 Go to www.eduplace.com/kids/hme/ for graphic organizers.

Developing the Plot

The Beginning

Catch your audience's interest. A good beginning makes your audience wonder what's going to happen. Here are some ideas for how to begin.

Describe a character.	Lily Pad had just finished changing from a tadpole to a frog. She was very proud of her new legs.
Describe the setting.	The large green pond in City Park was the perfect home for a frog.
Describe an action.	A tiny frog hopped from rock to rock across the pond. Then, with one big leap, she was out!

The Middle

Include only the important events that tell how the main characters solve the problem. Tell the events in an order that makes sense.

Use time clues to make the order of events clear. Some time clues are *after, that night, soon, the next day.*

more ▶

Focus Skill continued

Use dialogue to show the exact words your characters say.
What are your characters like? Let your readers hear their voices.
Compare the weak example below to the strong example from "The Billy
Goat and the Vegetable Garden." Start a new paragraph each time a new
character starts speaking.

Weak: Without Dialogue	Strong: With Dialogue
The old man said that he would say nice things to the billy goat to make him go away.	"Don't worry," said the little old man. "I can make him go away if I speak to him very, very nicely."

The Ending

Show how the problem works out. Reread the last four paragraphs of
"The Billy Goat and the Vegetable Garden" on page 290. These
paragraphs tell how the problem in the story worked out.

Think and Discuss

- With some classmates, list a few important events for a story that has one of the beginnings on page 301.
- With the same group, brainstorm a different ending for "The Billy Goat and the Vegetable Garden."

▶ Draft Your Story

❶ **Write** your story. Use your story map to
help you. Include any new ideas that
come to you.

❷ **Skip** every other line so that you can
make changes later. Don't stop to correct
any mistakes. Just keep writing.

HELP
? **Can't Get Started?**

If you can't decide
how to begin, try
writing the middle
or ending of your
story first.

Evaluating Your Story

▶ **Reread** your story. What do you need to do to make it better? Use this rubric to help you decide. Write the sentences that describe your story.

Rings the Bell!

- ■ The beginning catches the interest of my audience. It introduces the characters, the setting, and the problem.
- ■ The middle shows how the characters try to solve the problem.
- ■ The ending tells how the problem works out.
- ■ All the events are important and in order.
- ■ Details and dialogue bring the story to life.
- ■ *There are almost no mistakes.*

Getting Stronger

- ☐ The beginning could be more interesting.
- ☐ I don't tell how the characters try to solve the problem.
- ☐ The ending doesn't make the story feel finished.
- ☐ Some events are not important to the story.
- ☐ My story needs more details and dialogue.
- ■ *There are a few mistakes.*

Try Harder

- ☐ The beginning is boring.
- ☐ There is no clear problem.
- ☐ The story just stops. How does the problem work out?
- ☐ Many events are unimportant, or the order is unclear.
- ☐ I haven't included details or dialogue.
- ■ *There are a lot of mistakes.*

▶ Revise Your Story

1 **Revise** your story. Use the list of sentences you wrote from the rubric. Work on the parts that you described with sentences from "Getting Stronger" and "Try Harder."

HELP
? **Revising Tip**

Put your story away for a while before you begin to revise it.

2 **Have a writing conference.**

When You're the Writer Read your story to a partner. Discuss any parts you're having trouble with. Take notes to remember what your partner says.

When You're the Listener Tell at least two things you like about the story. Ask questions about anything that is unclear.

What should I say?

The Writing Conference	
If you're thinking . . .	**You could say . . .**
The beginning is not very interesting.	**Could you begin by describing a character, the setting, or an action?**
What does this part have to do with the story?	**Is this part really important? Can you take it out?**
This part doesn't make sense.	**Can you add details or time clues to help your audience understand this part?**
I can't picture this character.	**How does this character look and act? What does the character say?**
The ending might leave the audience wondering what happens.	**How does the problem work out?**

3 **Make more revisions** to your story. Use your conference notes and the Revising Strategies on the next page.

Revising Strategies

Elaborating: Word Choice Exact words will help your audience picture your characters, setting, and actions clearly.

Without Exact Words	With Exact Words
The **bird** had **pretty** feathers.	The parrot had red, blue, and green feathers.

▶ Change at least three words in your story to be more exact.

📖 Use the Thesaurus Plus on page H60.

Elaborating: Details Add more information by using groups of words that begin with little words such as *on, at, in,* and *with*.

Without Details	Elaborated with Details
A boy arrived. The knights waited.	A boy arrived at the castle gate. The knights waited in the forest.

▶ Use groups of words to add details in at least two sentences in your story.

Sentence Fluency A stringy sentence has too many *and*'s. Break a stringy sentence up into shorter sentences.

Stringy Sentence	Smoother Sentences
Laura climbed the stone wall **and** peeked over **and** crept back down.	Laura climbed the stone wall and peeked over. Then she crept back down.

▶ Fix any stringy sentences in your story.

▶ Proofread Your Story

Proofread your story, using the Proofreading Checklist and the Grammar and Spelling Connections. Proofread for one skill at a time. Use a class dictionary to check spellings.

Proofreading Checklist

Did I
- ✔ indent all paragraphs?
- ✔ correct any run-on sentences?
- ✔ use verbs correctly?
- ✔ write dialogue correctly?
- ✔ correct any spelling errors?

📖 Use the Guide to Capitalization, Punctuation, and Usage on page H51.

Proofreading Marks
- ¶   Indent
- ∧   Add
- ✔   Delete
- ≡   Capital letter
- /   Small letter

Tech Tip
The spelling tool on your computer will not find a word that is misspelled if the letters spell another word.

Grammar and Spelling Connections

Verbs Be sure to use the right verb form to to show present, past, or future time.

Present	This summer Eliza **is** at camp.
Past	Last summer Eliza **was** at camp.
Future	Next summer Eliza **will be** at camp.

GRAMMAR LINK ▶ *See also page 108.*

Quotation Marks Put quotation marks around a speaker's exact words.
    "Look! Isn't this the missing key?" said Ahmed.

GRAMMAR LINK ▶ *See also page 194.*

Spelling the Vowel Sound in *brown* and *sound* The vowel sound in *brown* and *sound* may be spelled *ow* or *ou*.
    crown, down   mound, found   📖 See the Spelling Guide on page H56.

▶ Publish Your Story

❶ Make a neat final copy of your story. Be sure you formed all the letters in your words correctly and used good spacing. Check that you fixed all mistakes.

❷ Write a title for your story that makes your audience curious. For example, "The Hero" is a better title than "A Good Dog."

❸ Publish or share your story in a way that works for your audience.

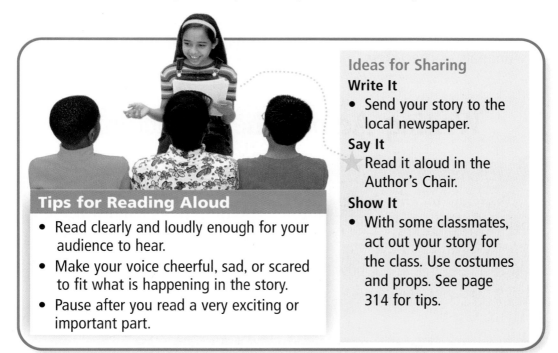

Ideas for Sharing
Write It
- Send your story to the local newspaper.

Say It
- Read it aloud in the Author's Chair.

Show It
- With some classmates, act out your story for the class. Use costumes and props. See page 314 for tips.

Tips for Reading Aloud
- Read clearly and loudly enough for your audience to hear.
- Make your voice cheerful, sad, or scared to fit what is happening in the story.
- Pause after you read a very exciting or important part.

▶ Reflect

Write about your writing experience. Use these questions to get started.

- What was easy to do? What was hard to do?
- What might you do differently the next time you write a story?
- Do you think this story is better than other papers you have written? Why or why not?

Writing Prompts

Use these prompts as ideas for a story or to practice for a test. Some of the prompts are about school subjects. Decide who your audience will be. Write your story in a way your audience will understand and enjoy.

1 Think about animals you know and the way they act. Write a funny story or an adventure story. Use these animals as characters.

2 Write a story about an eight-year-old detective who is hired to find something that's missing. What is it? How does the detective solve the case?

Writing Across the Curriculum

3 LITERATURE

Once upon a time, a king held a contest to find the smartest person in the land. Write a fairy tale about how a boy or girl won the contest.

4 SOCIAL STUDIES

Write a story that teaches a lesson, such as why it's better to share than to be selfish, or why it's better to work hard than to be lazy.

5 SCIENCE

While working on a science project, a student makes an amazing discovery. Then something goes wrong. Write a story telling what happens and how it all turns out.

6 PHYSICAL EDUCATION

Think about your favorite sport. Is it soccer? skating? Write an exciting story that includes this sport. Your characters can be superstars or ordinary people.

See www.eduplace.com/kids/hme/ for more prompts.

✓ Test Practice

This prompt to write a story is like ones you might find on a writing test. Read the prompt.

> **Think about animals you know and the way they act. Write a funny story or an adventure story. Use these animals as characters.**

Here are some strategies to help you do a good job responding to a prompt like this.

Remember that a story tells about a problem the characters have and how it all turns out.

❶ Look for clue words that tell what to write about. What are the clue words in the prompt above?

❷ Choose a topic that fits the clue words. Write the clue words and your topic.

Clue Words	My Topic
funny story or an adventure story Use these animals as characters.	I will write about a kitten that gets stuck inside a box and is carried to the dump.

❸ Plan your writing. Use a story map.

Beginning
Middle
End

❹ You will get a good score if you remember the description of what kind of story rings the bell in the rubric on page 303.

Writing a Play

A **play** is a story in which characters act out what is happening. Read the play below.

The Strongest Bird

Characters —
EAGLE
LOON
SWAN
HAWK
DUCK

Props —
Paper bag masks for each bird
A big soup pot
Large paper trees
Some twine (for a rope)

Scene ——————→ **SCENE ONE**

Setting — *(The setting is the woods. Five bird friends are sitting around a big pot, making soup.)*   Stage directions

EAGLE: *(To the other birds)* You know what? I think I'm the smartest bird around here!   Dialogue

LOON: Well, I think I'm the funniest bird in the whole forest.

SWAN: So? I think I'm the strongest bird in the entire world!

HAWK: *(Talking to herself)* Listen to my friends. They are bragging. It makes me sad when they act this way. Duck is the only one who isn't bragging! What a modest bird. Hey, I know! I have an idea!

HAWK: *(Speaking to* DUCK *so that the others cannot hear)* If you hold onto the roots of those trees at the pond, Swan won't be able to budge you, right? *(They both smile. Then* HAWK *talks to the others.)* I think that Duck is the strongest bird in the world.

SWAN: No way, Hawk! Look how tiny Duck is. I could pick that bird up, easy.

HAWK: Let's have a contest. If Duck wins, everyone has to promise to stop bragging. If Swan wins, Swan can decide what we will have for dessert tomorrow.

OTHERS: Good idea! Let's go!

DUCK: I'm ready. Let's go to the pond.

(They all leave the stage.)

SCENE TWO

(The setting is the pond. Only the edge of the pond can be seen. The rest is offstage. All the birds are present. SWAN holds one end of the twine.)

DUCK: Okay, give me the end of the rope. I'll tie it to my leg and then I'll dive into the pond and swim to the bottom. You pull on the other end, Swan. If you can pull me up, you win. If you can't, I win. Okay? *(Ties twine to ankle)*

SWAN: Okay. That sounds easy. Don't bother to take a deep breath, Duck. I'll pull you up so fast you won't need one!

HAWK: *(Points to* DUCK, *diving offstage)* There goes Duck, into the pond. Wait a second, Swan, so Duck can get settled down there on the bottom.

SWAN: Okay. I'll think about dessert.

EAGLE: Ready, Swan? You can start pulling.

LOON: Wow, look at Swan pulling and pulling on that rope.

SWAN: *(Pulling hard)* Gee, this is harder than I expected. Duck is stronger than I thought.

HAWK: *(Listening by the pond)* Duck wants to know when you are going to start pulling, Swan.

SWAN: I'm trying. I'm trying!

EAGLE: The soup is almost ready. Do you give up yet?

SWAN: No! Okay, yes! I guess I have to. I just can't do it. Maybe I'm not the strongest bird in the world after all. *(Scratches his head)*

(DUCK comes back onstage to stand by SWAN.)

DUCK: Don't worry about it, Swan. You tried your hardest. That's what's really important.

HAWK: This contest made me hungry. Is anybody else hungry? The soup's ready! I bet it's the best soup in the world!

OTHERS: Hawk! Now *you're* bragging! But let's eat!

(All of the birds run over to the soup pot.)

CURTAIN

Reading As a Writer

- The list of **characters** tells who is in the play.
  How many characters are in this play?
- The **props** are the things that the characters will use in the play.
  What props are used in this play?
- A **scene** is the setting, or place, where the action happens. Some plays have only one scene. Some plays have more.
  How many scenes does this play have?
- The **stage directions** tell the actors what to do.
  What are some of the things that the actors in this play are supposed to do?
- The **dialogue** is the talk between the characters in a play.
  How could you tell which character was speaking?

How to Write a Play

① **Choose** a story to write as a play. Think of a story that is simple and short. Be sure you can tell the story, using the characters' dialogue and actions.

② **Think** about your characters. Make some notes about what they are like, what they feel, and what kinds of words they use.

③ **Organize** your ideas about the events that will take place and where they will happen. Use a story map like the one on page 300 to plan the events.

④ **Write** your play. List the characters and props. Describe the setting. Then write dialogue to tell your story. Remember to include stage directions.

⑤ **Revise** your play. Read it aloud with a classmate. Talk about the order of events. Discuss any changes you may want to make.

⑥ **Proofread** for mistakes. Make sure you have used exclamation points and question marks correctly. Use a dictionary to check spellings.

⑦ **Make** a neat final copy of your play.

⑧ **Perform** your play for an audience.

 **Stuck for an Idea?**

Here are some suggestions.

- Turn a favorite tale into a play.
- Write about something fun that happened to you.
- Write about an important event.

? See pages 314–315 for tips on dramatizing.

 Tech Tip
If you use a computer to write, you can copy and paste the characters' names each time you write dialogue for them.

Dramatizing

Actors dramatize, or act out, characters from stories, poems, or plays. They speak and move the way they think the characters would. They use their voices to show feelings and to keep their listeners interested in what happens to the characters.

Start Thinking

Read each sentence below and think about the way you would say it. What facial expression would you use?

"I can't wait until tomorrow. We're going to the circus!"

"Oh, no. Mike lost the race."

"Watch out! There's a rattlesnake next to your foot!"

How would you describe the expressions on the faces in the photos? Would you have looked the same way if you had said these things?

Use these guides to help you act out a story, a poem, a play, or an experience you have had.

Guides for Dramatizing

1. Put yourself in your character's shoes. What is the character like? How would the character talk and move?

2. Use your speaking voice. Change the volume, rate, and pitch of your voice to show how your character feels. A high, fast voice might show excitement.

Using Your Voice	
volume	means loudness
rate	means speed
pitch	means how high or how low it sounds

3. Change the way your face looks to show different feelings.

4. Use your hands. Use movement to show a character's feelings. For example, walking slowly with your head down can show sadness.

5. Speak clearly but naturally. Be sure everyone can hear you.

6. Practice reading your lines. If you need help remembering them, write the most important words on note cards to use as hints or reminders.

Apply It

Choose part of a play or story to dramatize. You can also choose a poem or experience you have had. Follow the Guides for Dramatizing as you practice. Perform for your classmates or another audience, using simple props and costumes.

- Did you remember to speak clearly?
- Did the audience seem interested in your performance?
- What would you change to improve your performance?

Comparing Stories in Books and Movies

A good story in a book can sometimes make a good story for a movie. When a book is made into a movie, the story might change. That is because the way movies tell stories is different from the way books tell stories. The chart below shows how.

Reading the Story	Watching the Story
Books use words to tell a story. Readers make pictures in their minds. They use the words and their imaginations to think about what the characters and the setting are like.	Movies use pictures and sounds to tell a story. Movies show the audience what the characters and the setting are like.
The writer of a book uses words to tell the thoughts and feelings of the characters.	The actors in a movie show the thoughts and feelings of the characters. They do this by the way they look and by what they do and say.
People reading a book can read it as fast or as slowly as they like.	People watching a movie in a theater cannot make the movie go faster or slower. They must wait to see what happens.

Books can be long or short. Movies are usually about two hours long. To tell a story in that time, some characters may say a lot less. Other characters may be dropped altogether! Think of the ways that a story you like was changed when it became a movie.

Guides for Comparing Stories in Books and Movies

❶ Plot
- What happened in the book that did not happen in the movie? What happened in the movie that did not happen in the book?
- Did the movie end the same way as the book?

❷ Characters
- Were there characters in the book who were not in the movie?
- Were there any characters in the movie who were not in the book?

❸ Setting
- Was the book's setting the same as the movie's?
- If the setting was different, did it change the story in any way?

Apply It

Choose a book that you have read that has been made into a movie. Write a paragraph or more to describe how the book and movie are different. Use the guides above and these questions to help you.

- Did the movie characters look and act the way you imagined from reading the book?
- What were the biggest differences between the book and the movie?
- Which did you like better, the book's story or the movie's?

Books with Movie Versions
- *Balto*
- *Heidi*
- *Winnie the Pooh*
- *The Incredible Journey*
- *The Phantom Tollbooth*

Explaining and Informing

What You Will Find in This Section:

Listening for Information

When you listen to a news report or to someone giving directions, you are listening to facts. A **fact** is a piece of information that can be proved true. Your purpose for listening is to gain information. These guidelines will help you listen well.

Guidelines for Listening for Information

▶ Listen for the topic. What is the author talking about?
▶ Listen for the main idea. What does the author want to say about the topic?
▶ Listen for facts. What do they tell about the main idea?

Try It Out Listen as your teacher reads aloud this detailed description of bats from *Bats: Night Fliers,* by Betsy Maestro. Listen for facts. They will help you answer the questions below.

- What is the topic?
- What is the main idea?
- What are some facts the author uses to tell about the main idea?

 See www.eduplace.com/kids/ for information about Betsy Maestro.

Writing Informational Paragraphs

A paragraph that gives facts is an **informational paragraph**. An informational paragraph has a topic and a main idea. The **topic** is the subject of the paragraph. The **main idea** is what the writer wants to say about the topic. What is the topic of the informational paragraph below? What is the main idea?

Remember to indent the first sentence of a paragraph.

Indent —————

Topic sentence

Supporting sentences

Closing sentence

> Kittens learn in two different ways. They watch what their mother does. They see her use the scratch post, and they try it also. When their mother is friendly to children and adults, they learn that people are safe. Kittens also learn from each other. They wrestle each other and bite, but not too much. If the play gets too rough, one will cry as if to say, "No fair!" Kittens are both good students and good teachers.

Topic Sentence

The topic is kittens. The main idea is that kittens learn in two different ways. Which sentence introduces the topic and the main idea?

Supporting Sentences

The labels show the parts of an informational paragraph.

Closing Sentence

- The **topic sentence** tells the subject and the main idea.
- **Supporting sentences** give facts that tell about the main idea.
- The **closing sentence** finishes the paragraph.

Think and Discuss In the paragraph about kittens above, what facts are in the supporting sentences?

The Topic Sentence

You have learned that the **topic sentence** of an informational paragraph names the topic and the main idea. A good topic sentence catches the reader's interest too.

Topic   Main idea

Example: Kittens learn in two different ways.

What is the topic of each of these topic sentences? What is the main idea?

- Scientists are finding new kinds of dinosaur bones in Africa.
- Your tongue has different areas for tasting different flavors.

Try It Out Read the paragraphs below. They are missing the topic sentence. On your own or with a partner, write the topic and the main idea of each paragraph. Then write a topic sentence for each.

1. _____Topic sentence_____. Long ago, the Aztecs made a drink with chocolate, warm water, and hot chili peppers. In the 1500s, the Spanish borrowed chocolate from the Aztecs and replaced the spicy peppers with sugar. More than 300 years later, the Swiss learned about chocolate. They added powdered milk to make milk chocolate. Today there are all types of chocolate for the world to enjoy.

2. _____Topic sentence_____. There is soil under trees and under your feet. There is soil at the bottom of lakes and rivers. There is soil beneath lawns, roads, and sidewalks. Bare rocks and the tops of some rocky mountains are the only places on land that have no soil.

Supporting Sentences

Supporting sentences usually follow the topic sentence. They give details that tell about the main idea. Some details are **facts**, information that can be proved true. Read the paragraph below.

When water "cooks" inside the earth, the result may be a geyser. Water drains into cracks in the earth's surface. If the water hits heated rock, it becomes hotter and hotter. Soon the water turns into steam. The steam pushes back up the crack. It carries water and mud with it. The steam, water, and mud shoot out of the ground right into the air. A geyser's powerful blast is like a small volcano.

Think and Discuss What facts do the supporting sentences give?

Ordering Details Supporting sentences can be arranged in time order, the order in which things happened. They can also be arranged in another order that makes sense. **Order words**, such as *first, then,* and *later,* help the reader follow the main idea. What order words can you find in the paragraph below?

In a factory, a gooey liquid called latex is turned into balloons. First, color is added to the latex. Then balloon-shaped molds are dipped into the latex, and the balloons are allowed to dry. Next, stiff brushes push down the opening of each balloon to make the rolled lip. Finally, the balloons are ready to help you celebrate!

See page 16 for tips on ordering facts. See page 18 for more order words.

more ▶

Try It Out Read the topic sentence below, and look at the picture. On your own or with a partner, use the details shown to write some supporting sentences for the topic sentence. Put the details in an order that makes sense.

Topic Sentence: A table of contents is a map for finding information in a book.

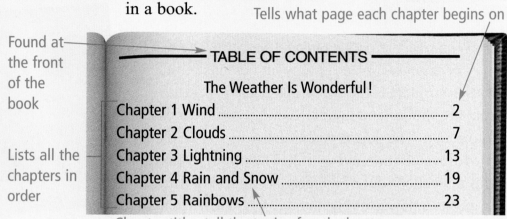

Tells what page each chapter begins on

Found at the front of the book

TABLE OF CONTENTS

The Weather Is Wonderful!

Chapter 1 Wind 2
Chapter 2 Clouds 7

Lists all the chapters in order

Chapter 3 Lightning 13
Chapter 4 Rain and Snow 19
Chapter 5 Rainbows 23

Chapter titles tell the topic of each chapter.

GRAMMAR TIP A complete sentence has a subject and a predicate and tells a complete thought.

The Closing Sentence

The **closing sentence** makes the paragraph feel finished. It can make a final comment or repeat the main idea in a new way. In the paragraph about geysers on page 323, the closing sentence makes a final comment.

Try It Out Read the paragraph below. It is missing the closing sentence. On your own or with a partner, write two different closing sentences.

Fire is both dangerous and helpful. Fire can burn forests. It can also burn houses, stores, and cars. On the other hand, fire can heat homes and cook food for people. In addition, fire can create light to help people see. _____Closing sentence_____.

Write Your Own Informational Paragraph

Now it's your turn to write an informational paragraph. Think of something you know about. You might write about your favorite animal or about something you like to do. Make a list of details. Put them in an order that makes sense. Then share your ideas with a partner. After that, write your paragraph!

Checklist for My Paragraph

✔ My **topic sentence** tells the topic and the main idea of my paragraph.

✔ My **supporting sentences** all tell about the main idea. They are in an order that makes sense.

✔ My **closing sentence** repeats the main idea in a new way or makes a final comment.

Looking Ahead

Now that you can write an informational paragraph, writing a longer informational essay will be easy. The chart below shows how an informational paragraph has the same parts as a longer essay.

Informational Paragraph   **Informational Essay**

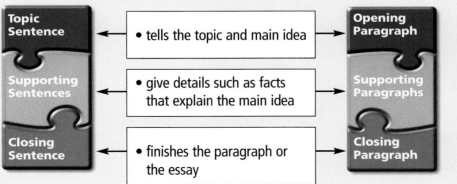

Informational Paragraph		Informational Essay
Topic Sentence	• tells the topic and main idea	Opening Paragraph
Supporting Sentences	• give details such as facts that explain the main idea	Supporting Paragraphs
Closing Sentence	• finishes the paragraph or the essay	Closing Paragraph

Unit 9

Writing Instructions

Don't just dream about castles. Build one! Here's how. . .

Here are some instructions that explain how to make a bird feeder. What steps do the writers say to follow?

Build a Bird Feeder

from *Science Wizardry for Kids,* by Margaret Kenda and Phyllis S. Williams

This bird feeder is easy to make, and it will last all year round.

Here's what you need:

- a one-gallon plastic bottle with a screw cap
- scissors
- a piece of rope or twine

Here's what you do:

1. Wash out the bottle. Rinse until the bottle is clean.

2. With the scissors, cut an opening in the side of the bottle opposite the handle. Start the cut about $1\frac{1}{4}$ inches from the bottom of the bottle. The opening ought to measure about 5 inches by 4 inches. Caution: You need an adult to help you with the cutting.

3. Tie a piece of rope or heavy twine around the neck of the bottle just below the bottle cap.

4. Hang the bottle from a limb of a tree, and KEEP IT FULL OF SEEDS.

THE BIRDS WILL LOVE THEIR BOTTLE FEEDER.

more ▶

Reading As a Writer

Think About the Instructions

- What are the steps in making the bird feeder?
- Look at step 3. Which details tell where to tie the rope or twine?
- What information do the writers include after the last step? Why is this better than just stopping with the last step?

Think About Writer's Craft

- Look at the headings, which are in bold print, and the step numbers. Why are they helpful?

Think About the Pictures

- How do the photos help you better understand how to make a bird feeder?

Responding

Write responses to these questions.

- **Personal Response** Explain why a bird feeder is or is not something you would want to make.
- **Critical Thinking** Which parts of these instructions would be easy to follow? Which parts would be hard?

What Makes Great Instructions?

Instructions explain how to do something.

Remember to follow these guidelines when you write instructions.

▶ Begin with an interesting topic sentence that states the main idea.

▶ List all the materials that will be needed.

▶ Include all the steps. Leave out anything that doesn't belong.

▶ Put the steps in the correct order. Use order words.

▶ Include details that make each step clear.

▶ End with a closing sentence that wraps up the instructions.

GRAMMAR CHECK

Use a comma after each item in a series.

WORKING DRAFT

Each winter, Selena Wilke loves to make snowmen. She wanted to teach her friends how to do it. Selena decided to write down the instructions so her friends could learn. She wrote this draft of her instructions.

Selena Wilke

How to Make a Snowman

Here's how to make a snowman. Get a hat, a scarf, mittens, a carrot, ~~some~~ six pieces of charcoal, and two almost even sticks. Put the items on the ground outside. If you want to make a snow fort, bring a shovel. Now you're ready to begin.

First, make three balls of snow. ~~Have really deep snow.~~ Roll small snowballs on the ground to make them bigger. Next, stack them on top of each other. Stack the medium ball on the big one. Make one very big ball, one medium ball, and one small ball. Stack the small ball on the medium one to make a head.

> You've listed all of the materials. Good!

> Is this step in the right order?

Add the arms and face. ~~Put~~ Push the sticks into the medium ball. ~~Sometimes my sister helps me with this.~~ Take two pieces of charcoal, and put them in the head for the eyes. Take the extra four pieces of charcoal for the mouth.

Dress the snowman. Now you're done.

What do I do with the carrot?

I'm not sure how to dress the snowman. Could you add some details?

Reading As a Writer

- What did Sal like about Selena's instructions? What were Sal's questions? What changes could Selena make to answer them?
- Look at the first paragraph on page 330. Which step does not belong?
- What questions would you like to ask Selena about her instructions?

Selena revised her instructions after discussing them with a classmate. Read her final paper to see what changes she made.

Make a Frosty Friend
by Selena Wilke

If you're bored on a cold, snowy day, making a snowman is a fun and easy thing to do. Get a hat, a scarf, mittens, a carrot, six pieces of charcoal, and two almost even sticks. Put the items on the ground outside. Now you're ready to begin.

First, make three balls of snow. Roll small snowballs on the ground to make them bigger. Make one very big ball, one medium ball, and one small ball. Next, stack them on top of each other. Stack the medium ball on the big one. Then stack the small ball on the medium one to make a head.

Now add the arms and face. Push the sticks into the sides of the medium ball to make the arms. Then take two pieces of charcoal, and put them in the head for the eyes. Take the extra four pieces of charcoal, and put them in a curved

> The steps are in the right order now.

> You've added more order words. Great!

line for the mouth. Get the carrot, and stick it in the middle of the head for the nose.

Now I know what to do with the carrot!

Finally, dress the snowman. Wrap the scarf around the bottom of the head. Put the hat on top of the head. Put the mittens on the sticks. Now you've got a supreme snowman!

The instructions feel finished. Good!

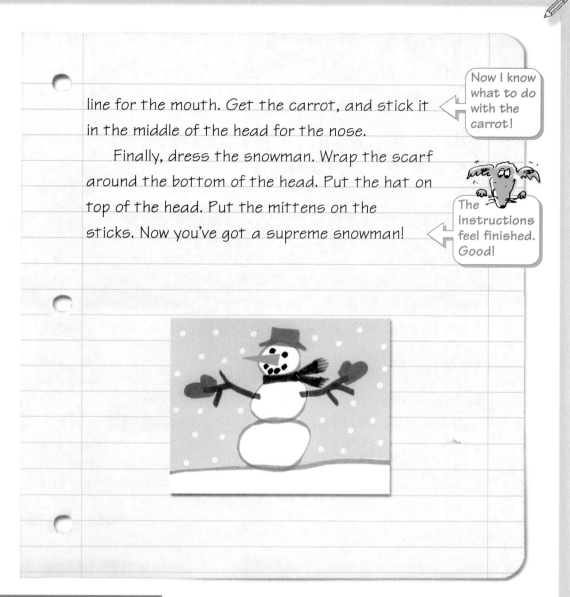

Reading As a Writer

- What changes did Selena make to answer Sal's questions? What else did she do that Sal liked?
- What changes did Selena make to the beginning of her final copy? Why is it better?
- What new details did Selena add about making the arms and face? Why did she add them?

Write Instructions

▶ Start Thinking

Make a writing folder for your instructions. Copy the questions in bold print, and put the paper in your folder. Write your answers as you think about and choose your topic.

- **Who will be my audience?** Will it be a friend? my family? a younger child?
- **What will be my purpose?** Do I want to teach how to do something that's useful? that's just for fun?
- **How will I publish or share my instructions?** Will I write an instruction booklet? put on a "How-To" TV show? make a poster?

▶ Choose Your Topic

① **List** three things you might like to teach. Selena got some ideas by thinking about what she does in different places.

> the park—play tag, build a snowman
>
> my room—make my bed, feed my hamster
>
> the kitchen—set the table, wash the dishes

HELP
? **Stuck for a Topic?**

Use these questions.
- What can you make?
- What do you do just for fun?
- What can you teach a five-year-old?

See page 344 for more ideas.

② **Discuss** your topics with a partner. Do you know all the steps? Would this be interesting or useful to your audience?

③ **Ask** yourself these questions about each topic. Then circle the topic you will write about.

- Would I enjoy explaining how to do this?
- Can I explain it in a few paragraphs?

▶ Explore Your Topic

1 **Think** about your topic. Picture the steps in your mind.

2 **Draw** pictures of the steps. Write a few words about the pictures.

Dress snowman.

Stack snowballs.

Add arms and face.

Make balls of snow.

3 **Use your pictures** to explain each step to a partner. Does your partner have any questions?

HELP ? See page 14 for other ideas for exploring your topic.

Focus Skill

Organizing Your Instructions

Good instructions are like signs on a highway. Don't let your readers get lost!

Put the steps in the right order. If you don't, your audience might get mixed up, or your instructions might not work out.

Use order words. Order words tell when the steps should be done. *First, second, next, now, then,* and *finally* are order words.

Selena numbered her pictures. Then she made a Steps Chart. Here is part of Selena's chart.

You need: snow, charcoal, carrot, two sticks, hat, scarf, mittens	
Steps	Details
1. First, make balls of snow.	
2. Next, stack them.	

Think and Discuss Look back at Selena's pictures on page 335.

- What other steps should she add to her chart? in what order?
- What order words could she use?

▶ Plan Your Instructions

❶ Number your pictures in the order the steps should be done.

❷ Use your pictures to help you make a Steps Chart. List what you need. List all your steps with order words.

 Go to www.eduplace.com/kids/hme/ for graphic organizers.

Focus Skill

Using Details

Give exact details for each step so that your audience won't make a mistake. Be sure to include all the important details.

Without Exact Details	With Exact Details
Make the snowman's eyes.	Take two pieces of charcoal, and put them in the head for the eyes.

Think and Discuss Compare the two examples above.

- What exact details did Selena include about the snowman's eyes?
- What mistake might someone make without those details?

▶ Draft Your Instructions

❶ **Add** details to your Steps Chart. Here is part of Selena's chart.

You need: snow, charcoal, carrot, two sticks, hat, scarf, mittens	
Steps	Details
1. First, make balls of snow.	roll balls one small, one medium, one large

❷ **Use** your chart to help you write your instructions. It's never too late to add more details if you need them.

HELP
?
Paragraph Tip

If a step has a lot of details, make it a separate paragraph.

❸ **Skip** every other line so that you can make changes later. Don't stop to correct any mistakes.

❹ **Read** your instructions to a partner. Have your partner act out the steps.

Focus Skill

Good Beginnings and Endings

Begin your instructions with a topic sentence that states your main idea. Write something interesting to make your audience want to try out your instructions.

Weak Beginning	Strong Beginning
Here's how to dive right.	If your dives end up as belly flops, try this.

End with a closing sentence that wraps up your instructions. Write something that makes the instructions sound fun or useful.

Don't just stop with the last step.

Weak Ending	Strong Ending
Now you know the right way to dive.	You'll feel great when your next dive is a success, not a flop!

Think and Discuss

- What makes the strong beginning better than the weak one?
- What makes the strong ending better than the weak one?

▶ Draft Your Beginning and Ending

❶ **Write** two beginnings for your instructions. Then write two endings.

❷ **Choose** the better beginning and the better ending for your instructions.

Evaluating Your Instructions

▶ **Reread** your instructions. What do you need to do to make them better? Use this rubric to help you decide. Write the sentences that describe your instructions.

Rings the Bell!

- ☐ I begin with a topic sentence that states the main idea.
- ☐ I included all the steps and everything that is needed.
- ☐ The steps are in order. I used order words.
- ☐ Details make each step clear.
- ☐ The ending makes the instructions sound fun or useful.
- ☐ *There are almost no mistakes.*

Getting Stronger

- ☐ The beginning could be more interesting.
- ☐ A few steps or things that are needed are missing.
- ☐ A few steps are out of order. I could use more order words.
- ☐ A few steps need more details to make them clear.
- ☐ The ending doesn't make the instructions feel finished.
- ☐ *There are a few mistakes.*

Try Harder

- ☐ The beginning doesn't say what my topic is.
- ☐ A lot of steps or things that are needed are missing.
- ☐ The steps are in the wrong place. There are no order words.
- ☐ Most of the steps have very few details.
- ☐ The instructions just stop with the last step.
- ☐ *There are a lot of mistakes.*

▶ Revise Your Instructions

① **Revise** your instructions. Use the list of sentences you wrote from the rubric. Work on the parts that you described with sentences from "Getting Stronger" and "Try Harder."

② **Have a writing conference.**

When You're the Writer Read your instructions to a partner. Discuss any parts that need improving. Take notes to remember what your partner says.

When You're the Listener Tell at least two things you like about the instructions. Ask questions about any confusing parts. Use the chart below to help you.

Tech Tip
Save a copy of your writing before you revise it. Then try different changes. Decide which ones you like best.

What should I say?

The Writing Conference	
If you're thinking . . .	**You could say . . .**
The beginning is boring.	**You picked a great topic! Can you begin by saying something interesting about it?**
When should this step be done?	**Are you sure the steps are in order? Can you add some order words?**
I don't understand this step.	**Will your audience understand this step? Could you add some more details?**
The instructions just end with the last step.	**Is there something you can say to wrap up the instructions?**

③ **Make more revisions** to your instructions. Use your conference notes and the Revising Strategies on the next page.

Revising Strategies

Elaborating: Word Choice Use exact verbs to tell your audience exactly what to do.

Without Exact Verbs	With Exact Verbs
Put the two pieces together.	**Tape** the two pieces together.
Move your foot back.	**Slide** your foot back.

▶ Find at least two verbs in your instructions that you can replace with more exact verbs. 📖 Use the Thesaurus Plus on page H60.

Elaborating: Details Use adverbs to add helpful details to your instructions.

Without Adverbs	With Adverbs
Water the seeds.	**Lightly** water the seeds.
Stir the paint.	Stir the paint **well**.

▶ Add adverbs in at least two places in your instructions.

GRAMMAR LINK *See also page 156.*

Sentence Fluency Try to write sentences of different lengths.

All the Same Length	Different Lengths
Everyone walks around the chairs. The music suddenly stops. Then everyone tries to get a seat.	Everyone walks around the chairs **until** the music suddenly stops. Then everyone tries to get a seat.

▶ Find a group of three or more sentences in your instructions that are all the same length. Make them different lengths.

GRAMMAR LINK *See also page 181.*

PREWRITING · DRAFTING · REVISING · **PROOFREADING** · PUBLISHING

▶ Proofread Your Instructions

Proofread your instructions, using the Proofreading Checklist and the Grammar and Spelling Connections. Proofread for one skill at a time. Use a class dictionary to check spellings.

Proofreading Checklist

Did I
- ✔ indent all paragraphs?
- ✔ begin and end sentences correctly?
- ✔ use verbs correctly?
- ✔ use commas correctly?
- ✔ spell all words correctly?

📖 Use the Guide to Capitalization, Punctuation, and Usage on page H51.

Proofreading Marks

¶	Indent
∧	Add
ꝰ	Delete
≡	Capital letter
/	Small letter

Tech Tip
Scroll down until just the top line shows. Proofread one line at a time.

Grammar and Spelling Connections

Irregular Verbs Some verbs do not end with *-ed* to show the past time.

Present	Past	With *has, have,* or *had*
Grow a tree.	You grew the tree.	You have grown the tree.
Do a good job.	You did a good job	You have done a good job.

GRAMMAR LINK ▸ *See also pages 116 and 118.*

Commas Use a comma after each item in a series.

You need paper, a pencil, and a ruler. **GRAMMAR LINK** ▸ *See also page 190.*

Spelling Silent Consonants The letters *wr, kn,* and *tch* sometimes spell one consonant sound.

wrong   knot   stitch   📖 See the Spelling Guide on page H56.

▶ Publish Your Instructions

❶ Make a neat final copy of your instructions. Be sure you formed all the letters in your words correctly and used good spacing. Check that you fixed all mistakes.

❷ Write an interesting title that tells what your instructions are about.

> **GRAMMAR TIP** ▶ Begin the first, the last, and each important word in a title with a capital letter.

❸ Publish or share your instructions in a way that suits your audience.

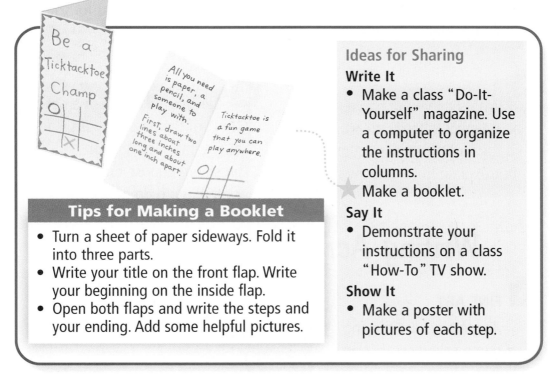

Be a
Ticktacktoe
Champ

All you need is paper, a pencil, and someone to play with.

First, draw two lines about three inches long and about one inch apart.

Ticktacktoe is a fun game that you can play anywhere.

Tips for Making a Booklet

- Turn a sheet of paper sideways. Fold it into three parts.
- Write your title on the front flap. Write your beginning on the inside flap.
- Open both flaps and write the steps and your ending. Add some helpful pictures.

Ideas for Sharing

Write It
- Make a class "Do-It-Yourself" magazine. Use a computer to organize the instructions in columns.
- Make a booklet.

Say It
- Demonstrate your instructions on a class "How-To" TV show.

Show It
- Make a poster with pictures of each step.

▶ Reflect

Write about your writing experience. Use these questions to get started.

- What part of your instructions did you do best?
- What are your goals for the next time you write instructions?
- How does this paper compare with others you have written?

✓ Writing Prompts

Use these prompts as ideas for writing instructions or to practice for a test. Decide who your audience will be. Write your instructions in a way your audience will understand and enjoy.

1 Think about the things you do before school each day. Do you brush your teeth? make your bed? Write instructions for one of the things you do.

2 Choose a special day, such as a birthday or a holiday. Write instructions on how to make a greeting card for that special day.

3 What can you draw well? an animal? a boat? a cartoon character? Write instructions that explain how to draw it.

4 Can you take care of a pet? Think of the different jobs, such as feeding, cleaning, or brushing. Choose one job and write how to do it.

Writing Across the Curriculum

5 FINE ART

These boys are playing a game called **snap the whip**. What games do you like to play outdoors? Choose a favorite game. Then write instructions, explaining how to play it.

Snap the Whip, by Winslow Homer (1836–1910)

Butler Institute of American Art, Youngstown, OH

✓ Test Practice

Sometimes on a test you will be asked to write a paper in response to a picture prompt like this one.

> Remember that instructions explain the steps for doing something.

These pictures show how to make a birthday crown. Look carefully at each picture. Then write instructions to go with the pictures that explain how to make a birthday crown.

Here are some strategies to help you do a good job responding to a prompt like the one on this page.

❶ Look at each picture and answer these questions.
  • What materials are shown?
  • What has been done with the materials in each picture?

❷ Plan your writing. Use the graphic organizer on page 337.

❸ You will get a good score if you remember the description of what kind of instructions rings the bell in the rubric on page 339.

Writing to Compare and Contrast

When you **compare**, you explain how two things are alike. When you **contrast**, you explain how two things are different. Rebecca compared and contrasted pencils and pens. Read what she wrote.

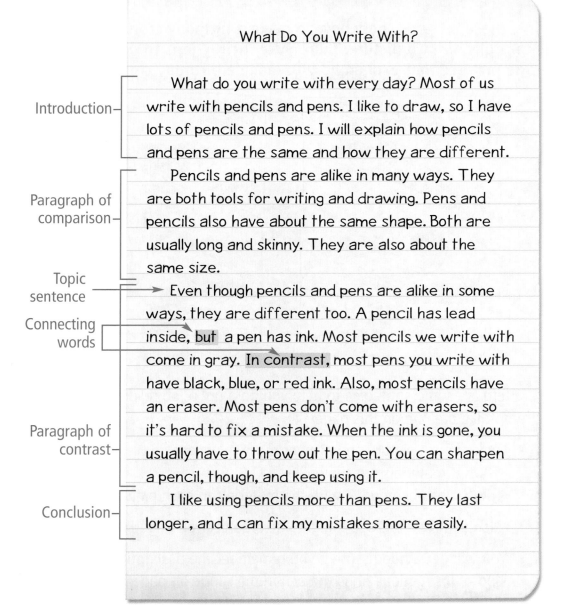

What Do You Write With?

Introduction—
What do you write with every day? Most of us write with pencils and pens. I like to draw, so I have lots of pencils and pens. I will explain how pencils and pens are the same and how they are different.

Paragraph of comparison—
Pencils and pens are alike in many ways. They are both tools for writing and drawing. Pens and pencils also have about the same shape. Both are usually long and skinny. They are also about the same size.

Topic sentence —
Even though pencils and pens are alike in some ways, they are different too. A pencil has lead

Connecting words
inside, but a pen has ink. Most pencils we write with come in gray. In contrast, most pens you write with have black, blue, or red ink. Also, most pencils have an eraser. Most pens don't come with erasers, so

Paragraph of contrast—
it's hard to fix a mistake. When the ink is gone, you usually have to throw out the pen. You can sharpen a pencil, though, and keep using it.

Conclusion—
I like using pencils more than pens. They last longer, and I can fix my mistakes more easily.

- The **introduction** tells you what is being compared and contrasted.

  What is Rebecca comparing and contrasting?

- The **paragraph of comparison** gives details that tell how the two subjects are alike.

  In what ways does Rebecca think pencils and pens are alike?

- The **topic sentence** gives the main idea for each paragraph.

  What is the topic sentence in the second paragraph?

- **Connecting words** help readers move from one idea to the next.

  What connecting words does Rebecca use?

- The **paragraph of contrast** gives details that tell how the two subjects are different.

  What differences does Rebecca describe?

- The **conclusion** sums up the likenesses and differences.

  What does Rebecca say in her conclusion?

more ▶

How to Write to Compare and Contrast

① **Think** about two subjects that are similar in some ways and different in other ways. You can choose people, places, animals, or things. Ask yourself these questions to help you choose two subjects to write about.

 Need a Topic?

Here are some ideas.
- birds and bats
- ice cream and cake
- watching TV and reading a book
- winter and summer
- two places I have visited

- Can I think of two ways these subjects are alike and two ways they are different?
- Can I explain those differences and likenesses clearly?
- Do I have enough to say about each subject?

② **List** details about each subject in a T-chart.

- Write the name of the subjects on each side of the chart. Then write details about each subject.
- Draw a line between a detail on one side that is the same as a detail on the other side.

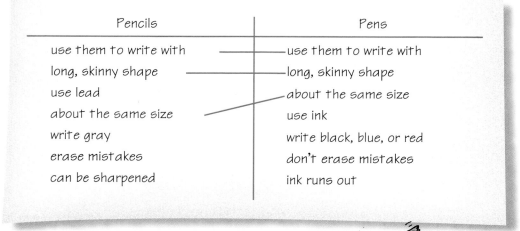

Pencils	Pens
use them to write with	use them to write with
long, skinny shape	long, skinny shape
use lead	about the same size
about the same size	use ink
write gray	write black, blue, or red
erase mistakes	don't erase mistakes
can be sharpened	ink runs out

Write as many details as you can!

3 **Organize** the details in your T-chart by putting them in a Venn diagram.

- Write the names of your subjects at the top of each circle.
- Write what is different about each subject in the outside sections.
- Write how the subjects are alike in the inside section. Use the lines you drew on your chart to help you.

Tech Tip
If you are using a computer, you can put your likenesses in one color and your differences in another.

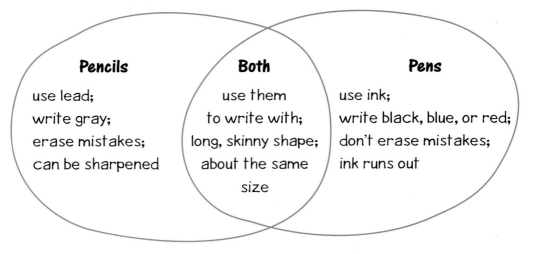

Pencils
use lead;
write gray;
erase mistakes;
can be sharpened

Both
use them
to write with;
long, skinny shape;
about the same
size

Pens
use ink;
write black, blue, or red;
don't erase mistakes;
ink runs out

4 **Write** an introduction to your two subjects. Tell something interesting that grabs your reader's attention.

more ▶

⑤ Write two paragraphs comparing and contrasting your subjects.

- Write one paragraph that compares your subjects by telling how they are alike. Use the inside section of your Venn diagram to help you.
- Write one paragraph that shows how your subjects are different. Use the outside sections of your Venn diagram.
- Begin each of your paragraphs with a topic sentence.
- Include connecting words to help your reader go from one idea to the next.

Connecting Words	
To Show Likenesses and Differences	**To Tell More**
in contrast even though while but although	also first second another

⑥ Conclude, or end, with a paragraph that sums up the likenesses and differences in an unusual way. You can also tell what you think about these likenesses and differences.

⑦ Revise your essay. Use the Revising Checklist to help you.

Revising Checklist

- ✔ Did I write a paragraph that introduces the two subjects?
- ✔ Did I put all the likenesses in one paragraph?
- ✔ Did I put all the differences in another paragraph?
- ✔ Did I use connecting words?
- ✔ Does my conclusion sum up the main points?

8 Hold a writing conference.
Remember to take notes on what the other person said about your writing. Add any changes or corrections that you want to make.

The Writing Conference	
If you're thinking . . .	**You could say . . .**
The two subjects are not different enough.	**Tell me more about how _____ is different from _____.**
The two subjects are not alike at all.	**Tell me more about how _____ is like _____.**
There are too many details—it's confusing.	**What is the main idea of this paragraph? Could you explain that in one sentence?**
That sentence is out of place.	**Does that sentence really belong in that paragraph?**

9 Proofread your essay. Use the Proofreading Checklist on page 342 to help you. Use a dictionary to check spellings.

10 Publish or share a final copy of your work in a way that suits your audience. You might make a poster or a collage to illustrate your subjects.

Giving and Following Instructions

When you explain how to do something, give your listeners clear instructions. Use these guides.

Guides for Giving Instructions

1. Explain the purpose for your instructions.
2. Tell one step at a time in the correct order.
3. Use hand gestures and movements to make each step easy to follow.
4. If needed, repeat steps for your listeners.

> Before you give your instructions, plan what you are going to say. List the steps in order.

When you follow instructions carefully, you'll make fewer mistakes. These guides can help you.

Guides for Following Instructions

1. Listen carefully. Take notes if you need to.
2. Listen for words like *first, then,* and *next* that tell you the order of the steps.
3. Picture each step in your mind. If the person is showing what to do, watch carefully.
4. Ask questions when you are unsure about a step.

Apply It

Choose a task, such as feeding a pet dog or making a bed. Give instructions to a classmate who will act them out. Then trade places.

- Were your instructions easy to follow?
- Were you able to follow the instructions yourself?
- What steps were left out?

Following Picture Directions

Have you ever made anything by following picture directions? These directions use pictures, such as drawings or photographs. Each picture shows one step of the directions. Steps are followed to finish the task.

Read the guides below to help you follow picture directions.

Guides for Following Picture Directions

▶ First, look at all the pictures. This will help you to know all of the steps before you start.

▶ Look for details about what to do in each step.

▶ Follow each picture in order.

▶ Finish each step before you go on to the next.

▶ Work slowly and carefully.

Apply It

Look at the picture directions below for making a paper airplane. Then use the Guides for Following Picture Directions. When you are finished making the airplane, see how well it flies.

- How well did your airplane fly?
- Are there any pictures you would change to make the directions easier to follow?
- Would it have been easier to follow written directions? Explain.

Make Your Own Model Airplane

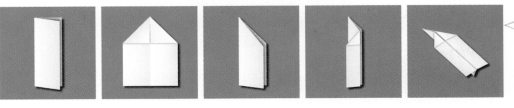

Writing a Research Report

Emperor penguin chicks hatch during the icy Antarctic winter. Their parents take care of them until summer.

Patricia Lauber did a lot of research about the octopus. She learned many facts about this sea animal. Read to find out how an octopus escapes being eaten.

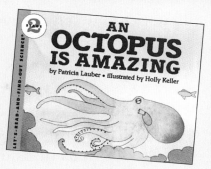

An Octopus Is Amazing

by Patricia Lauber

An octopus is an animal that lives in the sea. It has a soft, bag-shaped body and eight rubbery arms.

There are many kinds of octopus. The best-known is the common octopus. This octopus—like most others—lives alone. Its den is just big enough for its body. An octopus can squeeze into a small space because it has no backbone. In fact, it has no bones at all.

Go to www.eduplace.com/kids/ for information about Patricia Lauber.

more ▶

A Published Model **355**

An octopus can change color in a flash. Usually the octopus matches its surroundings and is hard to see. If it climbs into an empty shell, it turns pink and gray. If it crawls among rocks and seaweeds, it may turn brown and gray and green.

Changing color helps an octopus hide or escape from enemies. Its color may also show how an octopus is feeling. An angry octopus turns dark red. A frightened one turns pale.

An octopus has a big appetite. The common octopus likes crabs, lobsters, and clams best. Sometimes an octopus waits in its den until a crab or lobster passes by. Then it reaches out an arm and grabs its prey.

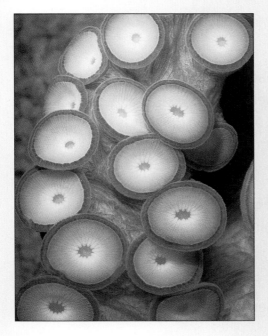

Each arm is lined with suckers. They work like little rubber suction cups. The octopus holds its catch with these suckers and examines it. Then the octopus carries the food toward its mouth, which is on the underside of its body. Inside its mouth is a hard, curved beak. The octopus uses this beak to crack the shell of its prey.

An octopus may leave its den and hunt for food. The octopus may crawl along, using its suckers to hold on to rocks and pull itself forward. Or it may move quickly, by shooting water out of its body through a tube called a siphon. With each spurt, the octopus jets through the sea.

Sometimes other animals try to eat an octopus. If a big fish attacks, the octopus changes colors and jets off. The octopus no longer looks like the animal the fish was going to attack. And so the fish is fooled.

An octopus can also give off an ink-black liquid through its siphon. The ink forms a blob that has the shape and smell of an octopus. The enemy attacks the blob, and the octopus escapes.

An octopus is truly amazing.

Reading As a Writer

Think About the Information

- Look at the third paragraph on page 357. What facts did you learn about how an octopus escapes being eaten?
- Now look at the third paragraph on page 356. What is the topic sentence? What are the supporting details?

Think About Writer's Craft

- In the first paragraph on page 356, the author wrote two sentences that begin with *If.* Why do you think she wrote both sentences in the same way?

Think About the Pictures

- How do the photos help you understand the information in this article?

Responding

Write responses to these questions.

- **Personal Response** What facts in the article did you find most interesting? Why?
- **Critical Thinking** How is the octopus similar to other sea creatures that you know about? How is it different?

What Makes a Great Research Report?

A **research report** gives facts about a topic. The facts are taken from different sources.

Remember to follow these guidelines when you write a research report.

▶ State the topic clearly in your opening. Say something interesting about your topic.

▶ Write a topic sentence that tells the one main idea of each paragraph. Use supporting details that tell about that main idea.

▶ Include only facts about the topic. Do not include your thoughts or opinions.

▶ Use your own words.

▶ Sum up the important points in the closing.

GRAMMAR CHECK

Add -s or -es to a verb when the subject is singular. Do not add -s or -es to a verb when the subject is plural.

WORKING DRAFT

Ashton Ray is interested in animals. She really likes frogs and has read all about them. She decided to share what she learned with her classmates. Ashton wrote this draft of her report.

Ashton Ray

Working Draft

Frogs

Here are some things I learned about frogs. Frogs are good jumpers. They are good swimmers too. Frogs do not walk very often. They hop. I love to watch frogs hop. Each back foot has five toes. They have thin webbing between them. Frogs use their feet as paddles. Now that we know about the legs, let's leap on to learn how they catch their prey.

The frog's tongue helps catch small insects. The frog sits very still. It waits for its dinner to arrive. An insect comes close. Then the frog attacks it. It does not miss its target very much. Let's jump to find out more about a frog's prey.

Frogs eat many different things. They eat moths, mosquitoes, mealworms, and

> The first sentence tells the main idea of this paragraph. Good!

> How does the frog attack it?

Working Draft

dragonflies. They also eat rats and mice. Frogs have really strong legs. Some frogs can even eat bees without being stung. Don't you think that's neat? Now jump with me to find out where frogs live.

Frogs are amphibians. Frogs live in woods, in swamps, and in ponds. Most frogs start life in water.

Now you can tell your friends and family all about frogs and say, "I know a lot of things about frogs."

Reading As a Writer

- What did Sal like about Ashton's report? What were Sal's questions? What changes could Ashton make to answer them?
- Which sentences tell Ashton's thoughts or opinions?
- What questions would you like to ask Ashton about her report?

FINAL COPY

Ashton revised her report after discussing it with a partner. Read the final paper to see what changes she made.

The Amazing Ways Frogs Survive
by Ashton Ray

What do you know about frogs? I am about to tell you something so wonderful you will not believe what you read. Leap with me to learn about frogs!

Frogs are good jumpers and swimmers. Their legs are so powerful! Frogs do not walk very often. They hop. Some kinds can leap twenty times their own body length! Each back foot has five toes. The toes have thin webbing between them. Frogs use their feet as paddles. Now that we know about the legs, let's leap on to learn how they catch their prey.

The frog's tongue helps catch small insects. The frog sits very still while it waits for its dinner to arrive. When an insect comes close enough, the frog attacks it. The frog shoots out its sticky tongue and strikes the creature. Then the frog flips its tongue back into its mouth with the next meal stuck to the tip. All this happens so fast that a

> That's an interesting fact!

person can hardly see it! The frog does not miss its target very often. It can even pick a fly right out of the air! Let's jump to find out more about a frog's prey.

Frogs eat many different things. They eat moths, mosquitoes, mealworms, dragonflies, rats, and mice. Some frogs can even eat bees without being stung. Now jump with me to find out where frogs live.

Frogs are amphibians, meaning "two lives." The frog does live two lives. One is on land, and one is in the water. Frogs live in woods, in swamps, and in ponds. Most frogs start life in water.

Now that you know about the body parts of frogs, their prey, and where frogs live, you can tell your friends and family all about frogs and say, "I know a lot of things about frogs."

Sources

Amphibian. Eyewitness Video Series. Co-Production of BBC Lionheart Television and Dorling Kindersley Vision, 1994.

Florian, Douglas. *Discovering Frogs.* New York: Scribner's, 1986.

Gibbons, Gail. *Frogs.* New York: Holiday House, 1993.

Reading As a Writer

- What changes did Ashton make after thinking about Sal's comments?
- What changes did Ashton make to the opening and closing of her final copy? Why are they better?
- What details did Ashton add about how a frog attacks its prey?

Write a Research Report

▶ Start Thinking

Make a writing folder for your research report. Copy the questions in bold print, and put the paper in your folder. Write your answers as you think about and choose your topic.

- **Who will be my audience?** Will it be my classmates? my younger brother or sister? a teacher?
- **What will be my purpose?** What topic would I like to explain?
- **How will I publish or share my report?** Will I read it aloud to a younger child? make an accordion book? present it with pictures?

▶ Choose Your Topic

❶ List four topics that you would like to learn more about.

❷ Discuss your ideas with a partner.

- Where can you find facts about them?
- Are any topics too big? Look at how Ashton broke her large topic, *animals,* into smaller ones.

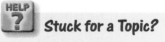

HELP ? Stuck for a Topic?

Here are some ideas.
- an insect
- an invention
- a bird
- a sport

See page 376 for more ideas.

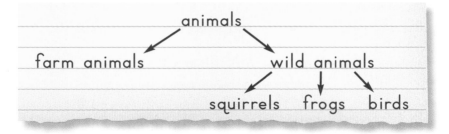

❸ Ask yourself these questions about each topic.

- Can I find facts about this topic from more than one source?
- Does this topic really interest me?

❹ Choose your two favorite topics. Circle the one you will write about.

Go to www.eduplace.com/kids/hme/ for topic links.

Explore Your Topic

1 **Think** about your topic as a riddle or a mystery. Write what you know about your topic on a chart like this one. Then write five questions you want to answer.

Topic: the planet Saturn

What I Know	What I Want to Learn	Possible Sources
Saturn is the closest planet to Jupiter.	What does Saturn look like?	books about planets, Internet articles about Saturn

2 **Choose** the three most interesting questions. Circle them.

3 **Look at your questions.** Be a detective. Where will you go to find the answers? Here are some possible sources.

People	teachers, librarians, experts about the topic
Print	nonfiction books, encyclopedias, magazines
Technology	the Internet, CD-ROM encyclopedias, CD-ROMs or videos about your topic

4 **Decide which sources are best for each question.** Beside each question, write two sources that you will try. If you cannot think of enough sources, go back to your list of topics.

Tech Tip
Before you use an Internet source, check with your teacher.

See Using the Library on page H21. Also see Using Technology: The Internet on page H39.

Focus Skill

Gathering Facts

Telling Fact from Opinion

When you look for information for your report, you will need to know the difference between facts and opinions.

Facts are statements that can be proved. You can check facts in an encyclopedia or in another nonfiction source.

Opinions tell what someone believes or feels. A research report should not include opinions. Look for words such as *I think, fun, worst,* and *good.* They often show opinions. Compare these facts and opinions.

Facts	Opinions
Ants have six legs.	Ants are better than wasps.
An ant's body has three separate parts.	I think ants are ugly.
Ants are insects.	Ants are cool!

Think and Discuss Read these sentences. Which ones tell facts? Which ones tell opinions?

- An ant has two stomachs.
- I think that ants are pests.
- Mosquitoes are even worse pests than ants.
- The queen ant is born with wings.
- An ant's head has two small eyes.
- Ants are interesting to study.

Taking Notes

Take notes to remember the facts you find. When you take notes, write only the main words to help you remember the important facts. Don't copy! List the sources for the facts you find.

This is how one student took notes to answer the question *What does the blue whale look like?* He found this information.

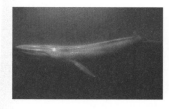

The largest whale is the blue whale. The body of a blue whale is slender. The overall color is blue-gray with light gray spots. A blue whale can be about 78 feet long.

Whales eat living things from the ocean. Some whales eat small fish, squid, and octopus. Other whales eat a mixture of plants and animals called plankton. They like small creatures called krill.

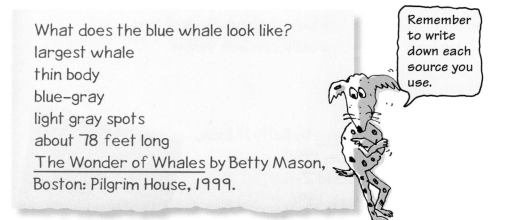

What does the blue whale look like?
largest whale
thin body
blue-gray
light gray spots
about 78 feet long
The Wonder of Whales by Betty Mason,
Boston: Pilgrim House, 1999.

Remember to write down each source you use.

Try It Out

- Work with a partner to take notes. Use the information above to answer the question *What do whales eat?*

▶ Explore Your Report

① **Write** each of your questions on a separate piece of paper. Look for facts that answer each question.

② **Then take notes** to help you remember. Write the name of each source you use on your paper.

📖 See page H26 for more help with taking notes.

Are you having trouble finding facts? Use more than one source.

▶ Plan Your Report

① **Organize** your notes. On each page, put a check mark next to all the facts that go together. Use one color for each type of fact.

Tech Tip
Use the Cut and Paste features to group facts that belong together.

Look at the notes below. The facts about the *color* of the whale have red check marks. The facts about the *size* of the whale have green check marks.

What does the blue whale look like?
✔largest whale   ✔babies about 24 feet long
✔thin body   ✔belly can look yellow
✔blue-gray
✔light gray spots
✔about 78 feet long
The Wonder of Whales by Betty Mason,
Boston: Pilgrim House, 1999.
Whale Watch by David Zeller,
Chicago: Bean Press, 1996.

② **Plan** which facts will come first, next, and last in your report. Number your questions in the order that you will write about them.

▶ Draft Your Report

❶ Leave five or six blank lines at the top of your paper. You will use this space to write an opening for your report later.

❷ Write one paragraph to answer each question.

- Write each question as a topic sentence.
- Use your notes to write the supporting details. Keep together the groups of facts that you circled in the same color. Write the details in complete sentences.

> **HELP ?**
> **Topic Sentences**
> Your topic sentence does not have to be a question. You can write your question as a statement.
> *What does the blue whale look like?* or *The blue whale is huge.*

❸ Skip every other line to leave room for changes if you are not using a computer. Do not worry about mistakes.

This paragraph was written from the notes on page 368.

> What does the blue whale look like? It's blue-gray in color with light gray spots. Sometimes its belly can look yellow. The blue whale is the largest whale. It's long and thin. A baby is about twenty-four feet long, and an adult whale is about seventy-eight feet long!

GRAMMAR TIP ▶ <u>It's</u> means "it is." <u>Its</u> means "belonging to it."

Focus Skill

Good Openings and Closings

Good Openings

A good opening tells what your topic is about and makes your readers want to read about it. Here are two ways to begin.

Start with an interesting fact about the topic.

Weak Opening	Strong Opening
I am going to tell you about bees. Here we go.	One beehive can have thousands of bees living and working inside!

Ask a question that makes your audience curious.

Weak Opening	Strong Opening
Did you know that bees are insects?	Did you ever wonder how honey is made?

Good Closings

A good closing sums up the main ideas.

Weak Closing	Strong Closing
Bees do different things. They have many different jobs. Well, that's all I have to say about bees.	Bees help flowers grow, and they make honey! They have many different jobs inside the beehive. Next time you eat honey, think of this amazing insect.

Think and Discuss

● Why are the strong openings and closings better?

▶ Draft Your Opening and Closing

Write an opening and a closing for your report.

Evaluating Your Research Report

▶ **Reread** your report. How can you make it better? Use this rubric to help you decide. Write the sentences that describe your report.

Rings the Bell!

- The opening states the topic in a clear and interesting way.
- Each paragraph has a main idea with many supporting details.
- My report has only facts.
- I use my own words.
- My closing sums up all the important points.
- There are almost no mistakes.

Getting Stronger

- My opening could be clearer and more interesting.
- I need more details to support some of the main ideas.
- I need to take out my opinions.
- I could write more of the report in my own words.
- My closing does not sum up the important points.
- There are a few mistakes.

Try Harder

- My opening is boring.
- I have very few details to support the main ideas.
- My report has more opinions than facts.
- I do not use my own words.
- The report just stops.
- There are a lot of mistakes.

▶ Revise Your Research Report

❶ **Revise** your report. Use the list of sentences you wrote from the rubric. Work on the parts that you described with sentences from "Getting Stronger" and "Try Harder."

HELP ? **Revising Tip**

To make sure each paragraph has a topic sentence, highlight your topic sentences with a colored marker.

❷ **Have a writing conference.**

When You're the Writer Read your report aloud to a partner. Talk about any trouble spots. Take notes to remember what your partner says.

What should I say?

When You're the Listener Tell at least two things you like about the report. Ask questions about any parts you think are confusing. Use this chart to help you.

The Writing Conference	
If you're thinking . . .	**You could say . . .**
The opening is a little dull.	**Could you begin with a question or an interesting fact about your topic?**
I don't understand some of these special words.	**It would help your readers if you explained some of the special words about your topic.**
The facts are interesting, but the report doesn't seem finished.	**Can you sum up the important points at the end?**
This report doesn't sound like you.	**Can you write more of the report in your own words?**

❸ **Make more revisions** to your research report. Use your conference notes and the Revising Strategies on the next page.

Revising Strategies

Elaborating: Word Choice Explain the meanings of special words about your topic that your audience might not know.

Without a Definition	With a Definition
Whales use their **flukes** to help them swim and dive.	Flukes are the flat parts of a whale's tail. Whales use their flukes to help them swim and dive.

▶ Find at least one place in your report where you can explain a special word about your topic.

Elaborating: Details Add details to help make the information clear.

Few Details	Elaborated with Details
Bees have different jobs.	Bees have different jobs. The queens lay eggs. Workers gather food and care for the young.

▶ Find at least two places in your report where you can add details.

Sentence Fluency Your writing will be more interesting to your readers if you begin your sentences in different ways.

Same Beginnings	Different Beginnings
An ant has no nose. An ant can still smell, though. An ant uses its antennae to smell.	An ant has no nose. It can still smell, though. Ants use their antennae to smell.

▶ Make sure the sentences in your report begin in different ways.

▶ Proofread Your Research Report

Proofread your research report, using the Proofreading Checklist and the Grammar and Spelling Connections. Proofread for one skill at a time. Use a class dictionary to check spellings.

Proofreading Checklist

Did I
- ✔ indent all paragraphs?
- ✔ use correct verb forms?
- ✔ use capital letters correctly?
- ✔ correct any run-on sentences?
- ✔ spell all words correctly?

📖 Use the Guide to Capitalization, Punctuation, and Usage on page H51.

Proofreading Marks

¶ Indent
∧ Add
⌐ Delete
≡ Capital letter
/ Small letter

HELP ? **Proofreading Tip**

Read your paper from right to left so you focus on each word by itself.

Grammar and Spelling Connections

Verb Forms When the noun in the subject is singular, add *-s* or *-es* to the verb. When the noun is plural, do not add *-s* or *-es* to the verb.

Singular Subject	Plural Subject
The ant eats insects.	The ants eat insects.
A seal catches fish.	Seals catch fish.

GRAMMAR LINK ▶ See also pages 100 and 102.

Spelling Vowel + *r* The sound of the vowel + *r* in *chair* or *care* may be spelled *air* or *are*.   fair   hair   rare   dare

📖 See the Spelling Guide on page H56.

 Go to www.eduplace.com/kids/hme/ for proofreading practice.

▶ Publish Your Research Report

1 **Make a neat final** copy of your report. Be sure you formed all letters correctly and used good spacing. Check that you fixed all mistakes. If you used a computer, print out a correct final copy.

2 **Write** a title that grabs your readers' attention.

3 **Include** a list of your sources at the end of your final copy. See Ashton's sources on page 363.

4 **Publish** or share your report in a way that suits your audience.

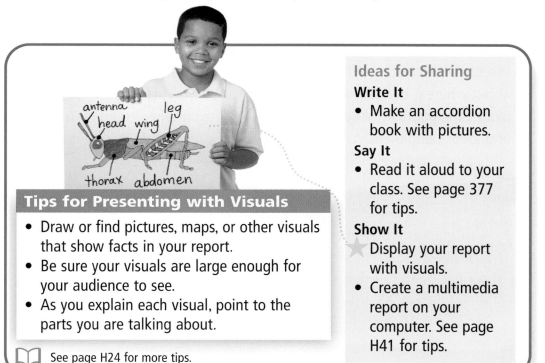

antenna · leg · head · wing · thorax · abdomen

Tips for Presenting with Visuals

• Draw or find pictures, maps, or other visuals that show facts in your report.
• Be sure your visuals are large enough for your audience to see.
• As you explain each visual, point to the parts you are talking about.

📖 See page H24 for more tips.

Ideas for Sharing

Write It
• Make an accordion book with pictures.

Say It
• Read it aloud to your class. See page 377 for tips.

Show It
⭐ Display your report with visuals.
• Create a multimedia report on your computer. See page H41 for tips.

▶ Reflect

Write about your writing experience. Use these questions to start.

• What have you learned about writing a research report?
• What else would you like to find out about your topic?
• How does this report compare with other papers you have written?

Writing Prompts

Use these prompts as ideas for research reports. Some of the prompts may fit with other subjects you study. Think about your audience. Write your report in a way that will make your audience want to read it.

Writing Across the Curriculum

1 SOCIAL STUDIES

Choose a city, such as Orlando, Florida, that you would like to visit some day. Write about where it is, its famous places, the popular things to do, and foods people eat.

2 MUSIC

Choose a musical instrument that interests you. Write about how the instrument is made and how it is played. Include facts on where the instrument was first used.

3 PHYSICAL EDUCATION

Write about your favorite sport. Tell when and where the sport was first played and how the sport is played now.

4 SCIENCE

Write about your favorite wild animal. Tell where it lives, what it eats, and what it looks like.

5 SCIENCE

Write about one of the planets. Tell its location, what it looks like, and any other facts about that planet.

6 SOCIAL STUDIES

Choose a holiday or special custom. Write about where it is celebrated. Explain why it was first celebrated and how it is celebrated today.

  See www.eduplace.com.kids/hme/ for more prompts.

Giving an Oral Report

Giving an oral report is a good way to share information. Instead of reading to an audience about a topic, you talk mostly from memory. You can use pictures, maps, and other media to make your report more interesting.

Which Media?	
Models Models show how things look from different sides. Would making a model and showing it to your listeners help them understand your topic?	Dioramas, clay models, and papier-mâché objects
Photographs Photos can show the people, events, or details you are telling about. Can you use a photograph to help explain an idea from your report?	Posters, slides, pictures from newspapers, magazines, and catalogs 
Illustrations Charts and drawings can help explain ideas. Should you organize information into a chart?	Charts, graphs, maps, diagrams, and tables
Recordings Could you play a song or scene from a video on your topic?	Cassette tapes, CDs, and videotapes 

📖 See pages H41–H43 in the Tools and Tips Handbook.

more ▶

Getting Ready

Prepare your materials ahead of time. If you plan to show pictures from a book, use bookmarks to hold your place. If you play music or a recorded speech, get your equipment ready. Practice setting cassettes, CDs, or videos to the right spot.

Once you have practiced your report, you are ready to give it. Here are some guides to help you.

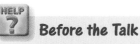

HELP

Before the Talk

- Write notes on cards.
- Practice your talk, using your notes.
- Say your report to a friend or in front of a mirror.
- Repeat words that may be hard to say.

Guides for Giving an Oral Report

▶ Stand up straight.
▶ Speak clearly and loudly enough for everyone to hear.
▶ Don't move around a lot.
▶ Be sure not to say *ah, well,* and *um.*
▶ Look at your listeners.

Apply It

Look at a report you have already written. Choose an interesting part to turn into an oral report. Select and prepare two types of media to add to your report. Give your report, using the guides above to help you. Then answer these questions.

- Which media did you choose for your report? Why?
- Was your audience interested in your report? How do you know?
- If you could give your report again, what would you do differently?

Knowing Facts from Opinions

Television and radio shows often include both facts and opinions. Some shows try to make opinions sound like facts. Some advertisements do too. How can you tell the difference?

Think About It

A statement that can be proved true is a fact. This is a fact: *Pianos are instruments.* A statement that tells what someone believes or feels is an opinion. This is an opinion: *Pianos are the best instruments.*

Read the guides below to help you know facts from opinions.

Guides for Knowing Facts from Opinions

► Find out from an expert whether a statement is true.
► Check a statement in an encyclopedia.
► Statements that use phrases like *always* and *never,* or *best* and *worst,* are usually not facts.
► Look and listen for phrases like *I feel, I think,* and *it seems.* These words show opinions.

Apply It

Read the statements below. Then use the Guides for Knowing Facts from Opinions to help you answer the questions. <kbd>HELP ?</kbd> See also page 366.

> Rainbow Park has ten acres of pond water. Five years ago there was twice as much.

> Our parks are the best in the county. Everyone can help protect them.

- Which do you think gives facts? Tell how you know.
- Which do you think gives opinions? Tell how you know.
- Could either example include both facts and opinions?

Section 3

Expressing and Influencing

What You Will Find in This Section:

380

Listening to an Opinion

An **opinion** is what someone thinks or feels about something. Opinions cannot be proved true or false, but they can be explained with reasons and facts or other details. When you listen to an opinion, what do you want to find out? These ideas will help you learn how to listen to opinions.

Guidelines for Listening to an Opinion

▶ Listen for the topic. What is the author talking about?

▶ Listen for words such as *I think, I feel, I like, good, bad, easy,* and *fun.* These are words that express opinions.

▶ Listen for the opinion. What does the author think about the topic?

▶ Listen for reasons. Why does the author feel the way he or she does?

▶ Listen for details. What does the author say to explain each reason?

Try It Out Listen carefully as your teacher reads aloud an opinion about cats by Andrew Clements. Then answer the questions below.

● What is the topic?

● What is the main idea?

● What reasons and details does Andrew Clements give to explain his opinion?

See www.eduplace.com/kids/ for information about Andrew Clements.

Writing an Opinion Paragraph

A paragraph that tells what someone thinks or feels is an **opinion paragraph.** An opinion paragraph has a topic and a main idea. The **topic** is the subject of the paragraph. The **main idea** is the writer's opinion on the topic. What is the topic of the paragraph below? What is the main idea?

Remember to indent the first sentence of a paragraph.

Indent ——————

Opinion statement

Supporting sentences

Closing sentence

Everyone in my class has fun singing "This Old Man," especially me. There are lots of silly hand movements. I know exactly when to do my part. Even better, sometimes we sing it really fast. Then I have to remember all the parts in a hurry. We laugh so hard! I really like to sing this song.

Opinion Statement

Supporting Sentences

Closing Sentence

The topic is singing the song "This Old Man." The main idea, or the writer's opinion, is that singing this song is really fun. Which sentence states the topic and the writer's opinion?

The labels show the three parts of an opinion paragraph.

- The **opinion statement** tells what the writer thinks or feels about a certain topic.
- **Supporting sentences** give reasons and details that explain the opinion.
- The **closing sentence** finishes the paragraph.

Think and Discuss Reread the song paragraph above.

- What are two reasons why the writer likes to sing the song?

The Opinion Statement

You know that a well-written paragraph begins with a sentence that states the topic and tells the main idea. In an opinion paragraph, this sentence is called the **opinion statement**. It tells what the writer thinks or feels about the topic.

Main idea   Topic

Example: Everyone in my class has fun singing "This Old Man," especially me.

Main idea

Try It Out Read the paragraphs below. They are missing the opinion statement. On your own or with a partner, write the topic and the main idea for each paragraph. Then write an opinion statement for each.

1. _Opinion statement_ . I cheered at Wendy's bravery when she learned to fly. She knew how to think too, and that helped the Lost Boys. Peter Pan was funny, and he was always having adventures. I also liked Tinkerbell, even though she was spoiled. *Peter Pan* is a movie I won't forget.

2. _Opinion statement_ . It's exciting when your turn comes to be at bat. Also, you don't get tackled like in football. Baseball is easy to play too. All you need is a bat, a ball, and a glove. Baseball is a really fun way to play with friends.

Supporting Sentences

The **supporting sentences** in an opinion paragraph tell the reasons for the writer's opinion. Details tell more about the reasons. The supporting sentences in the paragraph about *Peter Pan* give reasons and details about why the writer liked the movie.

Reason: Wendy was brave.
Detail: She learned how to fly.

Read the paragraph below. Look for reasons and details that explain the writer's opinion.

There's a lot to like about Thanksgiving. For one thing, dessert is awesome. I have so many bakers in my family that we usually have at least six different types of pie. Even better is seeing my relatives. About fifteen people crowd into our apartment. Best of all, everyone tells stories and laughs a lot! I wish Thanksgiving could happen every month.

Think and Discuss In the paragraph above, what reasons and details explain why the writer likes Thanksgiving?

Ordering Reasons and Details Supporting sentences are arranged in an order that makes sense. The best reason might be told last, for example. **Order words**, such as *first, another reason, better,* and *the best reason,* help connect the reasons and details. In the Thanksgiving paragraph above, what order does the writer use for the reasons? What order words do you find?

 See page 18 for more order words.

more ▶

Try It Out Look at the picture. Then read the opinion statement and the list of reasons and details. On your own or with a partner, write at least three supporting sentences to explain your opinion of soccer. You can use the list for help. Use an order word to link two of your sentences.

Opinion statement: I like (or don't like) to play soccer.

run a lot in soccer
learn to use your feet
get to kick the ball
play on a team
get really strong legs

GRAMMAR TIP ➤ *Use a comma after an introductory word that begins a sentence.*

The Closing Sentence

The **closing sentence** finishes the paragraph. It can repeat the writer's opinion in a new way or make a final comment. In the song paragraph on page 383, the closing sentence repeats the writer's opinion using different words.

Try It Out Read the paragraph below. It is missing the closing sentence. On your own or with a partner, write one for the paragraph.

I think the best part of the day is early morning. I can get up to see the sky just before the sun rises. Sometimes the sky changes from gray to purple to pink. I can also be by myself for a little while. I like to read or color before my sisters and brothers get up. Sometimes I just lie under the covers and daydream. _____*Closing sentence*_____.

Write Your Own Opinion Paragraph

Now you can write your own opinion paragraph. Think of something you feel strongly about. Do you love summer? spaghetti? What do you think is unfair? Write your topic. Then write your reasons in a list. Think of details to make your reasons clear. Practice telling your opinion, reasons, and details to a partner. Then begin to write!

Checklist for My Paragraph

✔ My **opinion statement** tells what I think or feel about the topic.

✔ I wrote **supporting sentences** that give reasons and details to explain my opinion.

✔ My **closing sentence** repeats my opinion or makes a final comment about my topic.

Looking Ahead

Now that you know how to write an opinion paragraph, writing an opinion essay will be easy. The diagram below shows how the parts of an opinion paragraph do the same jobs as the parts of an opinion essay.

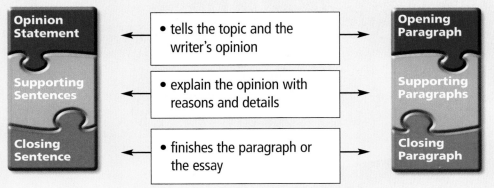

Opinion Paragraph

- Opinion Statement
- Supporting Sentences
- Closing Sentence

- • tells the topic and the writer's opinion
- • explain the opinion with reasons and details
- • finishes the paragraph or the essay

Opinion Essay

- Opening Paragraph
- Supporting Paragraphs
- Closing Paragraph

Writing to Express an Opinion

I have a plateful of reasons for liking spaghetti.

Brian Pinkney wrote this essay to explain what he thinks about baseball caps. What is his opinion of them?

Baseball Caps Rule

by Brian Pinkney

The best type of hat to wear on your head is a baseball cap. Ever since I was a little kid, I have loved to wear baseball caps. It does not matter if it's summer, fall, winter, or spring. There is always room on my head for a good baseball cap.

A baseball cap with a nice size brim is the perfect hat to wear in summertime. I'm the kind of guy who hates to wear sunglasses. I like to see the world in all of its brightness. A nice brim on a baseball cap keeps the glare out of my eyes and protects me from the harmful rays of the sun. Also, if I bend the brim a little, the baseball cap looks quite stylish.

Even though I'm not in school anymore, I still like to shop for new clothes in the fall. Baseball caps come in many colors and logos to complement my clothes. My favorite baseball cap colors

more ▶

See www.eduplace.com/kids/ for information about Brian Pinkney.

are blue, burgundy, or gray. My favorite baseball cap logos are from the Negro League teams from the 1940s and 1950s.

A baseball cap is also wonderful to wear in the winter. If I get a baseball cap with ear flaps, I can stay nice and warm on a cold and blustery day. If my baseball cap doesn't have flaps, a pair of earmuffs can keep the chill out with a snug fit over my baseball cap.

In the spring a new baseball cap makes me feel good. With my new cap on, I'm full of hope and ready for the new season to begin. Baseball caps with the adjustable strap in the back are the best for those windy March days.

Therefore, whatever the season I'm in, if it's for protection from the sun, looking stylish, warmth in the cold, or just feeling good, there is always a baseball cap on my head. The only time I take my baseball cap off is to put on a new one.

Reading As a Writer

Think About the Opinion Essay

- Reread the first paragraph on page 389. What is the author's opinion of baseball caps? Why do you think he tells his opinion in the first paragraph?
- Reread the second paragraph. What reason does the author give for his opinion of baseball caps? What details does he give to support this reason?
- Where does the author sum up his reasons for liking baseball caps?

Think About Writer's Craft

- In the first full paragraph on page 390, what exact words does the author use to help you "feel" what he is describing?

Think About the Pictures

- What things can you see in the photos that are also described in the text?

Responding

Write your answers to these questions.

- **Personal Response** Think about a hat you like. Which of your reasons for liking the hat are similar to the author's? Which of your reasons are different?
- **Critical Thinking** What reasons might someone have for *not* liking to wear baseball caps?

What Makes a Great Opinion Essay?

An **opinion essay** tells what the writer thinks about a topic.

Remember to follow these guidelines when you write an opinion essay.

► Introduce your topic in the opening. Say something interesting to get your audience curious.

► Include strong reasons to support your opinion.

► Write a paragraph for each reason. Include a topic sentence that states the reason.

► Give details that will help explain your reasons.

► Sum up the important points in the closing.

GRAMMAR CHECK

Be sure to use the pronouns *I* and *me* correctly.

WORKING DRAFT

Cody Reid thinks recess is an important part of the school day. He wrote this draft to share his opinion with other students.

Cody J. Reid

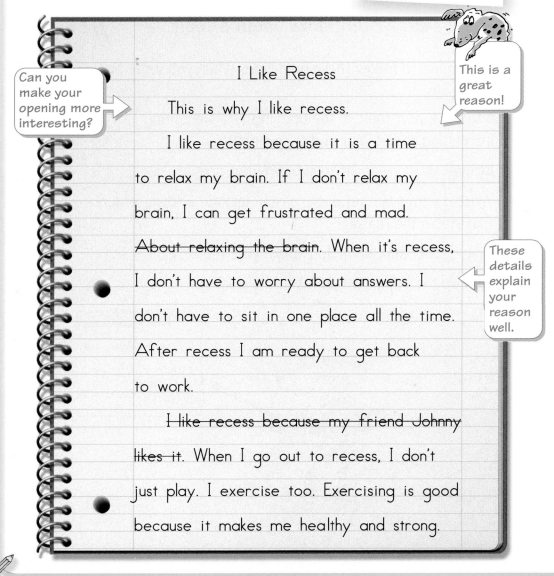

I Like Recess

This is why I like recess.

I like recess because it is a time to relax my brain. If I don't relax my brain, I can get frustrated and mad. ~~About relaxing the brain.~~ When it's recess, I don't have to worry about answers. I don't have to sit in one place all the time. After recess I am ready to get back to work.

~~I like recess because my friend Johnny likes it.~~ When I go out to recess, I don't just play. I exercise too. Exercising is good because it makes me healthy and strong.

Can you make your opening more interesting?

This is a great reason!

These details explain your reason well.

Healthy snacks are good for me too.

Recess is a time to learn important lessons like friendship and taking turns.

I hope that I gave you enough reasons why I like recess.

Reading As a Writer

- What did Sal like about Cody's opinion essay? What were Sal's questions? What changes could Cody make to answer them?
- Why did Cody cross out a reason in the third paragraph on page 394?
- What questions would you like to ask Cody about his opinion?

FINAL COPY

Cody revised his opinion essay after discussing it with a partner. Read his final copy to see what changes he made.

My Favorite Part of the Day
by Cody Reid

Most days I just can't wait for recess! It's the best part of my day.

I like recess because it is a time to relax my brain. If I don't relax my brain, I can get frustrated and mad. When it's recess, I don't have to worry about answers. I don't have to sit one place all the time. After recess I am ready get back to work.

When I go out to recess, I don't just play. I exercise too. Exercising is good because it makes me healthy and strong. I can have races with my friends, climb on the jungle gym, or practice any sport that I like.

Recess is a time to learn important lessons like friendship and taking turns. The other day, my friends and I played kickball together. We made

> Your new opening is interesting!

> You took out the detail about snacks. Good! It wasn't important.

fair teams. We waited our turns to kick, and we told each other to try our best.

I like recess because it's a time to take a break, exercise, and get along with my friends.

These details make this reason much stronger.

Now I really understand why you like recess!

Reading As a Writer

- What changes did Cody make after thinking about Sal's questions?
- What details did Cody add in the last paragraph on page 396?
- What changes did Cody make to the closing of his final copy? Why is this closing better?

Write an Opinion Essay

▶ Start Thinking

Make a writing folder for your opinion essay. Copy the questions in bold print, and put the paper in your folder. Write your answers as you think about and choose your topic.

- **Who will be my audience?** Will it be my parents? my classmates? the principal?
- **What will be my purpose?** Do I want my essay to be serious or funny?
- **How will I publish or share my opinion essay?** Will I send it to a newspaper? read it to my friends? make a comic strip?

▶ Choose Your Topic

1 **List** three or four topics that you have an opinion about. Do not list people. Cody made a chart to help him think of topics.

Things I Like	Things I Don't Like
band practice	homework
recess	chores
my parakeet	getting up early

HELP
? **Stuck for a Topic?**

Here are some ideas.
- a club or activity
- a season of the year
- watching television
- a kind of music

See page 410 for more ideas.

2 **Discuss** your topics with a partner. What are your reasons for liking or not liking each topic you listed?

3 **Ask** yourself these questions about each topic. Then circle the topic you will write about.

- Do I feel strongly about this topic?
- Can I think of enough reasons to support my opinion?

Focus Skill

Choosing Strong Reasons

Reasons help your audience understand why you think or feel a certain way. To help you think of reasons, imagine your audience asking you *Why?* about your opinion.

Choose reasons that are important enough to support your opinion. Make sure your reasons are clear and exact. Compare the weak and strong reasons below.

Opinion: *I do not like playing softball.*

Weak Reasons	Strong Reasons
It's not a fun sport.	You don't get to move around much in softball.
The uniforms are ugly.	You have to wait too long for the exciting parts.

Think and Discuss

- Why are the strong reasons better than the weak ones?
- Work with a partner. Think of two more strong reasons for not liking softball.

more ▶

► Explore Your Reasons

1 **Make a chart** like Cody's chart below.

- Think of sentences like the ones in the picture to help you fill in your chart.
- Write your opinion. Then write three or four reasons on the lines next to your opinion.

I like _____ because _____ .

I don't like _____ because _____ .

I like recess because	learn important lessons
	can exercise
	allowed to yell
	relaxes my brain

▲ Cody's chart

HELP ?

Need More Reasons?

If you cannot think of enough reasons, choose a new topic.

2 **Put a star** next to two or three of your strongest reasons.

HELP ? See page 14 for other ideas for exploring your topic.

Elaborating Your Reasons

You know that you need strong reasons to support your opinion. You also need strong details to support each reason. Look at how reasons and details support the opinion on the banner below.

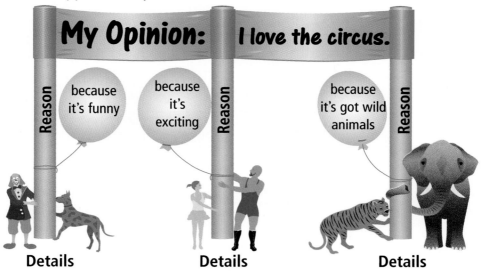

My Opinion: I love the circus.

Reason — because it's funny — because it's exciting — Reason — because it's got wild animals — Reason

Details   Details   Details

Include enough details to explain your reasons clearly. Give examples. Suppose your opinion is *I like summer vacation.* Compare the weak and strong details below.

Reason: *I get to visit my grandparents' farm.*

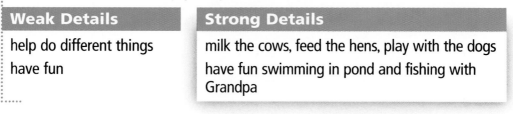

Weak Details	Strong Details
help do different things	milk the cows, feed the hens, play with the dogs
have fun	have fun swimming in pond and fishing with Grandpa

Think and Discuss Compare the weak and strong examples above.

- Why are the strong details better than the weak details?
- What other strong details can you think of to support the reason?

more ▶

▶ Explore and Plan Your Essay

❶ Add details to your chart. Draw lines from the reasons you starred. Then write details for these reasons. Here's an example from Cody's chart.

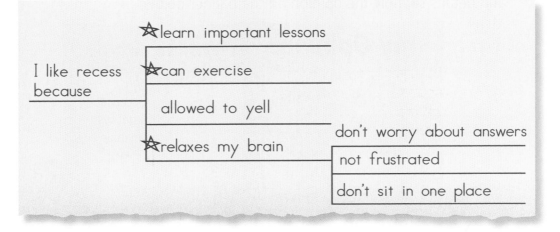

I like recess because

☆learn important lessons

☆can exercise

allowed to yell

☆relaxes my brain — don't worry about answers
not frustrated
don't sit in one place

❷ Number your reasons to show the order in which you will write about them.

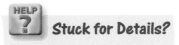

Stuck for Details?

If you can't think of details for a reason, work on another reason first.

Go to www.eduplace.com/kids/hme/ for graphic organizers.

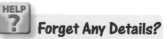

Draft Your Opinion Essay

❶ Write your draft. Use the reasons and details from your chart.

- Write a paragraph for each reason. Each paragraph should include a topic sentence that states the reason.
- Use the details to write supporting sentences for each reason. Add more details as you think of them.

HELP ? **Forget Any Details?**
Place a check mark next to each detail on your chart as you use it. This will help you see if you included everything.

❷ Skip every other line so that you can make changes later. Don't worry about mistakes now.

❸ Tell your audience how you really feel. Let them hear your voice. Compare one student's working draft and final copy.

Working Draft	Birthdays are nice. I have macaroni and cheese for dinner and chocolate cake for dessert. Chocolate cake tastes good.

Final Copy	Birthdays are great because I get to pick whatever I want to eat for dinner. I always ask for macaroni and cheese because it's my favorite dinner in the whole wide world! The best part of the meal is the chocolate cake I have for dessert. It's moist and gooey and tastes delicious!

Tech Tip
You may want to use a computer to draft your essay.

> This one lets me know how the writer really feels!

Focus Skill

Good Openings and Closings

Good Openings

A good opening gives a hint about your topic. It should get your audience interested in your opinion right away.

Weak Opening

There are lots of reasons why I like to go hiking with my family.

Strong Opening

I am the first one out of bed and ready for a great day! It's the day I get to go hiking with my family.

Good Closings

A good closing sums up the important points. Don't just end with your last reason.

Weak Closing

Now I've told you why I like to hike.

Strong Closing

I like hiking because I get to be out in the fresh air. I see lots of different animals, and I get to dip my tired feet in the cold stream.

Think and Discuss Compare the weak and strong examples above.

- Why is the strong opening better than the weak opening?
- Why is the strong closing better than the weak closing?

▶ ## Draft Your Opening and Closing

Write an opening and a closing for your opinion essay.

Evaluating Your Opinion Essay

▶ **Reread** your opinion essay. What do you need to do to make it better? Use this rubric to help you decide. Write the sentences that describe your essay.

Rings the Bell!

- ☐ The opening introduces the topic in a way that gets my audience curious.
- ☐ Each paragraph has a topic sentence that states a reason.
- ☐ I have strong reasons for my opinion.
- ☐ Details help my audience understand my reasons.
- ☐ The closing sums up the main points.
- ☐ There are almost no mistakes.

Getting Stronger

- ☐ My opening could be more interesting.
- ☐ Some paragraphs need topic sentences.
- ☐ I could include another reason for my opinion.
- ☐ I need more details to support my reasons.
- ☐ My closing does not sum up the main points.
- ☐ There are a few mistakes.

Try Harder

- ☐ The opening is boring.
- ☐ Where are the topic sentences?
- ☐ My reasons are weak or unclear.
- ☐ I have very few or no details to support my reasons.
- ☐ My essay just stops.
- ☐ There are a lot of mistakes.

▶ Revise Your Opinion Essay

❶ Revise your essay. Use the list of sentences you wrote from the rubric. Work on the parts that you described with sentences from "Getting Stronger" and "Try Harder."

Tech Tip
Boldface words or sentences in your essay that you want to remember to revise.

❷ Have a writing conference.

When You're the Writer Read your essay aloud to a partner. Ask questions about any problems you are having. Take notes to remember what your partner says.

When You're the Listener Say at least two things you like about the essay. Ask questions about any parts that are unclear. Use the chart below for help.

What should I say?

The Writing Conference	
If you're thinking . . .	**You could say . . .**
Your essay is really interesting, but the opening doesn't tell what your topic is.	**What is your topic? What do you think or feel about _____?**
This reason isn't important.	**Can you take it out? What other reasons do you have for your opinion?**
Some reasons aren't clear.	**Did you include enough details? Could you give some examples to support the reasons?**
The essay just stops.	**Can you sum up the important points?**

❸ Make more revisions to your opinion essay. Use your conference notes and the Revising Strategies on the next page.

Revising Strategies

Elaborating: Word Choice **Synonyms** are words with almost the same meaning. Instead of using the same word over and over, use synonyms.

Without Synonyms	With Synonyms
I love to take trips with my family. Once we took a trip to Alaska by boat. It was a long trip!	I love to take trips with my family. Once we took a cruise to Alaska. It was a long journey!

▶ Replace two or three repeated words in your essay with synonyms.

📖 Use the Thesaurus Plus on page H60. See also page H12.

Elaborating: Details Add details to your sentences, or add more sentences.

Without Details	With Details
I like to draw pictures.	I like to draw pictures of wild animals. Mom says my lions look real!

▶ Add details in at least two places in your essay.

Sentence Fluency Groups of short sentences sound choppy. Try making your sentences different lengths.

Choppy Sentences	Smoother Sentences
Carrots are yucky. Cooked carrots are squishy. They don't taste good.	Carrots are yucky. Cooked carrots are squishy, and they don't taste good.

▶ Find a group of short sentences in your essay. Make the sentences different lengths.

GRAMMAR LINK *See also page 47.*

▶ Proofread Your Opinion Essay

Proofread your opinion essay, using the Proofreading Checklist and the Grammar and Spelling Connections. Proofread for one skill at a time. Use a class dictionary to check spellings.

Proofreading Checklist

Did I
- ✔ indent all paragraphs?
- ✔ begin and end each sentence correctly?
- ✔ use *I* and *me* correctly?
- ✔ write contractions correctly?
- ✔ spell all words correctly?

📖 Use the Guide to Capitalization, Punctuation, and Usage on page H51.

Proofreading Marks
¶	Indent
∧	Add
℘	Delete
≡	Capital letter
/	Small letter

HELP ? **Proofreading Tip**

Touch each word with your finger.

Grammar and Spelling Connections

I and *me* Use *I* as the subject of a sentence. Use *me* as an object pronoun. Name yourself last when you talk about another person and yourself.

Using *I* Correctly	Using *me* Correctly
I enjoy swimming.	Dad takes me to the town pool.
Anna and I enjoy swimming.	Dad swims with Anna and me.

GRAMMAR LINK *See also page 222.*

Spelling Words Ending with -*ed* or -*ing* When a word ends with *e*, drop the *e* before adding -*ed* or -*ing*.

baked chased   joking waving   📖 See the Spelling Guide on page H56.

▶ Publish Your Opinion Essay

① **Make a neat final copy** of your essay. Be sure you formed all your letters correctly and used good spacing. Check that you fixed all mistakes. If you used a computer, print out a correct final copy.

② **Write a title** for your essay that will grab your audience's attention. "King of the Keyboard" is better than "Why I Like the Piano."

GRAMMAR TIP ▶ Begin the first, the last, and each important word in a title with a capital letter.

③ **Publish** or share your essay in a way that your audience will enjoy.

For fun in the water, a beach is the best place!

I love to play in the waves! You can dive into them or jump over them.

Tips for Making a Comic Strip

- Plan the number of frames you will need. Draw a rough sketch of your comic strip.
- Tell your opinion, reasons, and details in speech balloons.
- Draw pictures to show some of your details.

Ideas for Sharing
Write It
- Send your essay to a children's magazine.
- Create a class book with pictures for each essay.

Say It
- Read your essay and discuss your opinion in a small group.
- Make a tape recording of your essay.

Show It
★ Make a comic strip.

▶ Reflect

Write about your writing experience. Use these questions to get started.

- What was easy about writing an opinion essay? What was hard to do?
- What are your goals for the next time you write an opinion essay?
- How does this paper compare with other papers you have written?

Writing Prompts

Use these prompts as ideas for opinion essays or to practice for a test. Decide who your audience will be. Write your essay in a way that they will enjoy.

1 A friend asks your opinion about a new place to visit in town, such as a museum, a park, or a zoo. Is this place boring or lots of fun? Write your opinion.

2 Write your opinion about a movie or a TV program you have seen lately. Tell what you liked about it. Tell what you didn't like about it. Include strong reasons and details.

3 Think about a game that you have played. Write your opinion of the game. Tell what you like or don't like about it.

4 Do you ever wear dressy clothes to special events? Write an opinion essay. Tell why you like to dress up, and why you do not like to dress up.

Writing Across the Curriculum

5 FINE ART

Do you think the person in this picture likes getting a haircut? Do you like to get your hair cut? Write an opinion essay. Tell why you like or don't like getting your hair cut.

The Museum of Modern Art, New York.

Barber Shop, by Cundo Bermudez (1942)

 **Test Practice**

This prompt to write an opinion essay is like ones you might find on a writing test. Read the prompt.

> **Think about a game that you have played.** Write your opinion of the game. **Tell what you like or don't like about it.**

Here are some strategies to help you do a good job responding to a prompt like this.

Remember that an opinion essay tells what the writer thinks about a topic.

1 Look for clue words that tell what to write about. What are the clue words in the prompt above?

2 Choose a topic that fits the clue words. Write your clue words and your topic.

Clue Words	My Topic
a game that you have played what you like or don't like about it	I will write about why I like to play tag.

3 Plan your writing. Use a chart.

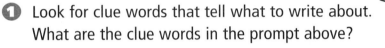

```
                                    details
                    reason    ┌──────────────┐
                              └──────────────┘

                                    details
    Opinion _____   reason    ┌──────────────┐
                              └──────────────┘

                                    details
                    reason    ┌──────────────┐
                              │              │
                              └──────────────┘
```

4 You will get a good score if you remember the description of what kind of opinion essay rings the bell in the rubric on page 405.

Writing a Book Report

A **book report** tells about a book you have read. It should also tell whether or not you liked the book. Read Milena's book report.

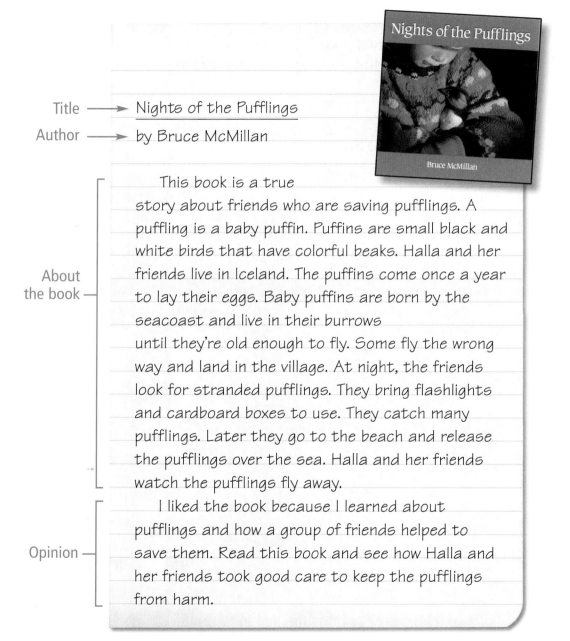

Title → Nights of the Pufflings

Author → by Bruce McMillan

About the book —

    This book is a true story about friends who are saving pufflings. A puffling is a baby puffin. Puffins are small black and white birds that have colorful beaks. Halla and her friends live in Iceland. The puffins come once a year to lay their eggs. Baby puffins are born by the seacoast and live in their burrows until they're old enough to fly. Some fly the wrong way and land in the village. At night, the friends look for stranded pufflings. They bring flashlights and cardboard boxes to use. They catch many pufflings. Later they go to the beach and release the pufflings over the sea. Halla and her friends watch the pufflings fly away.

Opinion —

    I liked the book because I learned about pufflings and how a group of friends helped to save them. Read this book and see how Halla and her friends took good care to keep the pufflings from harm.

 See www.eduplace.com/kids/hme/ for more examples of book reports.

- The **title** gives the name of the book.
  What is the title of this book?
- The **author** is the person who wrote the book.
  Who is the author?
- The writer tells **about the book**, giving information about the important people and main events in the book.
  What did Milena tell about?
- An **opinion** explains what the writer thought about the book.
  Why did Milena like this book?

How to Write a Book Report

1 **List** the title of the book and the author's name.

2 **Summarize**, or tell about, the book. Tell where the events take place. Give details about the people and the things that happen, as well as your opinion of the book.

3 **Revise and proofread** your book report. Use the Proofreading Checklist on page 408. Use a dictionary to check your spelling.

4 **Display** a neat final copy of your book report in your classroom's reading center. You can also place it in the school library for others to read.

HELP
? **Tell About This!**

Ask yourself these questions.
- Is the book a true story?
- Is the book a made-up story?
- What happens in the story?
- Did the pictures help tell the story?

Writing a Poem

In poetry, words can make music. Poets think about the sound of each word as they write. Their words might sound like soft whispers or loud bangs.

One way to make "word music" is to use many words that all begin with the same sound. What sounds does the poet repeat at the beginnings of words in "The Whales off Wales"?

The Whales off Wales

With walloping tails, the whales off Wales
Whack waves to wicked whitecaps.
And while they snore on their watery floor,
They wear wet woolen nightcaps.

The whales! the whales! the whales off Wales,
They're always spouting fountains.
And as they glide through the tilting tide,
They move like melting mountains.

X. J. Kennedy

Some sounds make special effects. Repeating *s, z,* and *sh* sounds makes a poem hiss. Lots of *b, p, k,* and *g* sounds add bumps and bounces. You can repeat vowel sounds too. What sounds does José Tablada repeat in "The Toad"?

The Toad

Mud lump bumped
    In the shadow
    Toad
    Tiptoed

José Juan Tablada
Translated by Eliot Weinberger

Some words sound like what they mean. *Thump* and *squirt* are two examples. In the following poem, which words sound like what they mean? Which sounds get repeated?

OPEN HYDRANT

Water rushes up
and gushes,
cooling summer's sizzle.

In a sudden whoosh
it rushes,
not a little drizzle.

First a hush and down
it crashes,
over curbs it swishes.

Just a luscious waterfall
for
cooling city fishes.

Marci Ridlon

Reading As a Writer

- In "The Whales off Wales" and "The Toad," find at least three words that sound like what they mean.
- In "Open Hydrant," which words have the *sh* sound?
  Why do you think the poet repeats this sound so many times?
- Compare the punctuation in "The Whales off Whales" and "The Toad." *How does it differ?*
- Compare the use of capital letters in "The Toad" and "Open Hydrant." *How does it differ at the beginning of lines?*

more ▶

How to Write a Poem

1 **Plan to write** a poem that has interesting sounds. Choose the sound effects you want to use in your poem. Use the chart below, or make a chart of your own. Think of topic ideas for the sounds you want to use.

Sound Effects	Topic Ideas
hissing or splashing sounds, such as *s, z,* and *sh*	water-skiing, rain, ducks, doing the dishes, snakes, fire, fishing, puddles, swimming
chunky, bumpy sounds, such as *k, b, g, ch,* and *d*	basketball, drums, hiking, fireworks, cooking or eating, trucks, thunder, bears
smooth sounds, such as *oo,* long *o, l,* and *m*	snowfall, singing, swans, skating, a river, the wind, deer, the ocean at night

2 **Make a details chart.** On one side, write notes about your topic. Does it include actions, colors, shapes, tastes, sounds, or feelings? List the details.

Think of words with interesting sounds that describe each detail. Write them on the other side of your chart. Here is part of one student's chart.

My Topic: The Most Amazing Salad Ever

Details	Words
I picked out the food. I felt like an artist.	green, red, orange
I made the salad.	scrape, tear, chop, toss, giant white bowl
I ate a lot. It tasted great.	munch, crunch, gobble, grin

You can also use words that sound like what they mean. Here are examples.

Words That Sound Like What They Mean

ripple	screech	moan
growl	boom	crunch
chirp	clap	rattle
bark	zip	hum

Hoot! Flutter! That sounds like me!

3 **Write** your poem, using the best words from your chart. Then think about how you want to end each line. The lines can be different lengths. You can also break lines where you would like your reader to pause a little. Add words that rhyme if you want to.

more ▶

④ Reread your poem. Do you like the way it sounds? Do you want to add new ideas? Read it to a partner. Make any changes you want.

⑤ Proofread your poem. Use a class dictionary to check spellings. Poets can capitalize and punctuate their poems in different ways. Look back at the models for ideas.

In poetry, you don't always have to write complete sentences.

⑥ Share your poem by reading it aloud to the class or to a small group. Make a neat copy of your poem for others to read.

- Add a picture to your poem, and put it on a bulletin board.
- Make a book or tape recording of class poems. Play the recording to a class of younger children.

Tips for Reading a Poem Aloud

- Make your voice loud or soft to fit the words.
- Speak slowly so that the audience will enjoy every word.
- Pause a little between ideas. Your listeners will wait in suspense.

Writing New Words to a Song

Words to a song are called **lyrics**. They often have **rhyme**—repeated sounds at the ends of words, as in *green* and *bean*. Each line has a set number of beats. They match the notes in the tune.

It's fun to write new words to a song you know well. Here are some of the lyrics of a familiar song and a new set of words for the same tune.

The Star

Twinkle, twinkle, little star,
How I wonder what you are!
Up above the world so high,
Like a diamond in the sky.

Jane Taylor

Martin has a ticklish nose.
Once he sniffed a red, red rose.
Soon the petals made him sneeze
Loud enough to scare the bees!

Reading As a Writer

- Which line endings rhyme in the two lyrics?
- How many beats are in each line?

How to Write New Words to a Song

1 **Choose** a song, and write down the words.

2 **Check** the rhyme pattern. Underline the words that rhyme. Do every two lines end with a rhyme? Does every other line rhyme?

3 **Count** the beats in each line. Write the number next to each line.

4 **Write** your lyrics. Use rhyme, following the pattern in the song. The number of beats should match those in the song.

5 **Sing** your lyrics to the tune to make sure the words fit.

Finding the Viewpoint in Pictures

The pictures that you see every day have a viewpoint. A viewpoint is an idea or a way of thinking about something. "I like dogs!" is a viewpoint. If someone who likes dogs takes a picture of a dog, what message do you think that picture might have?

Think It Through

The purpose of a picture may be to capture a moment of fun. It may also be to teach, to show something that happened, or to sell a product. When you look at a picture, think about its purpose. Think about who made the picture and why.

The person who makes a picture is sending a message. The message of the picture above is that dogs can make us smile.

Look at the pictures below. Notice that both photographs show water. Think about the message that each photograph gives about water. In the flood photo, what might the photographer think about the power of water?

Here are some ideas to help you find the viewpoint in pictures.

Guides for Finding the Viewpoint in Pictures

❶ **Subject** • Look carefully at the picture. What part of it gets your attention first?

❷ **Details** • Look at the other parts of the picture. Can you tell from the details how people feel or what action is taking place?

❸ **Purpose** • Look at the whole picture. Is the picture meant to inform you or to sell you something?

❹ **Message** • Try to figure out what the picture is telling you.

❺ **Viewpoint** • The person who made the picture believes something about the subject. What do you think he or she believes?

Apply It

Look at different kinds of photographs in a newspaper. If you can, find pictures of children your age. Choose one picture. Then find its viewpoint. Use the guides to help you.

Write a paragraph to explain what you think the picture is telling. Then ask yourself these questions.

- Do things such as books and movies have a viewpoint? Why do you think so?
- Why do you think finding the viewpoint is important?

> The picture is about a real school. It is not about milk or toys to buy. Girls and boys are playing drums and things. I think the picture is saying it is a good time.

Unit 12

Writing to Persuade

What's the latest cool way to keep warm? It's cloth made from recycled plastic bottles. Recycling makes good sense.

In this story by Beverly Cleary, a girl named Beezus doesn't like having her hair cut at home. What does Beezus want to persuade her mother to do?

The Great Hair Argument

from *Ramona and Her Mother,* by Beverly Cleary

"I want to get my hair cut in a beauty shop," said Beezus. "Like all the other girls."

"Why Beezus, you know we can't afford a luxury like that," said Mrs. Quimby. "Your hair is sensible and easy to care for."

"I'm practically the only girl in my whole class who gets a home haircut," persisted Beezus, ignoring her mother's little speech.

So began the great haircut argument.

❖   ❖   ❖

One evening, to distract her family from hair, Ramona was telling how her teacher had explained that the class should not be afraid of big words because big words were often made up of little words: *dishcloth* meant a cloth for washing dishes and *pancake* meant a cake cooked in a pan.

"But I bake cakes in pans—or used to—and this does not make them pancakes," Mrs. Quimby pointed out. "If I bake an angelfood cake in a pan, it is not a pancake."

See www.eduplace.com/kids/ for information about Beverly Cleary.

more ▶

A Published Model   423

"I know," said Ramona. "I don't understand it because *carpet* does not mean a pet that rides in a car. Picky-picky is not a carpet when we take him to the vet." At this example her parents laughed, which pleased Ramona until she noticed that Beezus was neither laughing nor listening.

Beezus took a deep breath. "Mother," she said in a determined way that told Ramona her sister was about to say something her mother might not like. The words came out in a rush. "Some of the girls at school get their hair cut at Robert's School of Hair Design. People who are learning to cut hair do the work, but a teacher watches to see that they do it right. It doesn't cost as much as a regular beauty shop. I've saved my allowance, and there's this lady named Dawna who is really good and can cut hair so it looks like that girl who ice skates on TV. You know, the one with the hair that sort of floats when she twirls around and then falls in place when she stops. Please, Mother, I have enough money saved." When Beezus

had finished this speech she sat back in her chair with an anxious, pleading expression on her face.

Mrs. Quimby, who had looked tense when Beezus first began to speak, relaxed. "That seems reasonable. Where is Robert's School of Hair Design?"

"In that new shopping center on the other side of town," Beezus explained. "Please, mother, I'll do anything you want if you'll let me go."

Ramona did not take this promise seriously.

In the interests of family peace, Mrs. Quimby relented. "All right," she said with a small sigh. "But I'll have to drive you over. If you can hold out until Saturday, we'll go see what Dawna can do about your hair after I drive your father to work."

"Oh, thank you, Mother!" Beezus looked happier than she had since the beginning of the great hair argument.

Ramona was pleased, too, even though she knew she would have to be dragged along. Peace in the family was worth a boring morning.

more ▶

Reading As a Writer

Think About the Story

- What is Beezus's goal in this story?
- Look at the second paragraph on page 424. What reasons does Beezus use to try to persuade her mother?
- What example does Beezus give to show what a good haircutter Dawna is?

Think About Writer's Craft

- Reread the sentence on page 424 in which Beezus describes the ice skater's haircut. Which words does the author use to make the skater's hair sound beautiful?

Think About the Picture

- Look at the picture on page 424. What is the family talking about? a haircut for Beezus or words such as *carpets*? Why do you think so?

Responding

Write your answers to these questions.

- **Personal Response** What did you learn from this story about persuading someone to do what you want?
- **Critical Thinking** What do you think was the best reason Beezus used to persuade her mother? Why?

What Makes a Great Persuasive Essay?

In a **persuasive essay,** a writer tries to persuade an audience to do something.

Remember to follow these guidelines when you write a persuasive essay.

► Start by telling your goal. Your goal is what you want your audience to do.

► Write a separate paragraph for each reason. State the reason in the topic sentence.

► Give strong reasons that support your goal.

► Support your reasons with facts and examples.

► Write in a voice that sounds like you.

► Sum up your goal and your reasons in the closing.

GRAMMAR CHECK

Use singular pronouns to take the place of singular nouns. Use plural pronouns to take the place of plural nouns.

WORKING DRAFT

Nikos loves to play ice hockey, and he wants his classmates to learn the game. He wrote this draft to persuade his principal to make ice hockey a school sport.

Nikos Polis

> You started by telling your goal. Good!

Why Our School Should Have Ice Hockey

I think it would be a great idea to have ice hockey as a school sport. Many of the kids in my class and all of my teachers love to ice skate. Playing ice hockey is the most fun thing you can do on skates!

> You really sound like you care about hockey.

The main reason I want my school to have ice hockey is so ~~everyone~~ all of my friends can learn to play. I play baseball at school. When I play ice hockey at Floyd Hall Arena, none of my friends are ever there. They want to come, but they don't know how to play.

~~The skates and other stuff you need for ice hockey cost a lot of money. If we had~~

ice hockey as a school sport, the school could pay for everything instead of our parents.

You get a lot of exercise playing ice hockey. We all know that when you run around a lot, your legs get stronger. Ice hockey is running on skates on the ice. I like skating better than running because it is more fun. My last reason is that I really think that ice hockey is a great team sport.

So please try to make ice hockey our new school sport. I think it would be great!

Is this a fact or your opinion?

Could you add some facts or examples to support this reason?

Reading As a Writer

- What did Sal like about Nikos's essay? What were his questions? What changes could Nikos make to answer them?
- What are Nikos's reasons for wanting his school to have ice hockey?
- Look at the second paragraph on page 428. What example did Nikos use to support his reason?

FINAL COPY

Nikos revised his essay after discussing it with his classmates. Read his final paper to see the changes he made to improve his essay.

A Cool New Sport
by Nikos Polis

I think it would be a great idea to have ice hockey as a school sport. Many of my friends and all my teachers love to skate. Playing ice hockey is the most fun thing you can do on skates!

The main reason I want my school to have ice hockey is so all of my friends can learn to play. I play baseball with my friends at school. When I play ice hockey at Floyd Hall Arena, none of my friends are ever there. They want to come, but they don't know how to play.

> Good! You've taken your opinion out of this paragraph.

Another reason is that you get a lot of exercise playing ice hockey. We all know that exercise is good for you. When you run a lot, your legs get stronger. Ice hockey is running on skates on the ice.

My last reason is that I really think ice hockey is a great team sport. When you join ice hockey, you get put on teams and get the same

> You've started a new paragraph for this reason. Great!

color jerseys. When you play and practice with the same kids, you see each other all the time and have fun and learn plays. It's great playing on a team because everybody helps everybody else. The coach always tells us there's no I in team.

> Nice work! You've added examples to this paragraph.

So please try to make ice hockey our new school sport. Then my friends can learn to play, everyone could get good exercise, and kids could have fun learning a great team sport.

Reading As a Writer

- What changes did Nikos make after thinking about Sal's questions?
- What changes did Nikos make to the closing of his final copy? Why is it better?

Write a Persuasive Essay

▶ Start Thinking

 Make a writing folder for your persuasive essay. Copy the questions in bold print, and put the paper in your folder. Write your answers as you think about and choose your topic.

- **What will be my** purpose **or** goal**?** What am I trying to persuade someone to do? Why do I care about this?
- **Who will be my** audience**?** Do I want to persuade my classmates? someone in my family? the school principal?
- **How will I** publish **or** share **my essay?** Will I post it on a bulletin board? make a photo essay? give a speech?

▶ Choose Your Goal

1 **List** three or four goals. Beside each goal, name the person or group you want to persuade. This is your audience.

2 **Discuss** each goal with a partner. Would this goal be interesting to your audience? Is this goal too big? Nikos broke one big goal into smaller parts.

Stuck for an Idea?
Think about these topics.
- I should get a pet.
- I should have a later bedtime.
- My class should go to the zoo.

See page 444 for more ideas.

> We should have more <u>sports</u> at school.
> swimming
> ice hockey
> in-line skating

3 **Ask** yourself these questions about each goal. Then circle the one you will write about.

- Do I really care about this goal?
- Can I think of enough reasons that will persuade my audience?

▶ Explore Your Goal

① Write your goal. Complete the sentence below.

I want (<u>audience</u>) to (<u>goal</u>).

② Turn your goal into a "why" question. Nikos's question was "Why should the principal make ice hockey a school sport?"

③ Imagine that your audience is asking you this question. What reasons might persuade your audience to do what you want?

④ Make a cartoon. Show your audience asking your question. Show yourself giving three or four reasons. Put each reason in a separate speech balloon.

Nikos made this cartoon to explore the reasons he would use in his essay.

HELP
? *Stuck for Reasons?*

If you can't think of enough reasons, choose a different goal.

Why should I make ice hockey a school sport?

It's good exercise.

The school could buy ice hockey stuff.

Everyone could learn to play.

It's a great team sport.

HELP
? See page 14 for other ideas for exploring your topic.

Focus Skill

Supporting Your Reasons

Think of your reasons as a bridge that will help you reach your goal. Bridges need strong posts to support them. Reasons need facts and examples to support them.

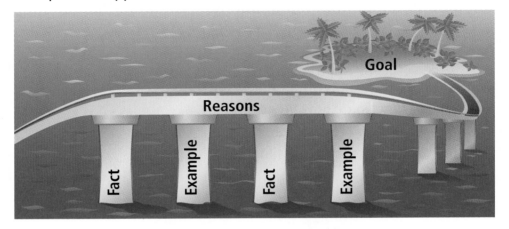

Support your reasons with facts, not opinions. Facts can be proved. Opinions tell how you think and feel. Suppose your goal is *I should have my own room.*

Reason: *I need more space.*

Weak Support: Opinion	**Strong Support: Fact**
I think the way Marie and I divide up the room is unfair.	Marie's bed, desk, dresser, and shelves take up more than half of the room.

Support your reasons with examples. An example tells about something that has happened or something that might happen.

Reason: *I need more space.*

Weak Support: Opinion	**Strong Support: Example**
I think it would be better for the whole family if I had more space.	I would have more places to put my things, so I wouldn't leave them around.

Think and Discuss Compare the weak and strong examples on page 434.

- Why are the strong examples better than the weak ones?
- With a partner, think of a fact and example to support the reason in this statement. Students should learn to use computers at school because computers are very helpful.

▶ Explore Your Reasons

Add facts and examples to each reason in your cartoon. Use a different color. Here is an example from Nikos's cartoon.

Think about your audience. Use facts and examples that will persuade them!

no friends at Floyd Hall Arena

don't know how to play

It's good exercise.

Everyone could learn to play.

The school could buy ice hockey stuff.

It's a great team sport.

Focus Skill

Organizing Your Essay

Make each of your reasons a paragraph. The sentence that tells your reason will be your topic sentence. The facts and examples will be your details.

Keep your mind on your goal. Leave out any reasons, facts, or examples that don't support your goal.

Topic Sentence	The main reason our school should collect toys is that we could help children in the hospital.
Facts and Examples	Foster Hospital has a special area for children, but it doesn't have many toys. Our toys could cheer up the children and help them get better.

Use connecting words. Connecting words such as *first of all, my second reason,* and *finally* help your audience move from one reason to the next.

When you use connecting words at the beginning of a sentence, don't forget to use a comma.

Think and Discuss Look at Nikos's working draft and final copy on pages 428–431.

- Which reason did Nikos cross out on his working draft? Why?
- What connecting words did Nikos use in his final copy?

▶ Plan Your Essay

❶ **Reread** your cartoon. Cross out any reasons, facts, or examples that don't keep to the topic. Put a star next to two or three of your strongest reasons.

❷ **Number** the reasons in an order that makes sense.

Focus Skill

Good Openings and Closings

Tell your goal clearly in your opening. Let your audience know exactly what you want them to do. Say something that will catch their interest.

Weak Opening	Strong Opening
There are hardly any trees on our street. It would be a lot nicer around here with more trees.	Picture our street with beautiful trees instead of just telephone poles. You can get these trees, and all it takes is a letter to the mayor.

Sum up your goal and reasons in your closing. Get your audience excited about doing what you want!

Weak Closing	Strong Closing
When I look out my window, I can't see a single tree. Other streets have a lot more trees.	If each family asks the mayor for trees, we'll have shade and chirping birds in the summer.

Think and Discuss Compare the weak and strong examples above.

- Why is the strong opening better than the weak one?
- Why is the strong closing better than the weak one?

▶ Draft Your Opening and Closing

➊ **Write an opening** for your essay that tells your goal. Try to catch the interest of your audience.

➋ **Write a closing** that sums up your goal and reasons.

Focus Skill

Writing with Voice

Let your audience hear your voice. Show that you care about your goal. This will make your essay more persuasive.

Weak Voice	Strong Voice
If we had a pet show, we could see each other's pets. It would be interesting to see them.	If we had a pet show, we could all show off our pets. Wouldn't you like to see Jack's cat or Ana's lizard? I certainly would!

Be positive! Being positive means thinking more about what is good than what is bad. In your essay, point out the good results your goal will bring. Don't sound angry or whiny.

Angry Voice	Positive Voice
If I can't go to Grandma's, I'll have a terrible summer. There's nothing to do here. I'll just be bored.	If I could spend the summer with Grandma, I would have tons of things to do! We would go to great parks and museums, and the public pool is huge.

Think and Discuss Compare each pair of examples above.

- What makes the strong voice better than the weak voice?
- Why is the positive voice better than the angry one?

▶ Draft Your Essay

❶ Write the rest of your essay. Use the reasons, facts, and examples from your cartoon. Skip every other line so that you can make changes. Don't worry about mistakes.

❷ Show your audience how you feel in a positive way.

Evaluating Your Persuasive Essay

▶ **Reread** your persuasive essay. What do you need to do to make it better? Use this rubric to help you decide. Write the sentences that describe your essay.

Rings the Bell!

- The opening tells my goal in an interesting way.
- Each paragraph has a strong reason that supports my goal.
- Facts and examples support each of my reasons.
- I show my feelings in a positive way.
- The closing sums up my goal and reasons.
- *There are almost no mistakes.*

Getting Stronger

- My opening could be more interesting.
- I need another strong reason to support my goal.
- One or more reasons need more facts and examples.
- In some places, my writing sounds angry.
- My closing does not remind my audience of my goal.
- *There are a few mistakes.*

Try Harder

- The opening does not tell what my goal is.
- My reasons are weak and unclear.
- I hardly used any facts or examples to support my reasons.
- I don't sound like I care about my goal.
- I forgot to write a closing.
- *There are a lot of mistakes.*

▶ Revise Your Persuasive Essay

1 Revise your essay. Use the list of sentences you wrote from the rubric. Work on the parts that you described with sentences from "Getting Stronger" and "Try Harder."

HELP ?

Revising Tip

Underline your reasons. Then check that each reason has facts or examples to support it.

2 Have a writing conference.

When You're the Writer Read your essay aloud to a partner. Ask questions about any problems you are having. Take notes to remember what your partner says.

When You're the Listener Tell at least two things you like about the essay. Ask questions about any parts that are unclear. Use the chart below for help.

What should I say?

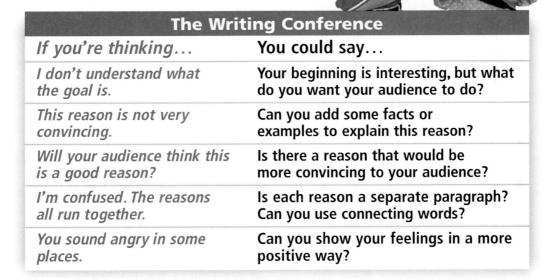

The Writing Conference

If you're thinking...	You could say...
I don't understand what the goal is.	**Your beginning is interesting, but what do you want your audience to do?**
This reason is not very convincing.	**Can you add some facts or examples to explain this reason?**
Will your audience think this is a good reason?	**Is there a reason that would be more convincing to your audience?**
I'm confused. The reasons all run together.	**Is each reason a separate paragraph? Can you use connecting words?**
You sound angry in some places.	**Can you show your feelings in a more positive way?**

3 Make more revisions to your persuasive essay. Use your conference notes and the Revising Strategies on the next page.

Revising Strategies

Elaborating: Word Choice Choose strong words such as *certainly, really, in fact,* and *of course* that will help persuade your audience.

Without Strong Words	With Strong Words
A class trip to the beach would teach us about the ocean.	A class trip to the beach would certainly teach us about the ocean.
I would pay for the game with my allowance.	Of course, I would pay for the game with my allowance.

▶ Find at least two places in your essay where you can add strong words.

Elaborating: Details Add details that will help make your sentences interesting and lively.

Few Details	Elaborated with Details
My **bed is warmer** when my dog, Buster, is allowed to sleep there.	My icy bed soon turns warm and cozy when my dog, Buster, is allowed to warm my feet.

▶ Find at least two places in your essay where you can add details.

Sentence Fluency Watch out for groups of words that begin with *because* or *since.* They must be added to a complete sentence.

Not a Complete Sentence	Complete Sentence
It would make sense for me to take piano lessons. **Since we have a piano.**	It would make sense for me to take piano lessons since we have a piano.

▶ Check your essay for groups of words that begin with *because* or *since.* Add each group to a complete sentence.

▶ Proofread Your Persuasive Essay

Proofread your essay, using the Proofreading Checklist and the Grammar and Spelling Connections. Proofread for one skill at a time. Use a class dictionary to check spellings.

Proofreading Checklist

Did I
- ✔ indent all paragraphs?
- ✔ write complete sentences?
- ✔ use pronouns correctly?
- ✔ use commas correctly?
- ✔ spell all words correctly?

📖 Use the Guide to Capitalization, Punctuation, and Usage on page H51.

Proofreading Marks
¶   Indent
∧   Add
⌐   Delete
≡   Capital letter
/   Small letter

Tech Tip
If you made the same spelling mistake a few times, fix it with the search-and-replace function on your computer.

Grammar and Spelling Connections

Pronouns Use singular pronouns to take the place of singular nouns. Use plural pronouns to take the place of plural nouns.

Singular Noun	A **playground** is needed.
Singular Pronoun	It is needed.
Plural Noun	More **playgrounds** are needed.
Plural Pronoun	They are needed.

GRAMMAR LINK *See also page 214.*

Spelling Words Ending with *y* When a word ends with a consonant and *y,* change the *y* to *i* and add *-es* or *-ed.*

study   stud**ied**   puppy   pupp**ies**   📖 See the Spelling Guide on page H56.

Publish Your Persuasive Essay

1 **Make a neat final copy** of your essay. Be sure you formed your letters correctly and used good spacing. Check that you fixed all mistakes. If you used a computer, print out a correct final copy.

2 **Write** a title that will catch your readers' interest.

> **GRAMMAR TIP** *Begin the first, the last, and each important word in a title with a capital letter.*

3 **Publish** or share your essay in a way that works for your audience.

Tips for Giving a Speech

- Speak with expression. Raise your voice at the end of a question. Say exclamations with feeling.
- Show your feelings with your face and hands. Use props to make your points clear.
- Speak so that your audience can hear you.

See page H5 for more tips.

Ideas for Sharing

Write It
- Send your essay in a letter.
- Post it on your school Internet site.

Say It
- Present your essay as a speech.

Show It
- Make a photo essay. Use real photos or draw pictures.
- Make a poster.

Reflect

Write about your writing experience. Use these questions to get started.

- What do you like the most about your essay? the least?
- What did you learn that will help you the next time?
- How does this paper compare with other papers you have written?

Writing Prompts

Use these prompts as ideas for persuasive essays or to practice for a test. Some of the prompts are about school subjects. Decide who your audience will be. Write your essay to persuade that audience.

1 Do you have a special wish for your next birthday? Would you like a hamster? a bike? a computer game? Persuade your parents to let you have your wish.

2 Should children have to work to get an allowance? Decide what you think. Then persuade your audience to agree with you.

Writing Across the Curriculum

3 **LITERATURE**

Have you ever read a book that a friend of yours might enjoy? What makes the book funny, exciting, interesting, or helpful? Persuade your friend to read the book.

4 **SCIENCE**

Think of a science activity you would like to do, such as setting up a fish tank or planting flowers. Persuade your teacher to let your class do the activity.

5 **PHYSICAL EDUCATION**

Think of all the reasons why everyone should learn to swim. Persuade your classmates to take swimming lessons.

6 **SOCIAL STUDIES**

Do you think your neighborhood needs a new park? a library? a public pool? Persuade your mayor to provide something your neighborhood needs.

Go to www.eduplace.com/kids/hme/ for more prompts.

 **Test Practice**

This prompt to write a persuasive essay is like ones you might find on a writing test. Read the prompt.

> **Do you have a special wish for your next birthday? Would you like a hamster? a bike? a computer game? Persuade your parents to let you have your wish.**

Here are some strategies to help you do a good job responding to a prompt like this.

Remember that a persuasive essay tries to persuade an audience to do something.

❶ Look for clue words that tell what to write about. What are the clue words in the prompt above?

❷ Choose a topic that fits the clue words. Write the clue words and your topic ideas.

Clue Words	My Topic
a special wish Persuade your parents	I will persuade my parents to give me a puppy for my birthday.

❸ Plan your writing. Use a chart.

My Goal		
reason	reason	reason
facts and examples	facts and examples	facts and examples

❹ You will get a good score if you remember what kind of persuasive essay rings the bell in the rubric on page 439.

Watching for Persuasive Tactics

The people who make ads on television know how to persuade. To persuade means to try to get someone to do something. Most television ads try to get people to buy a product. How do they do this?

Think About It

Think of an advertisement on television that you have seen a lot. Does it use music? Who is in it? What do you think about as you watch the ad? How does it make you feel?

Many ads use bright colors and fast action. Some have talking toys or animals. Even funny or cute ads can still use tactics, or ways, to persuade you. Look at the example below.

Everybody has one!

An ad that seems to say that "everybody" wears or uses the product plays on the viewer's feelings. This kind of ad wants to make you feel left out. It wants you to believe that if you buy the product, you'll be taking part in something special. Ask yourself: Does everybody really have this product? Will I really be happier if I buy it?

Some advertisers pay a sports star or a movie star to say something good about a product. When you see the product in a store, you may believe that the product is good because the star said so.

When you see an ad on television or in magazines, look for the ways it is trying to persuade you. Here are some guides to follow.

Guides for Looking at Media Advertising

▶ Look carefully at the advertisement. What does it want you to do?

▶ Think about how the ad is trying to make you feel.

▶ Check the ad to see whether it uses facts or opinions.

▶ Does the ad seem to say "everybody has one"? Does the ad include a sports star or other star?

▶ Ask yourself what the ad is trying to make you believe. Make up your own mind about what you see.

> Think about the product first. You might see that there are reasons not to buy it.

Apply It

Watch the ads that are shown during a television program you like. Videotape the program if you can. You can also look at the ads in children's magazines. Take notes on one ad, following the guides above. Then answer these questions.

- What is being advertised?
- Is the ad fun and entertaining? What do you like about it?
- If you could "talk back" to the ad, what questions would you ask?

Part

3

Tools
and
Tips

What You Will Find in This Part:

Taking and Leaving Messages

People use the telephone to keep in touch. If you answer a call for someone else, take a good message. If you make a call and no one answers, you can leave a message on an answering machine. Read this conversation and Madeline's message. What information did she write?

MRS. CROSBY: Hello, Madeline. This is Mrs. Crosby. May I speak to your mother?

MADELINE: I'm sorry, she can't come to the phone right now. May I take a message?

MRS. CROSBY: Yes, please ask her to call me at 555-0482.

MADELINE: I'll tell her to call Mrs. Crosby at 555-0482.

Madeline included the caller's name, the telephone number, and the message. She also gave the day and time of the call. When you take messages or leave messages, follow these guides.

Friday, 7:00 p.m.

Mom,
Please call Mrs. Crosby
at 555-0482.

Madeline

Guides for Taking and Leaving Messages

❶ Be polite. Speak slowly and clearly.

❷ When you take a message, write the caller's name and telephone number. Repeat the message to the caller to be sure it is correct. Write a clear message, and include the day and the time of the call.

❸ When you leave a message, give your name and telephone number. Leave a short message. Say when you called.

Apply It

A. Practice taking notes as your teacher reads a telephone message. Follow the guides.

B. Role-play giving and taking telephone messages with a classmate.

Giving a Talk

You talk every day. Talking is not the same as giving a talk to an audience. Follow these guides when you give a talk.

Guides for Giving a Talk

❶ Plan your talk.

- Know the group of people you will talk to.

- Choose a topic they can understand.

❷ Prepare your talk.

- Find the information you need.

- Find or draw any visual aids, such as pictures, maps, charts, or objects.

- Put your ideas in the correct order.

- Write notes on note cards.

> Camels
>
> a large, strong desert animal
> —6–7 feet tall
>
> can travel a long distance with little food or water
> —help people carry things in deserts
>
> have a food supply in their humps
> —hump is a large lump of fat

Giving a Talk *continued*

❸ **Practice** your talk.

- Give your talk to a friend or family member.

- Practice using notes and visual aids.

Tips for Using Visual Aids
• Make sure letters are large enough for people to read.
• Practice using machines you will need, such as an overhead projector.
• Make sure everyone can see the visual aids. Don't block the view!

- Practice how you say your words.

Speaking Tips
• Don't talk too fast or too slowly.
• Talk loudly enough to be heard.
• Speak with expression.

- Practice until you have almost memorized your talk.

❹ **Present** your talk.

- Remember to say everything just as you did when you practiced.

- Don't say *um, ah,* and *well.*

- Look at the people you are talking to.

- Use your face and hands to support your message.

HELP
? **Nonverbal Cues**
See page H7 for tips about using nonverbal cues.

See page H7 for tips about using nonverbal cues.

Apply It

Give a talk about a funny experience or something that interests you. Then follow the guidelines as you **plan**, **prepare**, **practice**, and then **present** your talk.

Understanding Nonverbal Cues

How does each student feel?

Each student is saying the same words, but each student feels a different way. How do you know? The nonverbal cues show how each student feels. A **nonverbal cue** is the look on a person's face. A person's body language, or movements, also sends nonverbal cues.

Using Nonverbal Cues

You can use nonverbal cues to support what you are saying. Here are some examples.

- Use facial expressions to match your message.
- Use your hands to show sizes and shapes.
- Point to show a direction or an object. (Don't point to people!)

more ▶

Understanding Nonverbal Cues **H7**

Understanding Nonverbal Cues continued

Nonverbal cues can send a message without using any words. Read the examples below and discuss what the pictures show.

- Smile and nod your head to show you are interested.
- Look puzzled when you don't understand something.
- Put your arm around family members to show you love them.
- Give a thumbs up to show support.
- Smile to show you are friends.

Watching for Nonverbal Cues

You should always pay attention to a speaker's nonverbal cues. They will help you better understand what the speaker is saying.

Watch for nonverbal cues that let you know how someone is feeling. If someone looks sad, you may have said something that hurt them. If someone looks down, the person might be embarrassed. If someone stares into space, the person may be bored.

Guides for Nonverbal Cues

▶ Always have good eye contact when you speak.

▶ Use nonverbal cues that match what you say.

▶ Use nonverbal cues to show how you feel.

▶ Watch for nonverbal cues from other people.

Apply It

With your class or in a small group, take turns demonstrating different nonverbal cues. Repeat each of the following sentences, using the feelings suggested. Discuss which nonverbal cues to use for each feeling.

What is your name? (Student looks puzzled, angry, or surprised.)
You can play soccer! (Student looks happy, surprised, excited.)

Interviewing

An **interview** is a kind of conversation. One person asks questions and the other person answers them. The **interviewer** is the person who asks the questions.

To get the facts you want when interviewing, you must ask the right questions. This takes careful planning. The guides below will help you.

Guides for Interviewing

1. Decide what you want to know.

2. Write questions that will help you get the information you want to know. Think of questions that begin with *Who, What, Where, When, Why,* or *How.* Do not ask questions that can be answered *yes* or *no*.

3. Write out your questions first. Leave space after each question for writing notes during the interview.

4. Before you ask your first question, tell the person the reason for your interview.

5. Ask your questions clearly and politely. Pay close attention to the answers.

6. Take notes to help you remember the answers.

7. If you don't understand something, ask more questions about it.

more ▶

Interviewing *continued*

The following notes were taken at an interview with a jeweler.

QUESTION: *What kinds of jewelry do you like to work on?*
—necklaces and bracelets
QUESTION: *How did you learn to make jewelry?*
—from my father
QUESTION: *When did you start working as a jeweler?*
—vacations from school
—full time after college
QUESTION: *Where do you do your work?*
—in our store
—sometimes at home
QUESTION: *Who comes to your store?*
—people who want to buy jewelry
—people who want to fix a piece of jewelry
QUESTION: *Why do you work with jewelry?*
—like working with my hands
—like creating things

Think and Discuss

- What kinds of questions did the interviewer ask?
- Work with a partner. Make up three more questions you could ask for the above interview. Share them with each other.

Apply It

A. Pair up with a classmate. Tell each other a topic that you know about. Write questions about the other person's topic. Interview each other by asking the questions. Follow the guidelines.
B. Interview a parent, relative, or neighbor about a job or hobby. Use the Guides for Interviewing.

Similes

Here is how one writer described the house shown above. The writer used words that describe exactly how the house looks.

The front of the house has a window on each side of the door. The window shades are down.

Another writer described the same house by showing how it was like something else. **A simile compares two different things using the word** *like* **or** *as*.

The front of the house looks like a face with closed eyes.

Here is another example using the word *as*.

The clouds above the house look as soft as cotton.

Apply It

Finish each sentence below with a simile.

1. The sun felt like _____.
2. The boy ran like _____.
3. From the airplane, the cars looked like _____.
4. The raindrops sounded like _____.
5. The squirrel balanced on the telephone wire like _____.

Synonyms

looked   searched

Words with almost the same meaning are synonyms.

The boys looked for their lost puppy.

They searched everywhere.

In the sentences above, *looked* and *searched* have almost the same meaning. They are synonyms.

Apply It

Replace each underlined word with a synonym from the word box.

1. We looked up at a noisy airplane.
2. Lisa did not see the big rock.
3. She tripped over it.
4. Lisa landed in a muddy puddle.
5. Her cap was crushed.
6. She got her boots wet.
7. I began to laugh.
8. Lisa looked awfully funny!

loud
silly
hat
soaked
huge
started
fell
dirty

Antonyms

Words that have opposite meanings are antonyms. Study the antonyms in each sentence.

One clown was happy, and the other was sad.

The big dog has a small tail.

In these sentences, *happy* is the opposite of *sad,* and *big* is the opposite of *small.*

Apply It

Replace each underlined word with an antonym from the word box. Write the new sentences so that the silly story makes sense.

1. A heavy rain began to <u>rise</u>.
2. Pepe's mother called him <u>outside</u>.
3. Pepe was very <u>happy</u>.
4. He could not <u>work</u> in the yard.
5. He could not climb <u>down</u> a tree.
6. His clothes would get <u>dry</u>.
7. It would not be <u>hard</u> to keep busy.
8. Pepe hoped the weather would get <u>worse</u>.

sad
up
easy
inside
better
play
wet
fall

Prefixes

tied   untied   retied

A prefix is a word part added to the beginning of a word.
A prefix changes the meaning of the word. Look at how the prefixes *un-* and *re-* change the meanings of words in the sentences below.

Dana helped me wrap the gifts. Which box do you want to unwrap first?

She quickly read the letter. Then she reread it more carefully.

Prefix	Meaning	Example	Meaning
un-	"not" or "opposite of"	unimportant	"not important"
re-	"again"	repack	"pack again"

Apply It

A. Complete each sentence by adding *un-* or *re-* to the word in ( ). Write the sentences.

1. He stayed in bed because he felt _____. (well)
2. She _____ the flat tire with air. (filled)
3. We were _____ of the address. (sure)
4. I _____ the old fence. (painted)
5. This knot is hard to _____. (tie)

B. Add *un-* or *re-* to each of these words. Then use each word in a sentence of your own.

    6. true   **7.** tell   **8.** known   **9.** build   **10.** kind

Suffixes

farm   farmer

A suffix is a word part added to the end of a word. A suffix changes a word's meaning. Look at how the suffixes *-er* and *-less* change the meanings of words in the sentences below.

That farm is owned by a skillful farmer.

The crowd screamed with fear, but the acrobat was fearless.

Suffix	Meaning	Example	Meaning
-er	"someone who does something"	painter	"someone who paints"
-less	"without"	scoreless	"without a score"

Apply It

Complete each sentence by adding *-er* or *-less* to the word in ( ). Write the sentences.

1. Is that stray kitten _____? (home)
2. My favorite _____ is giving a concert. (sing)
3. That broken baseball bat is _____. (use)
4. The blue sky is _____. (cloud)
5. Did your _____ give you a test today? (teach)
6. The woman felt _____ when her child fell. (help)
7. Is the _____ finished with the new home? (build)
8. Because she was _____, the dish broke. (care)

Using a Dictionary

Alphabetical Order

Words listed in the same order as the letters of the alphabet are in **alphabetical order.** This order helps you find words easily.

These rules will help you find words in alphabetical order.

Finding Words in Alphabetical Order
1. Look at the first letter of each word. Decide which of those letters comes first in the alphabet.   apple   cart   guide
2. When the first letter is the same, use the second letter of each word.   fall   field   float   fruit
3. When the first two letters are the same, use the third letter of each word.   package   page   paint   palace   parade

A dictionary gives the meanings of hundreds of words. The words are listed in alphabetical order. To find a word, think, *Where in the alphabet would the word come?*

a b c d e f g
beginning

h i j k l m n o p q
middle

r s t u v w x y z
end

Then look in that part of your dictionary. *Camera,* for example, would be at the beginning, with the other *c* words.

Entry Words and Guide Words

Entry Words The words in dark type on each dictionary page are called **entry words**. The first letter or two of all entry words on the page are usually the same.

Entry words ⟶

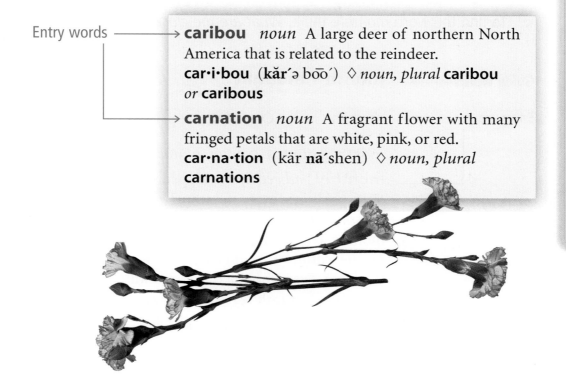

> **caribou** *noun* A large deer of northern North America that is related to the reindeer.
> **car·i·bou** (kăr′ə boō′) ◇ *noun, plural* **caribou** *or* **caribous**
>
> **carnation** *noun* A fragrant flower with many fringed petals that are white, pink, or red.
> **car·na·tion** (kär nā′shen) ◇ *noun, plural* **carnations**

Entry words are listed in simple forms. They do not have endings, such as *-ing, -s,* or *-es.* To find the entry word for a word with an ending, look for the simple form of the word.

To find:		**Look for:**	
	tossing		toss
	sharing		share
	shoes		shoe
	inches		inch

Guide Words At the top of each dictionary page are two **guide words**. The first guide word is the first entry word on the page. The second guide word is the last entry word. Every other entry word on the page comes in alphabetical order between the guide words. When you look up a word, find the guide words that are closest to the word you want.

. To find the word *monthly*, think, *What are the closest guide words?*

Guide words ⟶ **month ► moonlit**

Entry words ⟶ **month** *noun* One of the 12 periods that make up a year.
month (mŭnth) ◊ *noun, plural* **months**

monthly *adjective* **1.** Happening, appearing, or to be paid once every month: *The student council has monthly meetings.* **2.** Covering a period of a month: *The average monthly rainfall for this part of the country is approximately three inches.* ◊ *adverb* Every month; once a month.
month·ly (mŭnth′lē) ◊ *adjective* ◊ *adverb*

Monthly comes between *month* and *moonlit* in alphabetical order. *Month* and *moonlit* are the closest guide words.

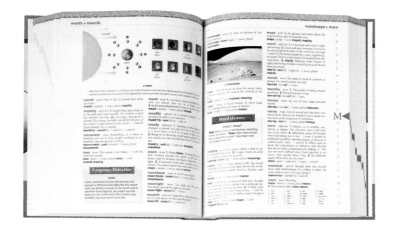

Definitions

A dictionary tells you the definitions of words. The **definition** is the meaning of a word. Sometimes there is more than one definition for a word. A number shows where each new definition begins. An **example sentence** helps make the meaning clear.

Entry word → **fork** *noun* **1.** A utensil with a handle and several prongs for use in lifting and eating food. **2.** A pitchfork. **3.** The place where ←—Definition something divides into two or more parts: Example → *Swallows built a nest in a fork of the tree.* sentence ◇ *verb* **1.** To pick up, carry, or pitch with a fork. **2.** To divide into branches: *If you look at the map, you'll see that the interstate highway forks here.* **fork** (fôrk) ◇ *noun, plural* **forks** ◇ *verb* **forked, forking**

There are three definitions for *fork* used as a noun. Which is the correct definition for *fork* as used in this sentence? Follow the guides below to decide.

She came to a fork in the road and went left.

Choosing a Definition

1. Read each of the definitions for the word.
2. Reread the sentence.
3. Choose the definition that makes the most sense in the sentence.

The third definition of *fork* makes the most sense. She came to a place where the road divided and went left.

Words That Are Spelled Alike Sometimes two entry words are spelled the same. However, they have very different meanings. To show that each word is a separate entry, a little raised number follows the word. In the part of a dictionary shown here, how many entries are there for *squash*?

Remember that an entry word appears in large, dark type. You can see that there are two entries for *squash—squash*[1] and *squash*[2].

> **squash**[1] *noun* Any of various fleshy fruits that are related to the pumpkins and the gourds and are eaten as a vegetable.
> **squash**[1] (skwŏsh) ◊ *noun, plural* **squashes** or **squash**
>
> **squash**[2] *verb* **1.** To press or be pressed into a flat mass or pulp; crush. **2.** To put an end to; suppress: *The revolt was quickly squashed.* ◊ *noun* A game played in a walled court.
> **squash**[2] (skwŏsh) ◊ *verb* **squashed, squashing** ◊ *noun*

Which is the correct meaning for *squash* as it is used in this sentence? Follow the guides below to decide.

The apples in the street were squashed by cars.

Choosing the Right Entry Word
1. Read the definitions after each entry word.
2. Reread the sentence.
3. Choose the definition that makes the most sense in the sentence.

The correct meaning is the second meaning. The apples in the street were pressed into a flat mass by cars.

Research and Study Strategies

Using the Library

How Libraries Arrange Books

You can easily find books in the library. There are places for fiction books, nonfiction books, and reference books.

Fiction Stories that are made up by the author are fiction. These books are in alphabetical order by the last names of the authors.

Nonfiction Books that contain facts are nonfiction books. These books tell about real people, animals, places, and events. Nonfiction books are grouped by subject. The subjects have certain numbers.

Reference Use reference books to find information. Reference books are all found in one section of the library. An atlas, a thesaurus, and an encyclopedia are reference books.

more ▶

How to Search for Books

Your library will have a card catalog or an electronic catalog. The catalog will help you find books in the library.

Card Catalog The card catalog is a chest of small drawers filled with cards. These cards list information about all the books in the library. They are arranged in alphabetical order.

If you know the author or title of a book, look for those cards. An **author card** lists the author's name at the top. A **title card** lists the title of the book first. These cards will give you the letters or call numbers to help you find the book.

To find a book about any subject, look for a subject card. For example, you can find a book about snow crystals listed under *snow* and under *weather*. A **subject card** lists the subject at the top. The letters or call numbers on the card will help you find the book.

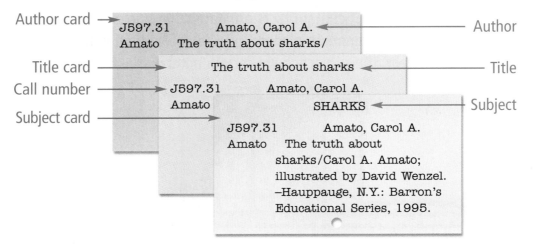

Author card →
J597.31   Amato, Carol A. ← Author
Amato   The truth about sharks/

Title card →   The truth about sharks ← Title
Call number → J597.31   Amato, Carol A.
Amato   SHARKS ← Subject

Subject card →
J597.31   Amato, Carol A.
Amato   The truth about
sharks/Carol A. Amato;
illustrated by David Wenzel.
–Hauppauge, N.Y.: Barron's
Educational Series, 1995.

Electronic Catalog Most libraries today have catalogs on computers. You can use the catalog to search for a certain book. You can also use it to look at a list of books.

A search in the electronic catalog is like looking in the card catalog. You can search by author or by title. You can also search by subject to find a book about a certain topic.

Reference Materials

Atlas An **atlas** is a book of maps. Some atlases give descriptions and facts about places. They may also tell about cities, rivers, mountains, weather, people, and animals.

There are many different kinds of atlases. A world atlas has maps of countries all over the world. There are also atlases of the solar system, the oceans, and world history.

Thesaurus A **thesaurus** is a book of words and their synonyms. A thesaurus may also list antonyms for some words. See page H60 for a helpful thesaurus.

Encyclopedia An **encyclopedia** is usually a set of books. Articles in these books tell about famous people, places, things, and events.

Encyclopedia articles are in alphabetical order. They are in books called **volumes**. Labels on each volume include one or more letters. The letters tell you the beginning letters of the articles found in that volume.

To find information, you must first think of a **key word**. The key word should name a subject that you can find in the encyclopedia.

You can also use an electronic version of an encyclopedia. There are CD-ROM and online versions. They include the entire set of volumes.

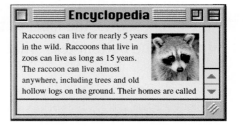

Using Visuals

Tables

A **table** is a chart that shows facts and compares information. Look at this table that the students at one school made about their activities.

After-School Clubs	
Club	**Number of Students**
Science Club	19
Art Club	11
Music Club	13
Gym Club	24

The title is at the top of the table. It tells the topic of the information in the table. The lines that go across are called **rows**. The lines that go up and down are called **columns**. Each column is labeled. The first column in this table names a club. The second column tells the number of students in the club.

Graphs

A **graph** is a drawing that compares different amounts. A graph puts information in picture form.

A graph that uses bars to stand for numbers is a **bar graph**. Look at this graph that the students in one class made about their favorite colors.

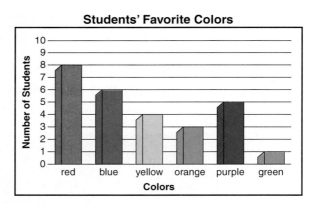

The labels on this graph explain the information. The title tells what the graph shows. The label at the side tells what the numbers mean. The label at the bottom tells what the bars stand for.

Maps

A **map** is a simple drawing of all or part of the earth. Most maps are flat. Others, called globes, are shaped like balls.

On this map of Alaska, broken lines show the border where this part of the United States meets the country of Canada.

A map key, or **legend**, explains what each symbol on a map means. For example, a black dot on this map stands for a city.

Another special symbol, the **compass rose**, shows directions on a map. This symbol points toward the north (**N**), east (**E**), south (**S**), and west (**W**).

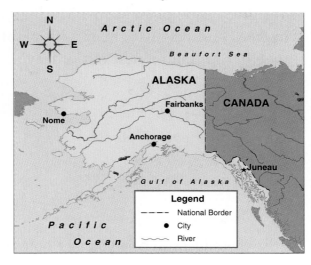

Diagrams

A **diagram** is a drawing that shows the different parts of something. A diagram can help you to understand how something works or how it is put together.

Look at the diagram of a kite. The title tells what the diagram shows. Labels name the different parts of the diagram. Lines connect the labels to the parts that they name.

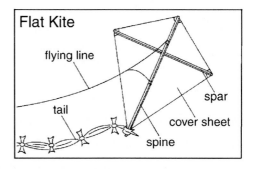

Research and Study Skills

Taking Notes

While Reading Taking notes is a good way to help you remember what you read. Read the paragraph below and the key words on the note card.

> Ants do not always live in nests underground. Doorkeeper ants live inside plant stems. Mudball ants build their nests in trees and disguise them with plants. Tailor ants work together to build a nest out of leaves.
>
> —from *Ants,* by Henry Pluckrose

Where do ants live?
- underground
- inside stems of plants
- in trees
- in nests of leaves

Use these ideas to help you take notes while you are reading.

How to Take Notes

- Don't copy what you read.
- Write your notes in your own words.
- Write words and phrases.
- Write main ideas. Then write details.
- Keep good records of the sources you use.

While Listening Don't write every word the speaker says. Write only the main ideas. Later, when you read your notes, you can add details.

While Viewing When you watch a video, write just the important words you hear. You can also draw simple pictures to help you remember the main ideas. Later, go over your notes and add more information.

Outlining

An **outline** is like a plan for your writing. It can help you organize your ideas and arrange them in order. You can write an outline from notes.

Here is another question and some additional notes about ants.

What do ants look like?
- three main body parts
- two eyes
- two feelers that look like long poles on their heads
- six legs

Order your notes in a way that makes sense. Follow these steps to create an outline.

How to Write an Outline

- Each question in your notes becomes a **main topic**. Write each main topic next to a Roman numeral. The first word begins with a capital letter.
- The notes that answer your question become the **subtopics**. Write each subtopic next to a capital letter. Indent them under the main topic. The first word begins with a capital letter.
- Each Roman numeral and capital letter is followed by a period.
- Write a title for your outline.

This outline has two main topics. They come from the questions that were asked. Each main topic has four subtopics. They come from the notes that were taken.

All About Ants
I. Where ants live
   A. Underground
   B. Inside stems of plants
   C. In trees
   D. In nests of leaves
II. What ants look like
   A. Three main body parts
   B. Two eyes
   C. Two feelers that look like long poles on their heads
   D. Six legs

more ▶

Summarizing

Summarizing an Article To help you remember information you read in an article, you can write a summary. A summary sums up the main idea and the important points of a selection in just a few sentences. Read "An Octopus Is Amazing" on pages 355–358. Decide what the main idea is. Then identify the most important points. Read the following summary of the article. The topic sentence is underlined.

An octopus is a sea animal with eight arms. It is unusual because it has no bones and it can change colors. Different colors can help the octopus hide or show how it is feeling. An octopus eats a lot. Suckers on the arms help hold food. The suckers also help the octopus to crawl. An octopus shoots water out of its body to help it move more quickly. An octopus can fool other animals by changing its shape or by giving off a liquid blob.

The main idea of the article is that an octopus is an animal that lives in the sea. The first sentence of the summary states this main idea as the topic sentence. The other sentences give the most important points about this main idea. Here are the steps to follow when you write a summary of an article.

How to Write a Summary of an Article

- Write the main idea in a topic sentence.
- Write sentences that support the main idea.
- Explain events or steps in the correct order.
- Keep the summary short.
- Use your own words.

Open-Response Questions

Sometimes tests ask you to read a passage and then write answers to questions. Use these guides to help you write a good answer.

Guides for Answering an Essay Question

1 Read the directions and the complete passage.

2 Read the question carefully. Look for clue words that tell what the answer should be about.

3 Write a topic sentence that uses words from the question. Write other sentences that give details to support the topic sentence.

4 Answer only the question that is asked.

Read the following part of a story and the question at the end.

As Ray rode his bicycle down the country road, he was happy. In two weeks, his grandmother would be celebrating her fiftieth birthday. He had been saving all summer, and now he had two dollars to spend on something special for her.

When he reached the center of town, he went straight to the nicest jewelry store. Instantly, he saw the perfect gift. It was a fancy ring set with five sparkling pink stones.

"How much?" he asked the clerk.

"Ten dollars," the clerk replied.

"Hmmm," said Ray, while wishing he could buy it. Then he spotted something a little plainer but still quite pretty. It was a short necklace of gleaming red beads.

"How much?" he asked.

more ▶

"Eight dollars," said the clerk.

"Well," said Ray, "I'll need some time to make up my mind." And he walked proudly out of the store.

Once outside, Ray had no energy to ride home. He plodded along the sidewalk, looking down. As he stepped across a sheet of newspaper, an ad caught his eye. "Newspaper needs delivery boy with a bicycle. Call 555-8973." Ray let out a whistle and hopped on his bike. Suddenly, he was full of energy. He started making plans.

Why did Ray take home the ad?

Read these two answers to the question. Which one is better? Use the Guides for Answering an Essay Question.

Ray likes to ride his bike. A newspaper put an ad in the paper for a delivery boy. He decided to take a job delivering newspapers on his bike because he loved to ride around town.

Ray took the ad home because he wanted to make some money. He wanted to buy his grandmother a birthday gift, but everything cost too much. He decided to earn money by delivering newspapers on his bicycle.

The first answer only partly explains why Ray took the ad home. It says that he wanted to deliver newspapers, but it does not say that he needed more money to buy his grandmother a special birthday gift. This answer also gives extra information that the question does not ask for.

The second answer uses words from the question in the topic sentence. The topic sentence and detail sentences list all the reasons Ray took home the ad. This answer gives only the information asked for.

Technology Terms

Computer Terms

The following terms will help you become familiar with using a computer.

CD-ROM A round disk on which information is stored and read with a laser.

cursor The marker on a computer screen that shows where the next letter will appear.

document A piece of writing created on a computer.

floppy disk A special plastic disk used to store information that can be read by a computer.

font Any one of many styles of letters a computer can make. Times, Geneva, *Brush,* and Tekton are fonts.

hard copy A computer document that is printed on paper.

hard drive A disk inside the computer that cannot be removed.

keyboard A part of the computer made up of a set of buttons called keys.

menu A list of computer commands shown on a monitor.

modem A part of a computer that allows it to communicate with other computers over telephone lines. A modem can be inside the computer, or it can be a separate device.

monitor A part of a computer system that shows information on a screen.

printer A part of a computer system that prints material.

software Programs that allow users to do things such as write and draw on computers.

Monitor

Printer

Hard drive

Floppy disk

Keyboard

more ▶

Word Processing Commands

These commands are often used in word processing. You can give each command by typing a key or series of keys or by selecting it from a menu.

Close	Closes the open document on the screen
Copy	Copies highlighted text
Cut	Removes highlighted text
delete	Removes text
Find	Locates specific words or phrases in a document
New	Opens a blank document
Open	Opens a selected document
Paste	Inserts copied or cut text in a document
Print	Prints the open document
Quit	Leaves the program
return	Moves the cursor to the beginning of the next line
Save	Stores a document for later use
shift	Allows you to type a capital letter
Spelling	Starts the spelling tool
tab	Indents the cursor to the right

Using Technology

Using E-mail

E-mail is a great way to communicate with people all over the world. Read this message that a girl sent to her friend.

---

e-mail

Subject: After School

Dear Sophia,

I read your first e-mail message this morning. I'm excited to have a new pen pal. I liked reading about your school day. What kinds of things do you like to do after school?

I usually play with my friends after school. Most of my friends live in my neighborhood, but not all of them. We like to ride bikes and play soccer. Sometimes, my mother drives me to my friend Emily's house. We are writing a play together.

Follow these tips for writing good e-mail messages.

Tips for Using E-mail

- Type a title in the subject line. The person who gets your message should know the subject before opening it.

- Keep your paragraphs short. Long paragraphs are hard to read on a computer screen.

- Skip a line instead of indenting when you begin a new paragraph. Your message will be easier to read.

- Remember that special type, such as italics or underlining, may not show up on the other person's screen.

- Follow the rules of good writing.

- Proofread your messages. Check for capital letters, end marks, and spelling mistakes.

Using a Spelling Tool

Your computer's spelling tool can help you proofread your writing. Even if you use a spelling tool, you still need to know how to spell.

Read this letter. Do you see any misspelled words? The spelling tool did not find the three mistakes that are highlighted.

A spelling tool cannot tell the difference between words that sound the same but are spelled differently.

Document 1

Deer Rosa,

How are you? It's Thursday night. I have to write a book report, but I decided to write a letter to you first. You're not going to believe what happened to day. I got the lead role in the school play, Annie. I hop you will be able to come.

Friends forever,
Jenny

A spelling tool does not know if two words should be one word.

A spelling tool cannot find a misspelled word that is the correct spelling of another word.

Think of a spelling tool as a proofreading partner. The spelling tool can help you find some mistakes in your writing, but you still need to proofread carefully.

Not all proper nouns are in the computer's database. You need to know the correct spelling for words like *Rosa* and *Annie.*

Computers and the Writing Process

You can use a computer to help you with your writing. Here are some ideas for using a computer in the writing process.

Using Technology

PREWRITING

Think Type your thoughts as you think of them. Do not worry about grammar and punctuation. You can make changes later.

Explore Dim the screen as you write so you don't worry about mistakes.

Plan Create lists or charts to help you plan your writing.

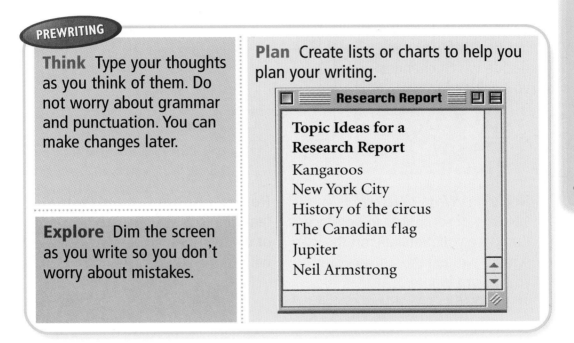

Research Report

Topic Ideas for a Research Report

Kangaroos
New York City
History of the circus
The Canadian flag
Jupiter
Neil Armstrong

DRAFTING

Set Spacing Double-space your draft so there is room to write changes when you print it.

Draft Print out your prewriting notes. Start a new document when you are ready to draft.

Save your document early and often!

more ▶

Computers and the Writing Process *continued*

REVISING

Conference Work with a partner right at the computer. Discuss any questions or problems you have. Then type your partner's comments in capital letters. Later you can decide which changes you will make.

Exact Words Use the electronic thesaurus to find synonyms. Be careful to choose a synonym that has the meaning you want.

Thesaurus: English (US)

Looked Up:
child

Meanings:
youth (noun)

Replace with Synonym:
youth

youth
young girl
infant
kid
young boy
youngster

Insert   Look Up   Cancel   Previous

Rewrite Write different versions of sentences in boldface. Compare your versions on the screen, and delete the version you do not want.

Revise Use the Cut and Paste features to make changes. Move or delete words or sentences with just a few clicks.

PROOFREADING

Check Spelling Use your word processor's spelling tool. Then check for errors a spelling tool will not catch! See "Using a Spelling Tool" on page H34.

Proofread Turn your sentences into a list.

Place·the·cursor·after·each·end·mark,·and· then·press·the·return·key.¶

Now·you·can·easily·spot·groups·of·words· that·are·not·sentences.¶

Make·sure·that·each·sentence·begins·with· a·capital·letter.¶

When·you're·finished·proofreading,·just· delete·the·extra·returns.¶

Using Technology

Computers make publishing your writing a snap. You can create final products that look professional by following these tips.

Choose Fonts Choose fonts that you like for your writing. Try to use no more than three fonts per page. If you use more than three fonts, your page will be hard to read.

This is Times.

This is Times italic.

This is Helvetica.

This is Helvetica italic.

Choose Type Sizes Choose a type size that can be read easily. Be careful not to use a type size that is too small to read. Twelve-point type is usually a good choice for papers and reports.

10-point font

12-point font (Best)

14-point font

Design Create a separate title page. Center the title, and below it type your name and the date.

Add Art Here are some ways to add art to your writing.

1. Use the Paint or Draw features to make your own picture.

2. Paste clip art into your document.

3. Use a scanner to copy an image, such as a photograph. Then insert it electronically into your document.

Using Technology

more ▶

Computers and the Writing Process *continued*

Using Technology

PUBLISHING

Print You may want to use colored paper or paper that already has a design on it.

Organize Sort your documents into electronic folders. Separate folders can store poems, stories, research reports, and letters.

Tables and Charts Create tables or charts to go with your writing. For example, you could make a graph to show the results of a class survey on pets.

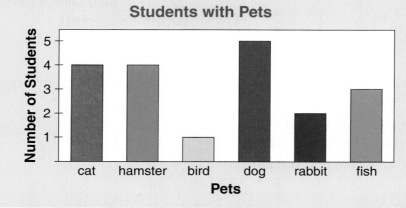

Students with Pets

(Bar graph — Number of Students vs. Pets)
- cat: 4
- hamster: 4
- bird: 1
- dog: 5
- rabbit: 2
- fish: 3

Saving Documents You can use your computer to organize and save your documents. When your writing is in electronic folders, it will be easy to find. You can create a separate folder for each kind of writing. You can even have a folder for writing that is not finished.

The Internet

The **Internet** is a network of computers that connects people and companies all over the world. It lets computer users communicate with each other quickly and easily. Here are some of the many things you can do on the Internet.

- Use a search engine to help you find Internet sites on a research topic or area of interest. Type in a key word or search by topics.

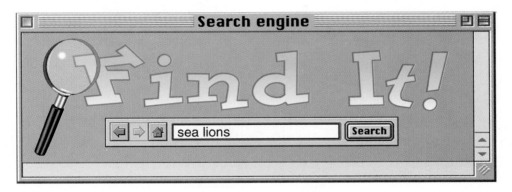

- Send e-mail to your friends and family. Anyone who is online can be reached. See "Using E-mail" on page H33.

- Use special software to create your own Web site. Design the page, write the text, and choose links to other sites. You can include interesting facts about yourself or your opinions about a specific topic. Your school may also have its own Web site where you can publish your work.

Tech Tip
Visit Education Place at www.eduplace.com/kids/hme/ for fun activities and interesting information.

more ▶

Using Technology

Tips for Using the Internet

Although the Internet can be a great way to get information, it can be confusing. Use these tips to make the most of the Internet!

Tips for Using the Internet

- Use a search engine, or tool, to help you find the topic you are interested in. Type in a key word or search by topics.

- Write down the source of any information you find on the Internet, just as you would for a book. List the author, title, date of the material, and online address (URL). Also include the date you found the information. Information on the Internet can change daily.

- Check your sources carefully. The Internet is full of information, but not all of it is correct. Check with your teacher before using any Internet source.

Making an Electronic Multimedia Project

An electronic multimedia project is a combination of words, pictures, and sounds. It lets you tell much more than you could with just words.

Equipment

You can use lots of different equipment. Check with your teacher, school librarian, or media specialist to find out what supplies your school has. Here is some equipment you can use.

- a computer with lots of memory
- a CD-ROM drive
- videotaping and recording systems
- a multimedia software program

Parts of an Electronic Multimedia Project

Text When you think of multimedia, you may think of pictures and sounds, but words are also an important part of your presentation. You may choose to write summaries, descriptions, or photo captions. Adjust the font, size, and color of your text so it is easy to see and to read.

Photos and Visuals Here are some ideas for ways to include pictures.

- Scan photos or artwork into your computer document.
- Make your own artwork, using a computer drawing program.
- Show a video you film yourself.

Animation Computer animation lets you create objects and then bring them to life. Here are some things you can do with animation.

- Tell a story with animated figures.
- Show an experiment being performed.
- Show how something is put together.
- Show how something grows.
- Display an object from all sides.

more ▶

Sound Sound can help make an image or text come alive. Here are some ideas for using sound.

- Add background sounds such as birds calling or water dripping.
- Use music to set a mood.
- Include songs that represent a time in history or a theme.
- Include a recording of yourself reading the text you wrote.
- Use video clips that include sound.

Designing an Electronic Multimedia Project

Using the writing process will help you plan and write the text for your multimedia project. In addition, you need to think about two other things. These are the types of media you can use and the order of your project.

Types of Media How will you present your words, pictures, and sounds? If you are planning a project on robins, you might make a list.

what robins look like
  outline of a robin, with labels
  a picture of a nest
  map of where robins live in the U.S. and Canada
  photographs of robins
  recording of robins singing
  recording of me reading my text

robin

Order In what order do you want users to go through your project? You can make them go in one order, from beginning to end. Another plan is to let them choose their own order as in the project below.

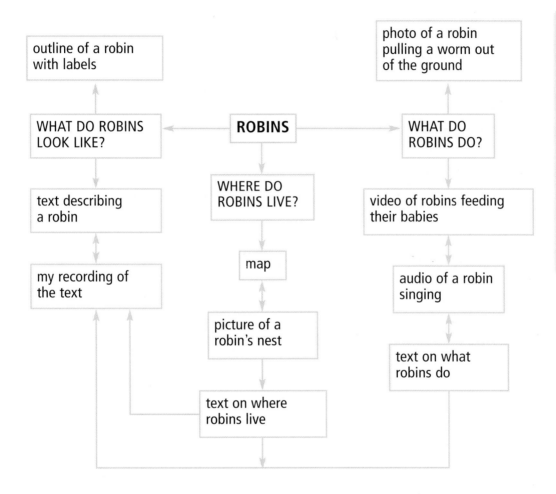

This student made her project in three parts: what robins look like, what robins do, and where robins live. She then arranged the media into these three categories. This gives the user a choice of several paths to follow.

Making an electronic multimedia project can be a lot of fun. Just as in writing, though, be sure to write any text in your own words. Always be sure to cite your sources.

Keeping a Learning Log

A **learning log** is a notebook for keeping track of what you learn. You can write facts about different school subjects. You can also write your own ideas. Use words, charts, or pictures to help you remember what you learned.

Here's an example from one student's learning log.

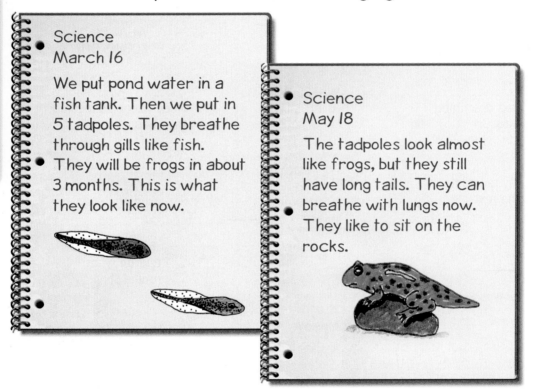

Science
March 16

We put pond water in a fish tank. Then we put in 5 tadpoles. They breathe through gills like fish. They will be frogs in about 3 months. This is what they look like now.

Science
May 18

The tadpoles look almost like frogs, but they still have long tails. They can breathe with lungs now. They like to sit on the rocks.

Try It Out Here are some suggestions for using a learning log.

- Make a vocabulary list for a subject.
- Make a chart to help you remember facts.
- Make a graph to show comparisons you have learned.
- Draw pictures to show ideas.
- Read a chapter of a book and take notes on the main ideas.

Keeping a Writer's Notebook

A **writer's notebook** is a place to keep ideas for your writing. Keep a list of words you like and notes to use for stories, essays, and poems. Then use your writer's notebook whenever you have a writing assignment. Pages from one student's notebook are shown below.

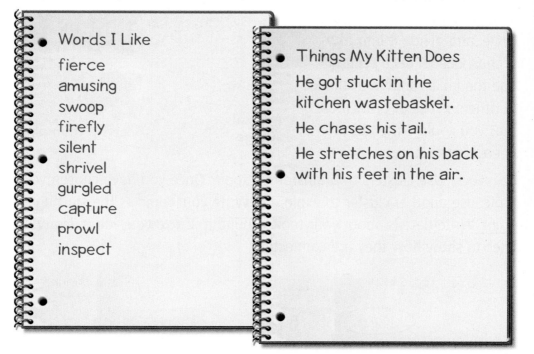

Words I Like
- fierce
- amusing
- swoop
- firefly
- silent
- shrivel
- gurgled
- capture
- prowl
- inspect

Things My Kitten Does
He got stuck in the kitchen wastebasket.
He chases his tail.
He stretches on his back with his feet in the air.

Jotting down notes about interesting experiences will come in handy later. You can use them when you need an idea for a writing assignment.

Try It Out Start your own writer's notebook. Try some of these suggestions.

- Write down funny things people say.
- Write details about people you know.
- Describe a place during a certain season or time of day.
- Describe something good or bad that happened recently.
- List things you wish would happen.

Graphic Organizers

Are you stuck for an idea to write about? Are you confused about how to organize your ideas? These graphic organizers can help!

Idea Wheels Use an idea wheel to help you think of ideas to write about. Draw a circle, and divide it into four sections. Label each section. Use the labels shown or think of others. Write or draw ideas that you could write about in each section.

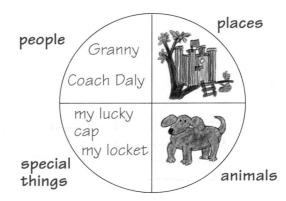

Clusters Use clusters to brainstorm a topic. Once you have chosen your topic, use another cluster to explore it. Write your topic as the starting point. Write details about your topic around it. Circle your ideas. Draw lines to show how they are connected.

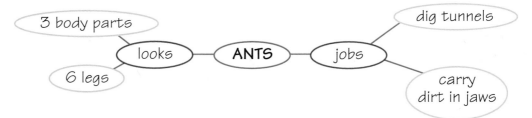

Idea Rakes Is your idea too big to write about in one paper? Use an idea rake to break it into smaller parts. Write your big idea at the top of the rake. Then write three smaller parts of that idea below it. Choose one small part to write about.

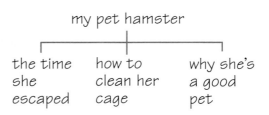

Planning Charts Use this chart for all of your writing. Fill it in before you write. Think about it while you write. Check it again after you write. Did you stick to your purpose? Did you write something your audience will enjoy?

My Topic _____

Purpose	Audience
Circle one. • to tell a real story • to tell a made-up story • to describe a person, place, or thing • to explain how to do something • to find something out • to give an opinion • to ask something • other _____ _____ _____	*Write answers to these questions.* 1. Who will read this? _____ 2. What do they already know about my topic? _____ 3. What do I want them to know? _____ 4. What part of my topic would interest them most? _____

Sense Charts Sense charts can help you remember details. Write your subject at the top of the chart. Try to list details for each of the five senses in separate columns. You may write more details in one column than another. You may leave a column blank if it does not apply.

Making Pizza

👁	👂	✋	👄	👃
tossing the pie	oven timer	squishy dough	hot and delicious	burning crust

Writer's Tools

Graphic Organizers *continued*

T-charts You can list details about two people, places, or things in a T-chart. Draw a large *T*. Write your two subjects at the top. Write details about each subject in the columns below it. You may want to match the information in the columns.

my brother	my sister
likes puzzles	likes video games
has a goldfish	wants a potbellied pig
plays outside	goes to the mall

Tree Charts Use a tree chart to show a main idea and its details. Write the main idea on the trunk. Write the details on the branches. Add as many branches as you need.

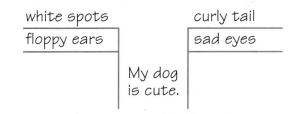

white spots
floppy ears
curly tail
sad eyes
My dog is cute.

Step Charts Make a step chart when you are writing instructions. List materials in the top section. Write each step in order in the left column. Include useful details in the right column.

Materials:_____

Steps	Details
Step 1:	
Step 2:	
Step 3:	
Step 4:	
Step 5:	

KWS Charts Before you begin your research report, write what you already **know** about your topic. Then write five questions you **want** to answer in your report. List **sources** you could use to find the answers.

Thomas Edison

What I Know	What I Want to Learn	Possible Sources
He was an inventor. He lived long ago.	Was he American? When did he live? What did he invent? What was his favorite invention? Did he get rich?	books about inventors, encyclopedias, the science museum, Internet articles

Time Lines A time line can help you remember when things happened. Draw an arrow. Write or draw events along it in order from left to right. Add dates for each event.

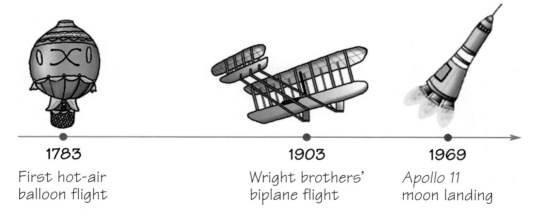

1783	1903	1969
First hot-air balloon flight	Wright brothers' biplane flight	Apollo 11 moon landing

Writer's Tools

Venn Diagrams Use a Venn diagram to compare two subjects. How are they alike? How are they different? List the differences in the outer parts of the circles. List the similarities where the circles overlap.

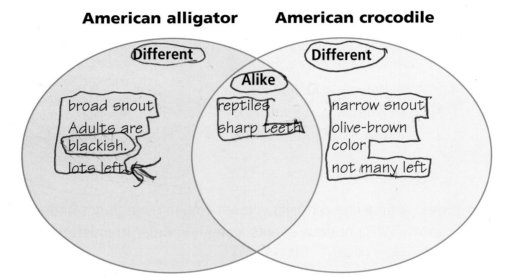

American alligator   **American crocodile**

Different
Alike
Different

broad snout
Adults are
blackish.
lots left

reptiles
sharp teeth

narrow snout
olive-brown
color
not many left

Story Maps Plan your story by making notes in a story map. In the **Beginning** box, tell where your story takes place. Name the main characters. Say what problem your story is about. In the **Middle** box, list what happens in order. In the **End** box, tell how your story works out.

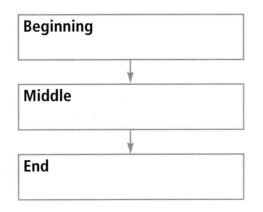

Beginning

Middle

End

Abbreviations

An abbreviation is a short way to write a word. Most abbreviations begin with a capital letter and end with a period.

Titles	Mr. Juan Albino	Ms. Leslie Clark
	Mrs. Frances Wong	Dr. Janice Dodds
	Note: *Miss* is not an abbreviation and does not end with a period.	
Days of the week	Sun. *(Sunday)*	Thurs. *(Thursday)*
	Mon. *(Monday)*	Fri. *(Friday)*
	Tues. *(Tuesday)*	Sat. *(Saturday)*
	Wed. *(Wednesday)*	
Months of the year	Jan. *(January)*	Sept. *(September)*
	Feb. *(February)*	Oct. *(October)*
	Mar. *(March)*	Nov. *(November)*
	Apr. *(April)*	Dec. *(December)*
	Aug. *(August)*	
	Note: *May, June,* and *July* are not abbreviated.	

Quotations

Quotation marks with commas and end marks	Quotation marks (" ") set off someone's exact words from the rest of the sentence. The first word of a quotation always begins with a capital letter. Use commas to separate the quotations from the rest of the sentence. Put the end mark before the last quotation mark. If the quotation does not end the sentence, use a comma before the last quotation mark.
	Linda said, "We don't know where Donald went."
	"Welcome to Chicago," announced the pilot.
	"What," asked Peggy, "should I do next?"

more ▶

Capitalization

Rules for capitalization	**Every sentence begins with a capital letter.** What a pretty color the roses are!
	The pronoun *I* is always a capital letter. What should I do next?
	Begin each important word in the names of particular persons, places, or things (proper nouns) with a capital letter. George Herman Ruth　　　Liberty Bell New Jersey
	Titles or their abbreviations when used with a person's name begin with a capital letter. Doctor Lin　　　　　　Mrs. Garcia
	Begin the names of days, months, and holidays with a capital letter. Labor Day is on the first Monday in September.
	The first and last words and all important words in the titles of books begin with a capital letter. Titles of books are underlined or italicized. The Hill and the Rock　　　The Bashful Tiger

Punctuation

End marks	**A period (.) ends a statement or a command. A question mark (?) follows a question. An exclamation point (!) follows an exclamation.** The scissors are on my desk. *(statement)* Look up the spelling of that word. *(command)* How is the word spelled? *(question)* This is your best poem so far! *(exclamation)*

Punctuation *continued*

Apostrophe	**Add an apostrophe (') and *s* to a singular noun to make it show ownership.**
	doctor**'s** father**'s** grandmother**'s** family**'s**
	For a plural noun that ends in *s*, add just an apostrophe to show ownership.
	sisters**'** Smiths**'** families**'** hound dogs**'**
	Use an apostrophe in contractions in place of missing letters.
	can**'**t (cannot) we**'**re (we are) I**'**m (I am)
Comma	**Use commas to separate a series of three or more words.**
	Rob bought apples**,** peaches**,** and grapes.
	Use commas after *yes, no, well,* and order words when they begin a sentence.
	First**,** set the table. No**,** it is too early.
	Use a comma to separate the month and the day from the year.
	I was born on June 17**,** 1951.
	Use a comma between the names of a city and a state and between the names of a city and a country.
	Chicago**,** Illinois Paris**,** France
	Use a comma after the greeting and after the closing in a letter.
	Dear Uncle Rudolph**,** Your nephew**,**

Capitalization / Punctuation / Usage

more ▶

Guide to Capitalization, Punctuation, and Usage   **H53**

Problem Words

Words	Rules	Examples
its	*Its* is a possessive pronoun.	The dog wagged its tail.
it's	*It's* is a contraction of *it is*.	It's cold today.
their	*Their* means "belonging to them."	Their coats are on the bed.
there	*There* means "at or in that place."	Is Carlos there?
they're	*They're* means "they are" (contraction).	They're going to the store.
two	*Two* is a number.	I bought two shirts.
to	*To* means "toward."	A cat ran to the tree.
too	*Too* means "also" or "more than enough."	Can we go too? I ate too many peas.
your	*Your* is a possessive pronoun.	Are these your glasses?
you're	*You're* means "you are" (contraction).	You're late again!

Adjective and Adverb Usage

Comparing with adjectives	To compare two people, places, or things, add *-er* to most adjectives.
	This plant is taller than the other one.
	To compare three or more people, places, or things, add *-est* to most adjectives.
	This plant is the tallest of the three.
Comparing with adverbs	To compare two actions, add *-er* to most adverbs.
	The clarinet sounded louder than the flute.
	To compare three or more actions, add *-est* to most adverbs.
	The drums sounded loudest of all.

Pronoun Usage

I, me	Use *I* as the subject of a sentence. Use *me* as an object pronoun. Name yourself last when you talk about another person and yourself.
	Beth and I will leave for school soon. Give the papers to Ron and me.
Subject and object pronouns	Use a subject pronoun as the subject of a sentence. He wrote many works for the piano. **Use an object pronoun after an action verb and after words like *to, for,* and *with*.** Let's share these bananas with her.
Possessive pronouns	Use possessive pronouns to show ownership. My dog is in the yard.

Verb Usage

Agreement: verbs in the present	Add *s* to a verb in the present when the noun or pronoun in the subject is singular. The child plays with the toy.
	Do not add *s* to a verb in the present when the noun or pronoun is plural. Some children run to the swings.
The verb *be*	Use *am, is,* and *are* to show present time. We are ready to play.
	Use *was* and *were* to show past time. The line was long. We were tired.
Helping verbs	Use *has* with a singular noun in the subject and with *he, she,* or *it*. Use *have* with plural nouns and with *I, you, we,* or *they*. Kip has phoned. I have taken a message.

Words Often Misspelled

You use many of the words on this page in writing. Check this list if you cannot think of the spelling of the word. The words are in *ABC* order.

A

again
a lot
always
am
and
another
anyone
anyway
around

B

beautiful
because
before
brought

C

cannot
can't
caught
coming
could

D

didn't
different
don't
down

E

every

F

family
favorite
for
found
friend
from

G

getting
girl
goes
going

H

have
here
his
how

I

I'll
I'm
into
it
its
it's

K

knew
know

L

letter
like
little

M

might
morning
mother
myself

N

now

O

off
other
our

P

people
pretty

R

really
right

S

said
school
some
started
sure
swimming

T

than
that's
their
them
then
there

they
thought
through
to
today
too
tried
two

V

very

W

want
was
where
whole
would
write

Y

you
your
you're

Spelling Guidelines

1. The short vowel sound in a word is usually spelled with just one letter: **a**, **e**, **i**, **o**, or **u**.

last	sand	best	chip	lot	club
flag	send	left	bit	pop	luck

2. Long vowel sounds may be spelled vowel-consonant-**e**.

s**a**m**e**	m**a**d**e**	m**i**n**e**	sm**i**l**e**	n**o**t**e**	h**o**m**e**

3. The long **a** sound may be spelled **ai** or **ay**. The long **e** sound may be spelled **ee** or **ea**.

p**ai**nt	tr**ay**	s**ee**m	sn**ea**k	r**ea**l
ch**ai**n	h**ay**	f**ee**l	tr**ea**t	

4. The long **o** sound may be spelled **o**, **oa**, or **ow**. The long **i** sound may be spelled **i**, **ie**, or **igh**.

s**o**ld	s**oa**p	bl**ow**	t**ie**	t**igh**t
c**oa**ch	**ow**n	k**i**nd	br**igh**t	

5. The vowel sound in **town** or **found** may be spelled **ow** or **ou**.

n**ow**	cr**ow**d	h**ow**	m**ou**th	l**ou**d	c**ou**nt

6. The vowel sound in **draw** or **walk** may be spelled **aw** or **a** before **l**.

str**aw**	cr**aw**l	s**aw**	t**a**lk	sm**a**ll	c**a**ll

7. The letters **wr**, **kn**, and **tch** sometimes spell one consonant sound.

wrap	**wr**ong	**kn**ow	**kn**ee	scra**tch**	pi**tch**

8. The vowel + **r** sounds in **harm**, **corn**, or **near** may be spelled **ar**, **or**, or **ear**.

smart	March	forty	year	fear
harm	storm	sport	clear	

9. The vowel + **r** sounds in **clerk**, **dirt**, or **burn** may be spelled **er**, **ir**, or **ur**.

serve	nerve	shirt	nurse	hurt
herd	thirsty	bird	church	

10. The vowel sound in **joy** or **oil** may be spelled **oy** or **oi**.

toy	boy	point	join	coin	broil

11. The consonant sound in **jeans** or **page** may be spelled **j** or **g**.

just	jump	gym	gentle	stage	huge

12. The sound of the vowel + **r** in **chair** or **care** may be spelled **air** or **are**.

hair	air	pair	bare	dare
fair	stair	scare	rare	

13. Two words that sound alike but have different spellings and meanings are called **homophones**.

knew new	our hour	pale pail

14. When a word ends with **e**, drop the **e** before adding **-ed** or **-ing**. When a word ends with one vowel followed by one consonant, double the consonant.

car**ed**	lik**ing**	chas**ed**	ste**pping**	tri**pping**	ta**pping**
wav**ing**	bak**ed**	jok**ing**	do**tted**	pa**tted**	gri**nned**

15. The vowel sound in **spoon** or **chew** may be spelled **oo** or **ew**.

| r**oo**t | ball**oo**n | t**oo**th | st**ew** | fl**ew** | dr**ew** |

16. A **prefix** is a word part added to the beginning of a word. A **suffix** is a word part added at the end of a word.

| **re**turn | **un**common | use**ful** | slow**ly** | help**er** |
| **re**join | thank**ful** | sad**ly** | teach**er** | |

17. When a word ends with a consonant and **y**, change the **y** to **i** and add **-es** or **-ed**.

| stor**ies** | famil**ies** | bab**ies** | hurr**ied** | stud**ied** |
| cherr**ies** | pupp**ies** | cr**ied** | dr**ied** | |

18. The spelling of the final **er** or **le** in a two-syllable word must be remembered.

| und**er** | lett**er** | gent**le** | unc**le** | ab**le** |
| summ**er** | matt**er** | app**le** | hand**le** | |

19. The consonant sound in **cent** or **space** may be spelled **c** or **s**.

| ni**c**e | **c**ity | pri**c**e | **c**enter | ba**s**e | **c**ase |

How to Use the Thesaurus Plus

Why do you use a thesaurus? One reason is to make your writing more exact. Suppose you wrote the following sentence:

I like my teacher.

Is *like* the most exact word you can use? To find out, use your Thesaurus Plus.

Look up Your Word Turn to the Thesaurus Plus Index on page H64. You will find

like, *v.*

Because *like* is in blue type, you can look up *like* in the Thesaurus Plus.

Use Your Thesaurus The main entries in the thesaurus are listed in alphabetical order. Turn to *like*.

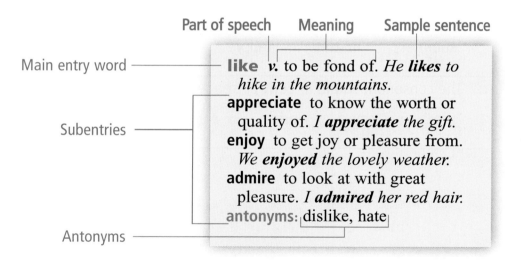

Part of speech   Meaning   Sample sentence

Main entry word —— **like** *v.* to be fond of. *He **likes** to hike in the mountains.*

Subentries —— **appreciate** to know the worth or quality of. *I **appreciate** the gift.*
enjoy to get joy or pleasure from. *We **enjoyed** the lovely weather.*
admire to look at with great pleasure. *I **admired** her red hair.*

Antonyms —— **antonyms:** dislike, hate

Which word might better tell how you feel about the teacher in the sentence above? Perhaps you chose *admire*.

Other Index Entries There are two other types of entries in your Thesaurus Plus Index.

❶ The slanted type means you can find other words for *tangy* if you look under *hot.*

❷ The regular type tells you that *tear* is the opposite of *repair.*

> *tan* brown, *adj.*
> *tangy* hot, *adj.*
> *tart* sour, *adj.*
> *task* job, *n.*
> tear repair, *v.*

Practice

A. Write each word. Look it up in the Thesaurus Plus Index. Then write the main entry word for each word.

1. kind
2. project
3. gold
4. last

B. Use the Thesaurus Plus to choose a more exact word to replace each underlined word. Rewrite the sentence, using the new word.

5. Our puppy is very <u>active</u>.
6. When he barks, he's really quite <u>loud</u>.
7. He sounds like he's <u>laughing</u>.
8. His coat is <u>brown</u>, like a nut.
9. I really <u>like</u> taking him for walks.
10. His fur is very <u>soft</u>.
11. Sometimes he is as <u>quiet</u> as a mouse.
12. Soon he's ready to <u>make</u> a fuss.
13. He's so <u>funny</u>!
14. We had a <u>party</u> for his birthday.

Thesaurus Plus Index

disappointed
    unhappy, *adj.*
discouraged
    unhappy, *adj.*
dislike like, *v.*
disturbing quiet,
    adj.
divide gather, *v.*
divide join, *v.*
divide mix, *v.*
downhearted
    unhappy, *adj.*
drop lift, *v.*
dull interesting, *adj.*

E

eager excited, *adj.*
employment job, *n.*
end, *v.*
endanger save, *v.*
energetic active, *adj.*
enjoy like, *v.*
enjoyable nice, *adj.*
enormous big, *adj.*
entertaining
    interesting, *adj.*
enthusiastic excited,
    adj.
errand job, *n.*
evil good, *adj.*
excellent nice, *adj.*
excited, *adj.*
experiment try, *v.*

F

facts information, *n.*
false real, *adj.*

familiar strange, *adj.*
fascinating
    interesting, *adj.*
fasten, *v.*
fasten join, *v.*
fearful brave, *adj.*
finally last, *adv.*
fine good, *adj.*
fine great, *adj.*
fine nice, *adj.*
finish end, *v.*
first last, *adv.*
form make, *v.*
free catch, *v.*
freezing cold, *adj.*
fresh new, *adj.*
friendly nice, *adj.*
frighten, *v.*
frightened brave, *adj.*
frosty cold, *adj.*
frown laugh, *v.*
frozen cold, *adj.*
fry cook, *v.*
funny, *adj.*

G

gather, *v.*
gaze look, *v.*
genuine real, *adj.*
get, *v.*
giggle laugh, *v.*
glad happy, *adj.*
glad sad, *adj.*
glad unhappy, *adj.*
glance look, *v.*
gleeful unhappy, *adj.*
gloomy sad, *adj.*
gloomy unhappy, *adj.*

gloomy happy, *adj.*
glum unhappy, *adj.*
gold yellow, *adj.*
good, *adj.*
goofy funny, *adj.*
grave funny, *adj.*
great, *adj.*
great nice, *adj.*
green, *adj.*
grieving unhappy,
    adj.
grown-up child, *n.*
guffaw laugh, *v.*

H

happen, *v.*
happy, *adj.*
hate like, *v.*
hazard danger, *n.*
heartbroken
    unhappy, *adj.*
heartless nice, *adj.*
heartsick unhappy,
    adj.
hike walk, *v.*
hilarious funny, *adj.*
hobble walk, *v.*
hot, *adj.*
hot cold, *adj.*
howl laugh, *v.*
huge big, *adj.*
humorous funny, *adj.*

Thesaurus Plus

Thesaurus Plus

protection danger, *n.*
proud, *adj.*
put, *v.*

Q

quiet, *adj.*
quiet loud, *adj.*
quit end, *v.*

R

race run, *v.*
raise lift, *v.*
ramble walk, *v.*
range walk, *v.*
rare unusual, *adj.*
raw cold, *adj.*
real, *adj.*
recover save, *v.*
red, *adj.*
regular unusual, *adj.*
release catch, *v.*
repair, *v.*
rescue save, *v.*
restless quiet, *adj.*
risk danger, *n.*
roam walk, *v.*
roar laugh, *v.*
roaring loud, *adj.*
roasting cold, *adj.*
rose red, *adj.*
ruby red, *adj.*
rude thoughtful, *adj.*
run, *v.*
rust brown, *adj.*

S

sad, *adj.*
safeguard danger, *n.*
sample try, *v.*
satisfied proud, *adj.*
save, *v.*
say, *v.*
scare frighten, *v.*
scarlet red, *adj.*
scatter gather, *v.*
scent smell, *n.*
seal fasten, *v.*
see look, *v.*
selfish thoughtful, *adj.*
separate join, *v.*
separate mix, *v.*
serious funny, *adj.*
set put, *v.*
sharp hot, *adj.*
shuffle walk, *v.*
silent quiet, *v.*
silly funny, *adj.*
slapstick funny, *adj.*
slow active, *adj.*
small big, *adj.*
smell, *n.*
sneak walk, *v.*
snicker laugh, *v.*
snort laugh, *v.*
sober funny, *adj.*
soft, *adj.*
soft loud, *adj.*
solemn funny, *adj.*
solid soft, *adj.*
soothe frighten, *v.*
sorrowful unhappy, *adj.*

sorry unhappy, *adj.*
sour, *adj.*
speak say, *v.*
spicy hot, *adj.*
spin twist, *v.*
stagger walk, *v.*
stale new, *adj.*
stalk walk, *v.*
stare look, *v.*
start end, *v.*
state say, *v.*
stiff soft, *adj.*
still quiet, *adj.*
stir mix, *v.*
stop end, *v.*
strange, *adj.*
stride walk, *v.*
stroll walk, *v.*
stumble walk, *v.*
superb great, *adj.*
superb nice, *adj.*
sweet nice, *adj.*
sweet sour, *adj.*

T

take place happen, *v.*
tan brown, *adj.*
tangy hot, *adj.*
tart sour, *adj.*
task job, *n.*
tear repair, *v.*
tell say, *v.*
tender soft, *adj.*
terrible great, *adj.*
terrible nice, *adj.*
terrific great, *adj.*
terrify frighten, *v.*
test try, *v.*

more ▶

Thesaurus Plus

A

active *adj.* moving about; busy. *He needed a rest after his **active** day.*

energetic full of strength and pep. *My **energetic** aunt exercises often.*

lively full of life and cheer. *The **lively** music kept us dancing.*

antonyms: lazy, slow

B

big *adj.* of great size. *It is easy to get lost in a **big** city.*

large bigger than average. *The **large** yard gave the children plenty of room to play.*

enormous very big. *A small boy fed that **enormous** elephant!*

huge giant-sized. *It took days to climb the **huge** mountain.*

tremendous great in size or amount. *A **tremendous** wind blew the roof off his house.*

antonyms: little, small, tiny

blue *adj.* having the color of a clear sky. *On a sunny day, the **blue** boat matched the sky.*

navy of a very dark blue. *The police wore **navy** uniforms.*

aqua of a greenish blue color. *Closer to shore, the water has a lovely **aqua** color.*

brave *adj.* having or showing courage. *The **brave** woman risked her life to help us.*

bold willing to take chances. *The **bold** man spoke out against the cruel leader.*

daring brave and adventurous. *The **daring** explorers set off into the unknown jungle.*

antonyms: cowardly, afraid, frightened, fearful

brown *adj.* of the color of wood or soil. *The leaves on the ground had all turned **brown**.*

tan of a yellowish brown. *The fawn was **tan** with white spots.*

beige of a pale brown. *The **beige** cottages matched the sand.*

chestnut of a deep reddish brown. *His **chestnut** hair glistened.*

rust of a very red brown. *The maple leaves turned **rust** in fall.*

C

catch *v.* to get hold of something that is moving. *I reached out to **catch** the ball.*

capture to take by force. *They **captured** and jailed the thief.*

trap to catch by closing off any way of escaping. *He **trapped** the air inside the balloon.*

antonyms: free, release

child *n.* a young boy or girl. *Marilyn is an only **child**.*

youth young people in general. *The **youth** of today are willing to work hard.*

more ▶

youngster a young person or child. *The **youngsters** sang well.*
tot a small child. *The **tots** raced around the playground.*
antonyms: adult, grown-up

How **Cold** Was It?
cold *adj.* without heat.

1. a little cold: *cool, crisp, fresh, brisk*
2. quite cold: *chilly, wintry, frosty, raw, nippy*
3. very cold: *icy, frozen, freezing, bitter*

antonyms: toasty, hot, roasting

cook *v.* to prepare food for eating by using heat. *We **cooked** corn.*
bake to cook in an oven with steady, dry heat. *The oatmeal bread **baked** in the oven.*
fry to cook in hot oil or fat. *The chicken **fried** to a golden brown.*
broil to cook under or over heat. *I **broiled** fish on the grill.*

— D —

danger *n.* the chance of harm. *The pioneers feared the **dangers** of the wild forest and the winters.*

hazard something that may cause injury or harm. *An old electric cord can be a fire **hazard**.*
risk the chance of trouble. *I **risked** my life to save the injured cat.*
antonyms: protection, safeguard

— E —

end *v.* to bring to a close. *The president **ended** the meeting.*
finish to reach the end of. *He **finished** the book.*
stop to cut off an action. *The fence **stopped** me from entering.*
complete to make or do entirely. *I **completed** the work in a day.*
quit to give up. *If you **quit** trying, you will never win.*
antonyms: begin, continue, start

excited *adj.* stirred up. ***Excited** teenagers waved to the rock star.*
eager filled with desire. *The **eager** crowd ran toward the exit.*
enthusiastic showing strong interest and liking. *The **enthusiastic** listeners clapped.*
antonyms: bored, uninterested

— F —

fasten *v.* to attach firmly. *She **fastened** the tag to her shirt.*
tie to fasten with a rope, string, or similar material. *She **tied** back her hair with a ribbon.*
bind to hold together. *Birds **bind** their nests with mud.*

Thesaurus Plus

close to shut. *Please close the lid.*

seal to close tightly with glue, wax, or other hardening material. *He sealed the letter so that no one would read it.*

antonyms: loosen, undo

frighten *v.* to make or become afraid. *The thunder and lightning frightened us.*

scare to startle or shock. *A door slammed, scaring the lazy cat.*

alarm to make suddenly very worried. *The storm alarmed me.*

terrify to frighten greatly. *The forest fire terrified the animals.*

antonyms: calm, soothe

Word Bank

funny *adj.* causing smiles or laughter; amusing.

merry	joking
playful	comical
jesting	silly
laughable	humorous
hilarious	joshing
goofy	amusing
jolly	witty
slapstick	

antonyms: serious, sober, grave, solemn, mournful

G

gather *v.* to bring together in one place. *He gathered a bunch of dandelions from the field.*

compile to put together into a single list or collection. *They compiled cards to make a set.*

assemble to put together the parts of. *The directions told how to assemble the parts.*

antonyms: divide, scatter

get *v.* to go after; fetch. *I will get the broom from the closet.*

collect to get payment of. *"Did you collect the money that he owes you?" Frank asked.*

good *adj.* right, or as it ought to be. *A rainy day is a good time for doing chores.*

fine very good; excellent. *The teacher gave her a high grade for her fine work.*

proper following social rules. *It is proper to say thank you for a gift.*

appropriate suitable. *The shoes looked great, but they were not appropriate for hiking.*

decent honest and thoughtful. *Returning the lost ring was a decent thing to do.*

antonyms: bad, evil, unsuitable

great *adj.* important; outstanding. *The statue in the park honored a great leader.*

terrific very good; very pleasing. *I was thrilled with my terrific new radio.*

fine enjoyable. *Fine weather helped make the picnic a success.*

wonderful marvelous. *I thanked them for the wonderful gift.*

superb grand; splendid. *The view from the mountaintop is **superb**.*
antonyms: awful, terrible

green *adj.* having the color of grass. *Some kinds of apples are still **green** when they are ripe.*

olive of a dull yellowish green. *The **olive** tent blended in with the surrounding bushes.*

jade having a deep green color named for a stone that is used for jewelry. *Rubber plants have shiny **jade** leaves.*

— **H** —

happen *v.* to come into being. *When did the flood **happen**?*

take place to come about. *The wedding will **take place** in May.*

occur to come to pass. *How did the accident **occur**?*

happy *adj.* very satisfied. *I was **happy** to hear the good news.*

glad pleased. *"I would be **glad** to help," said Vic.*

cheerful merry; lively. *The **cheerful** song helps him forget his worries.*

joyful showing, feeling, or causing great happiness. *The puppy galloped toward its owner with a **joyful** bark.*

jolly full of fun. *The **jolly** waitress liked making us laugh.*

lighthearted having no cares. *I felt **lighthearted** after I handed in my paper.*
antonyms: gloomy, miserable

hot *adj.* having flavorings that make the mouth feel warm. *Use only a little of that **hot** mustard.*

spicy tasting of pleasant, strong flavorings. *I like chili and other kinds of **spicy** food.*

sharp having a biting taste. ***Sharp** cheese adds zest to crackers.*

tangy pleasantly sharp in taste or smell. *I like the **tangy** smell of freshly picked apples.*
antonyms: mild, bland

— **I** —

information *n.* part of all that is known about something. *Do you have any **information** about Mrs. Lee's accident?*

news information about recent events. *The latest **news** is reported every hour.*

facts information known to be true. *The science book had many **facts** about the planets.*

knowledge understanding. *Her **knowledge** of French made her trip to France more interesting.*

interesting *adj.* getting and holding attention. *The **interesting** display brought many visitors to the new art museum.*

amusing interesting in a light and pleasant way. *Solving the puzzle was an **amusing** pastime.*

entertaining fun to watch, listen to, or take part in. *The movie's dancing was **entertaining**.*

Thesaurus Plus

fascinating very interesting. *She loves a **fascinating** mystery story.*
antonyms: boring, dull

J

Shades of Meaning

job *n.* work.

1. one piece of work: *chore, project, task, errand, assignment*
2. a general word for a person's work: *career, profession, employment, business*
3. a general job title: *position, post, office*

join *v.* to bring or come together. *Let's **join** hands in a circle.*
connect to serve as a way of joining things. *A wire **connects** the brakes with the wheel.*
unite to join in action for a certain purpose. *Neighbors **united** to repair the flood damage.*
fasten to attach firmly. *Please **fasten** all the pages together.*
bind to fasten together as if by tying. ***Bind** your hair with ribbon.*
antonyms: divide, part, separate

L

last *adv.* at the end. *Dessert is usually served **last**.*

finally at the end of a series. ***Finally**, frost the cooled cake.*
antonym: first

Shades of Meaning

laugh *v.* to make sounds in the throat that show amusement.

1. to laugh quietly:
   giggle
   chuckle
   titter
2. to laugh in a mean way:
   snicker
   snort
   cackle
3. to laugh very hard:
   howl
   roar
   guffaw

antonyms: frown, cry, weep

lift *v.* to pick up. *I tried hard to **lift** the heavy box.*
boost to give an upward shove or push. ***Boost** me into the tree.*
raise to move to a higher place. *He **raised** the ladder to the roof.*
antonyms: drop, lower

like *v.* to be fond of. *He **likes** to hike in the mountains.*
appreciate to know the worth or quality of. *I **appreciate** the gift.*
enjoy to get joy or pleasure from. *We **enjoyed** the lovely weather.*
admire to look at with great pleasure. *I **admired** her red hair.*
antonyms: dislike, hate

more ▶

Thesaurus Plus

look *v.* to use one's eyes. *I **looked** for my friend in the crowd.*

see to view. *Did you **see** the Thanksgiving parade?*

glance to look quickly. *He **glanced** at me as he ran by.*

gaze to look steadily and long. *For hours we sat **gazing** at stars.*

stare to look at steadily with wide, unblinking eyes. *She **stared** in wonder at the huge pumpkin.*

loud *adj.* having a high volume of sound. *A **loud** bang woke me up.*

noisy making or filled with loud sounds. *The fireworks are **noisy**.*

booming making a loud, hollow sound. *The **booming** voice of the giant scared the man.*

roaring making a loud, deep sound. *The car's **roaring** engine drowned out the radio.*

antonyms: quiet, soft

—————— M ——————

make *v.* to produce. *My mother bought meat to **make** stew.*

build to make by putting together materials or parts. *Birds **build** nests of mud, twigs, and straw.*

create to bring into being. *She **created** a design with leaves.*

mix *v.* to combine. ***Mix** the peanuts and raisins in a bowl.*

blend to combine completely. *To make the color orange, **blend** red and yellow together.*

stir to mix by using repeated circular motions. ***Stir** the soup to be sure that it heats evenly.*

antonyms: divide, separate

—————— 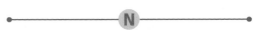 N ——————

new *adj.* having just come into being. *We started a **new** game.*

fresh just made, grown, or gathered. *I love **fresh** tomatoes.*

modern up-to-date. *The office replaced the old typewriters with a more **modern** kind.*

antonyms: old, outdated, stale

Shades of Meaning
nice *adj.*
1. kind: *friendly, sweet, caring, thoughtful, unselfish, understanding*
2. pleasing: *likable, delightful, enjoyable, charming, agreeable*
3. good: *great, fine, wonderful, excellent, superb*
antonyms: mean, cruel, nasty, heartless, unpleasant, disagreeable, bad, awful, terrible

O

orange *adj.* of a reddish yellow color. *The **orange** paint made the room look like a sunset.*

peach of a yellowish pink color named for the fruit. *Her **peach** dress matched the glow in her cheeks.*

carrot of a bright orange color named for the vegetable. *He had hundreds of freckles and short **carrot** hair.*

P

party *n.* a gathering of people for pleasure and fun. *All of her friends came to her birthday **party.***

celebration a party or other gathering for a special occasion. *The **celebration** for the town's hundredth anniversary lasted a week.*

proud *adj.* feeling good about oneself. *Kim was **proud** that she had won the prize.*

pleased feeling enjoyment. *I am **pleased** that you like my hat and scarf.*

satisfied feeling that one's needs have been met. *I wanted to win, but I was **satisfied** to come in second.*

antonym: ashamed

put *v.* to cause to be in a certain place. ***Put** some salt in the soup.*

place to put in a certain position or order. *I **placed** the index cards in alphabetical order.*

lay to put down in a flat or resting position. *He **laid** his coat and hat on the bed.*

set to put on a surface. *Please **set** that box on the table.*

Q

quiet *adj.* having very little noise and activity. *The busy street grew **quiet** after rush hour.*

calm having only smooth, gentle noise and activity. *As the wind died down, the water grew **calm**.*

silent completely without sound. *She listened for footsteps, but the night was **silent**.*

peaceful quiet in a pleasant, relaxing way. *In the **peaceful** meadow, two cows lay in the sun.*

still without any motion. *Keep **still** until I snap your picture.*

antonyms: disturbing, noisy, restless

R

real *adj.* truly existing. *You have a **real** talent for singing!*

actual not imaginary or make-believe. *The toy dog looked like an **actual** poodle.*

genuine not fake. *Is that stone a **genuine** diamond?*

antonyms: fake, false

Thesaurus Plus

Thesaurus Plus

Shades of Red

red *adj.* the color of strawberries.

rose: a deep pinkish red, like that of a red rose

scarlet: a bright orange red, like that of a ripe tomato

ruby: a deep red, like that of the gem called a ruby

crimson: a purplish red, like that of blood

maroon: a dark purplish red, like that of a red plum

cardinal: a deep clear red, like that of the bird called a cardinal

repair *v.* to fix something that is damaged. *Do you think that the shop can repair our TV?*

mend to repair a tear, hole, or crack. *Please mend the hole in my shirt.*

patch to repair by covering with a piece of material. *We patched the hole in the roof with tar paper.*

antonyms: break, tear

run *v.* to move quickly on foot. *I ran inside to answer the phone.*

race to rush at top speed. *As the bus pulled away, she raced to catch it.*

jog to run at a slow, steady speed. *He jogs around the block every day for exercise.*

S

sad *adj.* feeling or causing sorrow. *The teacher's illness was sad news for the class.*

unhappy without joy or pleasure. *She had an unhappy summer.*

gloomy mildly sad. *Losing made the team feel gloomy.*

antonyms: cheerful, glad

save *v.* to keep from danger or harm. *The canned food saved them from going hungry.*

rescue to remove from a dangerous place. *I rescued my cat from the tree.*

recover to get something back; to regain. *The police recovered the lost child and took him home.*

antonyms: endanger, lose

say *v.* to make known or put across in words. *What did your brother say in the letter?*

speak to say with the voice; talk. *The teacher spoke loudly.*

tell to describe. *Teresa told us what happened at the party.*

state to say in a very clear, exact way. *The rule states that dogs are not allowed here.*

smell *n.* what the nose senses. *I love the smell of apple pie.*

scent a light smell. *The woman had left, but the scent of her perfume remained.*

odor a strong smell. *The odor of mothballs clung to the coat.*

soft *adj.* not hard or firm. *The **soft** cheese spread smoothly.*

delicate very easily broken or torn. *A slight tug will snap the **delicate** chain.*

fluffy light and airy. *A puff of wind scattered the **fluffy** feathers.*

antonyms: solid, stiff

sour *adj.* having an acid taste. *Lemons are too **sour** to eat.*

tart sharp in taste. *I like **tart** apples better than sweet ones.*

bitter having a strong, unpleasant taste. *He hated to take the **bitter** medicine.*

antonym: sweet

strange *adj.* not ordinary. *The **strange** look on her face made me wonder what happened.*

odd somewhat out of the ordinary. *He had an **odd** habit of carrying an umbrella even on sunny days.*

weird strange in a frightening way. *A **weird** noise made us jump out of our chairs.*

antonyms: familiar, normal

————————— T —————————

thoughtful *adj.* caring about the feelings of others. *You were **thoughtful** to remember me!*

kind showing goodness, generosity, or sympathy. *It was **kind** to share your lunch.*

considerate helpful. *A **considerate** girl held the door for me.*

antonyms: mean, rude, selfish

trip *n.* a period of time spent going from one place to another. *When are you leaving for your **trip** to Canada?*

journey a long trip. *It took the pioneers months to make the **journey** across the plains.*

outing a short outdoor trip for pleasure. *We are going to the park for a family **outing**.*

try *v.* to put to use for the purpose of judging. *If you like apples, **try** these.*

test to use in order to discover any problems. ***Test** the brakes and the horn to be sure that they work.*

sample to test by trying a small part. *Before you serve a dish to your guests, **sample** it.*

experiment to do a number of tests to find out or prove something. *She **experimented** to find out which colors looked best in her design.*

tug *v.* to pull at strongly. *I **tugged** hard at the door handle.*

pull to apply force to draw toward the force. *The huskies **pulled** the sled.*

yank to pull with a sudden, sharp movement. *Sue **yanked** the doll from her sister's hand.*

twist *v.* to move in a winding path. *The road **twisted** through the mountains.*

turn to move around a center. ***Turn** the cap to the right to open it.*

Thesaurus Plus

twirl to cause to move quickly around a center. *The cowhand **twirled** the lasso.*

spin to move very quickly and continuously around a center. *The ice skater **spun** like a top.*

U

How Unhappy Were You?

unhappy *adj.* sad.

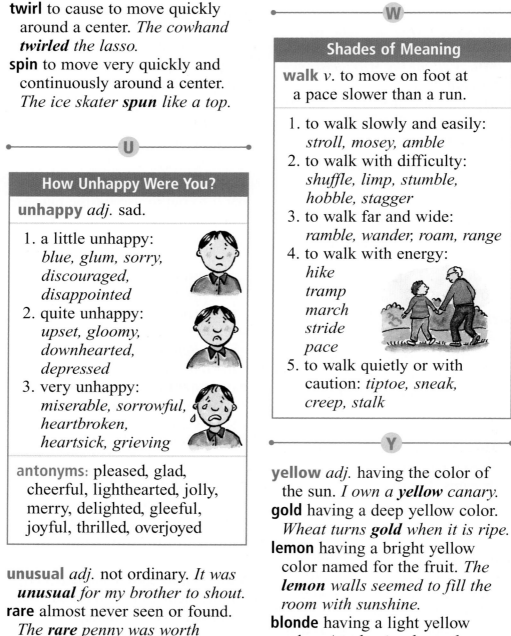

1. a little unhappy: *blue, glum, sorry, discouraged, disappointed*
2. quite unhappy: *upset, gloomy, downhearted, depressed*
3. very unhappy: *miserable, sorrowful, heartbroken, heartsick, grieving*

antonyms: pleased, glad, cheerful, lighthearted, jolly, merry, delighted, gleeful, joyful, thrilled, overjoyed

unusual *adj.* not ordinary. *It was **unusual** for my brother to shout.*

rare almost never seen or found. *The **rare** penny was worth thousands of dollars.*

unique being the only one of its kind. *Most dancers dressed alike, but Anne's costume was **unique**.*

antonyms: ordinary, regular

W

Shades of Meaning

walk *v.* to move on foot at a pace slower than a run.

1. to walk slowly and easily: *stroll, mosey, amble*
2. to walk with difficulty: *shuffle, limp, stumble, hobble, stagger*
3. to walk far and wide: *ramble, wander, roam, range*
4. to walk with energy: *hike tramp march stride pace*
5. to walk quietly or with caution: *tiptoe, sneak, creep, stalk*

Y

yellow *adj.* having the color of the sun. *I own a **yellow** canary.*

gold having a deep yellow color. *Wheat turns **gold** when it is ripe.*

lemon having a bright yellow color named for the fruit. *The **lemon** walls seemed to fill the room with sunshine.*

blonde having a light yellow color. *A palomino horse has a **blonde** mane and tail.*

mustard having a dark brownish yellow color named for the food. *Are your **mustard** pants made of khaki or cotton?*

Index

Index *continued*

Communication *continued*
electronic, 316–317,
377–378, 446–447,
H41–H43
nonverbal, 314–315
oral presentations, 285,
352, 377–378,
H41–H43
persuasive tactics in,
446–447
producing, 282–283,
310–313, 377–378
skills, 1–6, 285, 314–315,
316–317, 352–353,
379, 420–421, H4,
H5–H6, H7–H8,
H9–H10
See also Composition
using technology for,
377–378, H33,
H39–H40
visual, 353, 420–421,
H41–H43
See also Discussions;
Listening; Media;
Speaking
Comparison and contrast,
16, 150–151, 346–351
Compass rose, H25
Composition
classificatory, 398–409
comparison and contrast,
346–351
complete sentences,
32–33, 34–35, 46–47,
49
elaborated sentences, 17,
34–35, 47, 66, 146,
156, 277, 304–305,
340, 341, 372, 373,
406, 407, 441
evaluating, 275, 303, 339,
371, 405, 439
modes of
descriptive, 9–11, 13,
15, 17, 19, 21, 23, 25,

27, 41, 65, 119, 143,
151, 188, 219, 225,
229
expository, 33, 39, 45,
70, 73, 101, 103, 109,
113, 117, 121, 123,
145, 149, 151, 155,
183, 187, 189, 191,
197, 320–325, 327,
345, 346–347,
348–351, 364–365,
382–411, 412–413
expressive, 37, 39, 61,
63, 69, 75, 77, 105,
107, 115, 159, 179,
185, 187, 215, 231,
282–284, 412–413
narrative, 37, 43, 61,
63, 99, 153, 159,
189, 191, 195, 215,
217, 223, 253–257,
259–263, 264,
265–268, 269–279,
282–284, 297–309,
310–312, 313
persuasive, 48, 63, 71,
75, 143, 179, 229,
231, 423–426, 427,
428–431, 432–445
paragraph, 63, 189,
250–251, 253–257,
318–319, 321–325,
380–381, 383–387
purposes for writing
to compare/contrast,
113, 151, 219,
346–351
to create, 61, 69, 105,
159, 185, 187, 215,
227
deciding on, 269, 297,
334, 364, 432
to describe, 13, 41, 65,
119, 143, 225, 229
to entertain, 310–313
to explain, 103, 145,

183, 189, 334, 346
to express, 37, 115, 217
to influence, 432
to inform, 33, 39, 70,
101, 109, 117, 121,
149, 155, 191, 197,
321, 364
to narrate, 43, 99, 153,
195, 223, 253, 269,
297
to persuade, 63, 71, 75,
179, 398, 432
to record ideas and
reflections, 77, 107,
279, 307, 343, 375,
409, 443, H44
to summarize, 188
steps in writing
drafting, 18, 19,
272–274, 301–302,
337–338, 369–370,
403–404, 437–438
prewriting, 12, 13–17,
269–271, 297–300,
334–336, 364–368,
398–402, 432–436
proofreading, 24, 25,
278, 306, 342, 374,
408, 442
publishing, 26, 27, 279,
307, 343, 375, 409,
443
reflecting, 26, 279, 307,
343, 375, 409, 443
revising, 20, 21–23,
276–277, 304–305,
340–341, 372–373,
406–407, 440–441
types of
ad, 48, 71, 143, 229,
231
article, 117
book report, 413
book summaries, 188
caption, 65
cartoon strip, 231

Index

Index

Index *continued*

Index

Acknowledgments *continued*

From *Mrs. Mack* by Patricia Polacco. Copyright ©1998 by Patricia Polacco. Reprinted by permission of Philomel Books, a division of Penguin Putnam Inc.

From *An Octopus Is Amazing* by Patricia Lauber. Text copyright ©1990 by Patricia G. Lauber. Used by permission of HarperCollins Publishers.

Poetry

"Open Hydrant" by Marci Ridlon. Copyright ©1983 by Marci Ridlon. Used with permission of the author.

"The Star" by Jane Taylor.

"The Toad" originally published as "Los sapos" by José Juan Tablada. English translation copyright ©1994 by Eliot Weinberger. Reprinted by permission of Eliot Weinberger.

"The Whales off Wales" by X. J. Kennedy first published in *One Winter Night in August and Other Nonsense Jingles.* Copyright ©1975 by X. J. Kennedy. Published by Atheneum Books, a division of Simon & Schuster Books for Young Readers. Reprinted by permission of Curtis Brown, Ltd.

Book Report

Nights of the Pufflings by Bruce McMillan. Jacket photographs ©1995 by Bruce McMillan. Reprinted by permission of Houghton Mifflin Company. All rights reserved.

Student Handbook

Definitions of "caribou," "carnation," "collar," "collarbone," "croquet," "fork," "month," "monthly" "moon," "moonbeam," "moonlight" "moonlit" and "squash" from *The American Heritage® Children's Dictionary* by the Editors of the American Heritage® Dictionaries. Copyright ©1998 by Houghton Mifflin Company. Reproduced by permission of *The American Heritage® Children's Dictionary.*

Getting Started: Listening

BATS: NIGHT FLIERS by Betsy Maestro, illustrated by Giulio Maestro. Illustrations copyright ©1994 by Giulio Maestro. Reprinted by permission of Scholastic Inc.

IN MY MOMMA'S KITCHEN by Jerdine Nolen, illustrated by Colin Bootman. Illustrations copyright ©1999 by Colin Bootman. Used by permission of HarperCollins Publishers.

One Minute Warm-up

3/1 *Dogs* by Gail Gibbons, published by Holiday House, 1996. Used by permission.

3/1 *Iguana Beach* by Kristine Franklin, illustrated by Lori Lohstoeter. Illustrations copyright ©1997 by Lori Lohstoeter. Reprinted by permission of Random House Children's Books, a division of Random House, Inc.

3/2 *Big-Top Circus* by Neil Johnson, published by Dial Books for Young Readers, 1995. Used by permission.

3/2 *Martin's Mice* by Dick King-Smith, illustrated by Jez Alborough. Illustrations copyright ©1988 by Jez Alborough. Reprinted by permission of Random House Children's Books, a division of Random House, Inc.

3/2 *Mufaro's Beautiful Daughters* by John Steptoe, published by Lothrop, Lee & Shepard Books, 1987. Used by permission.

3/2 *Pet Parade* by Patricia Reilly Giff, illustrated by Blanche Sims. Text copyright ©1996 by Patricia Reilly Giff. Illustrations copyright ©1996 by Blanche Sims. Used by permission of Random House Children's Books, a division of Random House, Inc.

3/2 *When Jo Louis Won the Title* by Belinda Rochelle, illustrated by Larry Johnson, published by Houghton Mifflin Company, 1994. Used by permission.

3/3 *Hooray, A Piñata!* by Elisa Kleven, published by Dutton Children's Books, 1996. Used by permission.

Acknowledgments *continued*

3/3 *River Day* by Jane B. Mason, illustrated by Henri Sorensen. Text copyright ©1994 by Jane B. Mason. Illustrations copyright ©1994 by Henri Sorensen. Reprinted with the permission of Simon & Schuster Books for Young Readers, an imprint of Simon & Schuster Children's Publishing Division.

3/3 *Striking It Rich: The Story of the California Gold Rush* by Stephen Krensky, illustrated by Anna DiVito. Text copyright ©1996 by Stephen Krensky. Illustrations copyright ©1996 by Anna DiVito. Reprinted with the permission of Simon & Schuster Books for Young Readers, an imprint of Simon & Schuster Children's Publishing Division.

3/3 *Weather Words and What They Mean* by Gail Gibbons, published by Holiday House, 1990. Used by permission.

3/4 *Gabby Growing Up* by Amy Hest, illustrated by Amy Schwartz. Text copyright ©1998 by Amy Hest. Illustrations copyright ©1998 by Amy Schwartz. Reprinted with the permission of Simon & Schuster Books for Young Readers, an imprint of Simon & Schuster Children's Publishing Division.

3/4 *Manatees* by Emilie U. Lepthien, published by Children's Press, 1991. Used by permission.

3/4 *Red Bird* by Barbara Mitchell, illustrated by Todd L.W. Doney, published by Lothrop, Lee & Shepard Books, 1996. Used by permission.

3/4 *The Planets* by Gail Gibbons, published by Holiday House, 1993. Used by permission.

3/5 *Alexander and The Terrible, Horrible, No Good, Very Bad Day* by Judith Viorst, illustrated by Ray Cruz. Text copyright ©1972 by Judith Viorst. Illustrations copyright ©1972 by Ray Cruz. Reprinted with the permission of Atheneum Books for Young Readers, an imprint of Simon & Schuster Children's Publishing Division.

3/5 *Birthday Blizzard* by Bonnie Pryor, illustrated by Molly Delaney, published by Morrow Junior Books, 1993. Used by permission.

3/5 *City Green* by DyAnne DiSalvo-Ryan, published by Morrow Junior Books, 1994. Used by permission.

3/5 *Pepita Talks Twice/Pepita Habla Dos Veces* by Ofelia Dumas Lachtman, illustrated by Alex Pardo DeLange, published by Pinata Books, 1995. Used by permission.

3/5 *Yunmi and Halmoni's Trip* by Sook Nyul Choi, illustrated by Karen Dugan, published by Houghton Mifflin Company, 1997. Used by permission.

3/6 *Flash, Crash, Rumble, and Roll* by Franklyn M. Branley, illustrated by Ed Emberley, published by Thomas Y. Crowell, 1964. Used by permission.

3/6 *Radio Boy* by Sharon Phillips Denslow, illustrations by Alec Gillman. Text copyright ©1995 by Sharon Phillips Denslow. Illustrations copyright ©1995 by Alec Gillman. Reprinted with the permission of Simon & Schuster Books for Young Readers, an imprint of Simon & Schuster Children's Publishing Division.

Student Writing Model Contributors

Jermaine Boddie, Milena Carrese, Daniel Estavez, Nikos Polis, Ashton Ray, Cody Reid, Rebecca Silberman, Emily Smith, Selena Wilke

Credits

Illustrations

Special Characters illustrated by: Sal, the Writing Pal by LeeLee Brazeal; Pencil Dog by Jennifer Beck Harris; Enrichment Animals by Scott Matthews.

Yvette Banek: 42, 123 (bottom)

John Bendall-Brunello: 23, 71, 228

Gwen Connelly: 116, 188, 222

Chris Demarest: 230, 231 (center), 255, 272, 273, 301, 384, 386

Eldon Doty: 153, 189 (top), 195

Julie Durrell: H7, H8, H12, H68, H69, H71, H72, H74, H76

Kate Flanagan: 70 (top), 189 (center), 226 (bottom)

Jim Gordon: 196

Jennifer Harris: 118 (bottom), 194

Meg Kelleher Aubrey: H23

Jared Lee: 78

Andy Levine: 44 (bottom)

Rosanne Litzinger: 1-4, 6, 7

Steven Mach: 68

Bob McMahon: 114 (top)

Patrick Merrell: 142

Laurie Newton-King: 102 (top), 120 (top)

Chris Reed: 99, 106, 148

Scot Ritchie: 74, 120 (bottom), 216

Tim Robinson: 38

Ellen Sasaki: 62, 76, 218 (top)

Lauren Scheuer: 114 (bottom), 160, 169, 338, 345, 399, 400, 419, H5

Rémy Simard: 36, 226 (top)

Michael Sloan: 44 (top)

George Thompson: 108, 112

George Ulrich: 37, 70 (center), 102 (bottom), 154, 218 (bottom)

Matt Wawiorka: 336, 414, 415, 417, H15, H21

Bill Whitney: 118 (top)

Jean Wisenbaugh: H13, H14

Amy L. Young: 158

Mary Ellen Zawataski: H25

Debra Ziss: 161

Photographs

iv © Bill Brooks/Masterfile. v © Telegraph Colour Library/FPG International. vi © Alan Schein/The Stock Market. vii © Lori Adamski Peek/Tony Stone Images. ix © Art Wolfe/Tony Stone Images. xi (t) © Paul Barton/The Stock Market. (b) © Johnny Johnson/Tony Stone Images. xii © Donna Day/Tony Stone Images. xiii (t) © Ron Chapple/FPG International. (b) © Arthur Tilley/FPG International. 15 © Artville. 31 © Paul Chesley/Tony Stone Images. 32 © Mark Sherman/Photo Network. 34 (t) © Lawrence Migdale/Tony Stone Images. (b) © J. & P. Wegner/Animals Animals. 35 © Frans Lanting/Tony Stone Images. 36 © Jean Higgins/Unicorn Stock Photo. 37 © PhotoDisc, Inc. 38 © Charles Thatcher/Tony Stone Images. 39 © Jeffrey Sylvester/FPG International. 40 © Nancy Sheehan/PhotoEdit. 41 (t) © PhotoDisc, Inc. (b) © Margaret Ross/Stock Boston. 42 © Tom Prettyman/PhotoEdit. 43 © iSwoop/FPG International. 45 © Siede Preis/PhotoDisc, Inc. 47 (t) © Lori Adamski Peek/Tony Stone Images. (tm) © Myrleen Ferguson/PhotoEdit. (bm) © Stephen McBrady/PhotoEdit. (b) © Dan McCoy/Rainbow/Picture Quest. 50 © Peter Weimann/Animals Animals. 53 © Scott Barrow/International Stock Photo. 54 © PhotoDisc, Inc. 55 © PhotoDisc, Inc. 56 © Steve Smith/FPG International. 57 © PhotoDisc, Inc. 58 © Ellis Herwig/Stock Boston. 59 © Bill Brooks/Masterfile. 60 (t) © Comstock, Inc. (m) © CORBIS. (b) © Joanna B. Pinneo/Aurora/Picture Quest. 61 (t) © PhotoDisc, Inc. (b) © CORBIS. 62 © Cartesia. 64 © Jeff Greenberg/Unicorn Stock Photo. 65 © Ed Bock/The Stock Market. 66 (tl) © Karen Holsinger Mullen/Unicorn Stock Photo. (tr) © Tony Freeman/PhotoEdit. (bl) © Ariel Skelley/The Stock Market. (br) © Fabricius & Taylor/Photo Network. 67 © Bob Daemmrich/Stock Boston/Picture Quest. 71 (t) © Stuart Westmorland/Tony Stone Images. (b) Image provided by MetaTools. 72 © John Fortunato/Tony Stone Images. 73 © Comstock, Inc. 75 © PhotoDisc, Inc. 76 © PhotoDisc, Inc. 78 © Paramount/Picture Quest. 79 © Jack Hollingsworth/PhotoDisc,

Acknowledgments *continued*

Inc. **82** © PhotoDisc, Inc. **86** © Charles Gupton/The Stock Market. **87** © PhotoDisc, Inc. **88** (t) © Wolfgang Kaehler/CORBIS. (b) © David Wells/The Image Works. **89** © Musee d'Orsay, Paris/Giraudon, Paris/SuperStock. **90** © Joe McDonald/Animals Animals. **91** (t) © Bill Lai/The Image Works. (b) © CORBIS. **92** © Schenectady Museum; Hall of Electrical History Foundation/CORBIS. **93** © Ralph Reinhold/Animals Animals. **94** (t) © James Watt/Animals Animals. (m) (b) © PhotoDisc, Inc. **95** © PhotoDisc, Inc. **96** © Myrleen Ferguson/PhotoEdit. **97** © Telegraph Colour Library/FPG International. **98** © John Warden/Tony Stone Images. **100** © Jim Whitmer. **101** © PhotoDisc, Inc. **104** © Kindra Clineff/Tony Stone Images. **107** © David Young-Wolff/PhotoEdit. **108** © Bob Daemmrich/Stock Boston/Picture Quest. **109** © Cartesia. **110** © The Granger Collection, New York. **112** © Jennie Woodcock; Reflections Photolibrary/CORBIS. **116** © Bob Daemmrich/Tony Stone Images. **117** Courtesy of NASA. **119** © John A. Rizzo/PhotoDisc, Inc. **121** © PhotoDisc, Inc. **122** © Randall Hyman/Stock Boston. **130** (t) © R. Crandall/The Image Works. (b) © SuperStock, Inc. **131** © PhotoDisc, Inc. **132** © Rocky Jordan/Animals Animals. **133** © Bettmann/CORBIS. **134** © Archive Photos. **135** © Michael Gadomski/Animals Animals. **137** © Jeremy Woodhouse/PhotoDisc, Inc. **138** © Mark Scott/FPG International. **139** © Richard Day/Animals Animals. **140** © Robert Maier/Animals Animals. **141** © Claire Hayden/Tony Stone Images. **142** © Vince Streano/Tony Stone Images. **143** © PhotoDisc, Inc. **144** © Don Spiro/Tony Stone Images. **146** (tl) © Art Montes De Oca/FPG International. (tr) © SuperStock, Inc. (bl) © Anne-Marie Weber/FPG International. (br) © Archivo Iconografico, SA/CORBIS. (shell) © PhotoDisc, Inc. **148** © Peter Woloszynski/Tony Stone Images. **149** © Zefa/Herbert Spichtinger/The Stock Market. **150** Courtesy of NASA. **151** Courtesy of NASA. **152** © Michael Newman/PhotoEdit. **156** © Peter Menzel/Stock Boston. **157** (t) © Gavin Hellier/Tony Stone Images. (bl) ©

Michael Busselle/Tony Stone Images. (br) © Oliver Benn/Tony Stone Images. **160** © Spencer Grant/PhotoEdit. **163** © Joe McDonald/Animals Animals. **166** (t) © Roy Morsch/The Stock Market. (b) © Joe McDonald/Animals Animals. **167** (t) © Tom & Dee Ann McCarthy/The Stock Market. (b) © SuperStock, Inc. **168** © PhotoDisc, Inc. **170** © David Lawrence/The Stock Market. **171** © Adam Woolfitt/CORBIS. **172** Courtesy of NASA. **173** © Joe McDonald/Animals Animals. **174** (t) © Stouffer Prod./Animals Animals. (b) © Eastcott-Momatiuk/The Image Works. **175** © SuperStock, Inc. **176** (t) © Dean Abramson/Stock Boston/Picture Quest. (b) © Telegraph Colour Library/FPG International. **177** © Alan Schein/The Stock Market. **178** © Santow/Geocaris/Tony Stone Images. **182** © Timothy Shonnard/Tony Stone Images. **184** © Jeff Greenberg/The Picture Cube, Inc. **185** © Travelpix/FPG International. **186** © Mary Kate Denny/PhotoEdit. **188** © Eric R. Berndt/Unicorn Stock Photo. **190** © Mary Kate Denny/PhotoEdit. **191** (l) © Comstock, Inc. (tr) © Siede Preis/PhotoDisc, Inc. (br) © PhotoDisc, Inc. **193** © John Warden/Tony Stone Images. **196** © Myrleen Ferguson/PhotoEdit. **197** © PhotoDisc, Inc. **201** © PhotoDisc, Inc. **204** © SuperStock, Inc. **205** © PhotoDisc, Inc. **206** © Chuck Pefley/Tony Stone Images. **207** Image provided by MetaTools. **209** © Andrew Holbrooke/The Stock Market. **210** (t) © PhotoDisc, Inc. (b) © Aaron Horowitz/CORBIS. **211** © Robin L. Sachs/PhotoEdit. **212** © Clay Wiseman/Animals Animals. **213** © Lori Adamski Peek/Tony Stone Images. **214** © Ralph H. Wetmore, II/Tony Stone Images. **215** © Mark Downey/PhotoDisc, Inc. **216** © Comstock, Inc. **221** © Bob Daemmrich/Stock Boston. **224** Courtesy of The Gorilla Foundation/© Ron Cohn. **225** Courtesy of The Gorilla Foundation/© Ron Cohn. **227** © Myrleen Ferguson/PhotoEdit. **228** © Joan Clifford/The Picture Cube, Inc. **229** © John Terence Turner/FPG International. **230** © CORBIS. **237** © Myrleen Ferguson/PhotoEdit. **238** © A.

Ramey/PhotoEdit. **239** © George Shelley/The Stock Market. **240** © Ed Bock/The Stock Market. **241** (t) © Stockbyte. (b) © Robin L. Sachs/PhotoEdit. **242** © Lori Adamski Peek/Tony Stone Images. **243** (t) © Don Farrall/PhotoDisc, Inc. (b) © PhotoDisc, Inc. **244** Image provided by MetaTools. **245** © Digital Vision/Picture Quest. **246** © PhotoDisc, Inc. **250-1** © Art Wolfe/Tony Stone Images. **250** © Frans Lemmens/The Image Bank. **251** (b) © Rick Edwards/Animals Animals. **253** © Bob Daemmrich/Stock Boston/Picture Quest. **254** © Matthew McVay/Stock Boston. **256** © James L. Amos/CORBIS. **258** © Frans Lemmens/The Image Bank. **280** © *On The Rocks,* Anna Belle Lee Washington/SuperStock, Inc. **286** © Rick Edwards/Animals Animals. **318-9** © Paul Barton/The Stock Market. **318** © John Higginson/Tony Stone Images. **319** (b) © Johnny Johnson/Tony Stone Images. **320** (l) © Stephen Krasemann/Tony Stone Images. (r) © Art Wolfe/Tony Stone Images. **321** © Brent Peterson/The Stock Market. **322** © Tom Edwards/Animals Animals. **323** © Gary Randall/FPG International. **326** © John Higginson/Tony Stone Images. **344** © *Snap the Whip,* Winslow Homer (1836-1910), Butler Institute of American Art, Youngstown, OH./The Bridgeman Art Library. **354** © Johnny Johnson/Tony Stone Images. **355** © Jeffrey L. Rotman/CORBIS. **356** (t) © Stuart Westmoreland/CORBIS. (b) © Lawson Wood/CORBIS. **357** © Stuart Westmoreland/CORBIS. **361** © Zig Leszczynski/Animals Animals. **366** © David Overcash/Bruce Coleman/Picture Quest. **367** © Mike Johnson Photography. **368** © W. Perry Conway/CORBIS. **370** © Gary W. Carter/CORBIS. **375** © Paul Barton/The Stock Market. **377** © PhotoDisc, Inc. **380-1** © Ron Chapple/FPG International. **380** © Donna Day/Tony Stone Images. **381** (b) © Arthur Tilley/FPG International. **382** © Jon Crispin. **383** © Janice Rubin/Black Star/Picture Quest. **385** © Ariel Skelley/The Stock Market. **386** © Stephen Simpson/FPG International. **388** © Donna Day/Tony Stone Images. **402** © Syracuse Newspapers/The Image Works. **410** © Cundo Bermudez. *Barber Shop,* 1942. Oil on canvas, 25 1/8 x 21 1/8 (63.8 x 53.7 cm) The Museum of Modern Art, New York. Inter-American Fund. Photograph © 2001 The Museum of Modern Art. **420** (t) © Dennis Blachut/The Stock Market. (bl) © Ron Dahlquist/Tony Stone Images. (br) © A. Ramey/PhotoEdit. **422** © Arthur Tilley/FPG International. **437** (t) © Emma Lee/Life File/PhotoDisc, Inc. (b) © Bob Calhoun; Clara Calhoun/Bruce Coleman, Inc./Picture Quest. **446** © CMCD/PhotoDisc, Inc. **H10** © John Michael/International Stock. **H17** © C Squared Studios/PhotoDisc, Inc. **H23** © iSwoop/FPG International. **H25** © Cartesia. **H36** © Myrleen Ferguson/PhotoEdit. **H37** © SuperStock, Inc. **H42** © PhotoDisc, Inc.

Cover Photograph

Cover: John Higginson/Tony Stone Images.